Due

page 184

The HOME and Its FURNISHINGS

AMERICAN HOME AND FAMILY SERIES

CONSULTING EDITOR, Helen Judy Bond
HEAD, DEPARTMENT OF HOME ECONOMICS
TEACHERS COLLEGE, COLUMBIA UNIVERSITY

Carson: How You Look and Dress
Hurlock: Child Growth and Development
Kilander: Nutrition for Health
Landis: Your Marriage and Family Living
Morton: The Home and Its Furnishings
Pierce: Youth Comes of Age

(Other Books in Process)

Illustrations on the following two pages from Hedrich-Blessing Studio (*left*)
and *The Stylist Magazine* (*right*).

THE HOME
and Its
FURNISHINGS

by RUTH MORTON

ILLUSTRATOR AND COLLABORATOR
ERNA KAROLYI

McGRAW-HILL BOOK COMPANY, INC.

NEW YORK   TORONTO   LONDON

THE HOME AND ITS FURNISHINGS

Affiliations of Author and Collaborator:

Ruth Morton is a professional decorator and consultant who lectures at the University of Wisconsin Extension School, in vocational high schools, to women's clubs, school assemblies, department stores, and on radio and television.

Erna Károlyi is a teacher of design and home furnishings at Pratt Institute who has also taught both junior and senior high school classes.

Notes to the Teacher

The Home and Its Furnishings has been written especially as a textbook for girls studying home furnishings for the first time. Because there are so few textbooks for teen-age girls which are devoted exclusively to the subject of home furnishings, it is important that the teacher understand the purpose, approach, content and organization, illustrations, and study aids in this book so as to obtain the full value of the material when using it for the course in home furnishings.

Purpose. The purpose of this book is to give girls the basic principles of home furnishings and to show them how to make use of these principles in (1) decorating their own rooms; (2) practicing in the homemaking center of the home economics department; (3) helping to decorate community centers; (4) helping with the furnishing plans at home; and (5) furnishing their own homes in the future.

A definite effort has been made throughout to include only information and examples that are within the realm of possibility for young girls. They are shown how to make the most of what is available or what may be obtained easily, rather than stimulated to want or to buy something new or something that they cannot afford.

All discussions and examples are based on the idea that furnishings should be functional, beautiful, individual, and personally satisfying. A sufficient number of suggestions are given in connection with the presentation of each topic to show how these requirements may be fulfilled in a variety of ways. It is made clear that what is suitable or useful to one person may not be so to another.

Approach. *The Home and Its Furnishings* begins with a girl's personal and natural interests—color, dress, her own room, and her possessions. From these interests it is hoped that the girl's enthusiasm and attention will be aroused and channeled into an interest in the furnishings of the whole house.

Every principle of decorating is made tangible to girls by the use of analogies drawn from their own experiences—nature, clothes, make-up, places, people, interests, and hobbies. Only after the principles have been thus explained through things that are familiar to them has the application of these principles to home furnishings been shown.

The writing has been kept within the vocabulary level of young girls. When it has been necessary to use technical terms, they have been explained. A free and easy style of writing has been used to keep the subjects from seeming to be too rigid, too formal, or too technical. The spirit of the book is to help girls enjoy home decorating.

Content and organization. The subject matter is divided into six large sections, which are presented in the natural sequence for decorating a home—that is, the book begins with color and continues with furniture, fabrics, accessories, management, and making plans for a home. It was felt that girls are more interested now in knowing how to decorate their own rooms than they are in deciding whether to rent or to buy or what to consider in establishing a home. However, in order that the student will have some information that will be useful when the time comes for her to select a place to live, the general aspects of home planning are given at the end of the book.

The book comprises twenty chapters—each of the six sections containing from two to five chapters. Each chapter in a section contains a different application of the subject of the section, developed logically from the preceding chapter. For example, in Section One on "Color in the Home" the girl first learns about the theory of color; then she is shown how color may be applied to a room; next, to an apartment; and finally, to a whole house. Thus she begins with elementary information on color and its application and is gradually presented with more advanced information and application.

The chapters are well organized for easy reading, comprehension, and reference by divisions with large headings in sentence form. Most of these sentences are definite statements of principles of decorating. These divisions are broken down into smaller topics by run-in sideheads or by key words that indicate the topic that follows.

Illustrations. The book contains more than three hundred line drawings, which were prepared in as simple a form as possible and clearly labeled for easy identification. The photographs have been carefully selected to show the application of principles in actual settings and to prove the effectiveness of the procedures suggested in the text.

Only basic facts of decorating are emphasized in the illustrative material. Thus, no confusion is created by showing too much detail, current fads, or exceptions to principles which might be included in an adult book on this subject.

No piece of furniture, fabric, or accessory has been shown in drawings or photographs that is not now obtainable on the market.

Study aids. At the end of each chapter are two groups of activities for the use of the student. The first of these—"Checking Your Knowledge"—contains questions for review and motivation on the subject of the chapter. The second group—"Using Your Knowledge"—gives suggestions for actual application in the student's own room or in another room of her home, in the homemaking center, or in a community center. The projects also include suggestions for making use of the resources available in the community—such as the library, museums and galleries, stores, and building projects—in studying the subject of home furnishings and applying the knowledge learned.

Wherever it is helpful or necessary to give specific and detailed information, the material is presented in the form of a chart. There are sixteen charts distributed throughout the various chapters.

A glossary of more than two hundred words is given at the end of the book so that the student can refer to it for any technical word or term which is not understood.

The bibliography in the back of the book contains a general list of books and pamphlets on the subject of home decorating and also six separate lists of reference material on the specific subjects of the sections in the book.

In order to show the application of color and to illustrate further by visual means the principles discussed in *The Home and Its Furnishings*, a set of filmstrips in full color has been prepared to accompany this text. The names of the filmstrips that correlate with the sections of the book are given on page xii, as well as at the beginning of the sections to which they apply.

Perhaps one of the most outstanding features of *The Home and Its Furnishings* is its threefold emphasis on the importance of home furnishings to the success and happiness of the entire family. *A personalized home* encourages individual and family interests that stimulate personal growth. *A comfortable home* makes for more agreeable living and better family relations. *A beautiful home* is a social force of great value in providing pleasant surroundings for good human relations. It is, therefore, hoped that the girls who use this book as a textbook in their study of home furnishings will learn not only the principles of decorating but also the personal and social values of an attractive home.

Acknowledgments. The author wishes to express her deep appreciation and thanks to the following people, who contributed so generously to the content and writing of *The Home and Its Furnishings*.

Miss Florence E. Beatty, supervisor of home economics, Milwaukee Public Schools, checked the content outline for the text.

Edward A. Boerner, head of the art department, Rufus King High School, Milwaukee, member of the committee on curriculum planning for Wisconsin, president of Wisconsin Painters and Sculptors, helped with the technical content of the color chapters.

Mrs. Vera Ellwood, director of the home service department, Wisconsin Electric Power Company, Milwaukee, contributed information on lighting and household appliances.

Mrs. Elizabeth Gray, formerly associate professor of housing in home economics, Pratt Institute, Brooklyn, contributed ideas and suggestions in connection with the section on housing.

Miss Treva E. Kauffman, supervisor, bureau of home economics education, New York State Education Department, made suggestions for the text and for the activity material at the ends of the chapters.

Mrs. Elizabeth Wilson Machotka, former vice principal of the Girls' Trade and Technical High School, Milwaukee, participated in the original planning of the content.

The following people at the Milwaukee Public Library helped in the collecting of material and illustrations: Wilbert Beck, curator of the art and music department; Mrs. Hazel Medway Schmidt, adult readers' guide; Miss Mamie Renquist, chief of the reference department; Miss Helen Terry, chief of the literature department; and Paul Gratke, chief of the philosophy, education, and religion department.

Miss Catherine Morton, teacher of English, Rufus King High School, Milwaukee, suggested the writing of the book and gave constant encouragement and help in the writing and organization of the entire manuscript.

Dr. Paulena Nickell, head of the home management department, Iowa State College, made many helpful suggestions for Section Five on "Management of the Home."

Edward M. Tuttle, executive secretary of the National School Boards Association, encouraged the author to proceed with the writing of this textbook.

Miss Oma Umbel, assistant professor in home economics, University of Hawaii, read the entire manuscript and noted places which might be revised for clarity.

Miss Margaret Wernecke, formerly dean of women, Milwaukee University School, typed the manuscript and helped with finer points of technical presentation of the material.

The author also wishes to thank the following companies and magazines, which cooperated generously in loaning photographs for illustrating the book: Armstrong Cork Company, Bates Fabrics, Inc., *Better Homes and Gardens, Interiors, Popular Home,* and *The Stylist.*

Ruth Morton

McGraw-Hill Text-Films for *THE HOME AND ITS FURNISHINGS*

In order to illustrate further the basic principles of home furnishings, the following filmstrips have been prepared in full color to correlate with sections of *The Home and Its Furnishings:*

An Introduction to Color (Section One)

Color in the Girl's Room (Section One)

Selecting Furniture for the Girl's Room (Section Two)

Arranging Furniture in the Girl's Room (Section Two)

Fabrics in the Girl's Room (Section Three)

Accessories in the Girl's Room (Section Four)

Contents

Section Six: Plans for the Home

LIST OF CHARTS

Editor's Introduction

Nature has surrounded us with untold beauty. It is our responsibility to add to this beauty and not to detract from it—whether we are creating a garden, a public building, a farm, or a home.

Our immediate surroundings reflect our personality as much as does our personal appearance, and, as is true with good grooming, we can learn through study and observation how to make our environment one which will not only expand our personality and be pleasing to ourselves, but will attract others to us.

A knowledge of personal and family needs in respect to housing, and how these may be met, represents the first essential. Knowing the basic principles of art, developing the ability to create certain things for ourselves, learning how to choose wisely when purchasing, how to blend the old with the new, how to enhance our possessions by the use of correct colors and arrangements, how to care for and manage our homes so that time and energy are available for the enjoyment of other things in a pleasing atmosphere—all these contribute to efficient and effective living.

Miss Morton, through her splendid text, and Miss Károlyi, through her realistic drawings, have challenged young girls to make their own immediate surroundings more attractive and better suited to their needs. Through the careful presentation of basic elements, they have also given a background for meeting new situations with assurance. Such knowledge will be of great value to young people in helping to create homes of their own.

Helen Judy Bond

Notes to You

All your life you are going to be living somewhere. This year you probably have your own room or share a room with some member of the family. When you finish high school, you may remain at home with your family, live in a college dormitory, share an apartment, or have a part of a house.

If you are like most girls, you will want your surroundings to express your own personal taste as well as the tastes of the people who live with you. You will want the pictures on your walls, the draperies at your windows, and the accessories on your desk to be your own choice. When you know something about interior decoration, your choice will be based on knowledge as well as on personal taste, and the result should be artistic as well as individual.

You will find as you proceed with your study of this book that the amount of knowledge you have, rather than the amount of money you spend, determines whether or not your surroundings will be comfortable and satisfying to you and attractive to others. But studying this book is not enough. You must practice the knowledge that you will find in this book. It would be a very poor meal you served your husband if you waited until after you were married to learn about food and meal planning. Practice in interior decoration is equally important to success in furnishing an attractive home, and the time to begin is now, in your own room. Interior decorating is a homemaking skill of the greatest importance. The creation of a livable home is one of the most important jobs of your life, and *The Home and Its Furnishings* has been written to help you do it well.

Ruth Morton

SECTION ONE: *Color in the Home*

The color filmstrips "An Introduction to Color" and "Color in the Girl's Room" have been prepared to correlate with this section.

CHAPTER 1: Color in Your World

If you were asked, "What is the first thing you are conscious of about a dress, a room, or a scene?" undoubtedly your answer would be "color," because most of us see the world and everything in it in terms of color first. Even our mood is affected by the color in the world around us. When the sky is leaden and a driving rain makes the universe look dull and gray, our spirits droop. But when the sky is clear and the warm sun brings out the soft green of foliage and the brilliant colors of flowers, we feel that our lives, our friends, and our future are all good. We laugh easily, and our mood is gay.

The fact that color affects our choice of most things is proved beyond a doubt by research and sales records. Most items, from the salads on a cafeteria counter to the rubber mats in the hardware stores, sell or do not sell mainly because of their color. Merchants and theater managers recognize the value of color and spend large sums for expert help in the selection of the most attractive colors for salesrooms, lobbies, and lounges.

Stop for a moment and analyze your reactions to color in connection with your personal life. What actually was the reason you selected that sweater you just bought? What is one of the determining factors in the selection of the drugstore you and your friends patronize? The answer to both is probably "color." Of course you probably did not say or even think, "This bright red sweater will make me feel festive every time I wear it," or "The green walls in the corner drugstore make me think of grass and trees and so are more attractive to look at than the dull gray ones of the store across the street." But when you stop to consider your reactions

3

thoughtfully, you will probably realize that color was the most important factor in your decisions.

The importance of color in our lives is also shown by the way in which colors have become symbolic of our moods. Whether we live in Brooklyn or Birmingham, Salem or San Francisco, we "feel blue" when we are sad, we "see red" when we are angry, we "feel green with envy" when we long for something someone else has, or we "see the world through rose-colored glasses" when we are happy and our lives are going well.

Indeed, color is so important that it influences nearly everything we do and almost every reaction we have.

An understanding of color comes through experimenting with paint.

The easiest way to understand color is to experiment with paint. To do this, get a box of water colors, like those used in grade schools, that contains red, yellow, blue, and black paint. You will need several large pieces of water-color paper and a good-sized brush. Then make the following experiments.

Experiment 1. Brush clear water over one of the large pieces of paper, blotting off any excess moisture so the paper is evenly damp. Next, brush on large daubs of each of the red, yellow, and blue from your paintbox. Then add an equal quantity of yellow to the red, of blue to the yellow, and of red to the blue. [Note: Clean your brush before applying each color.] The resulting new colors will be orange, green, and violet—colors that are quite different from the red, yellow, and blue in your paintbox. These three colors, with the three in your box, make up the six colors shown in the small color wheel at the top of page 19.

Experiment 2. Repeat Experiment 1, but make two daubs of each of the color combinations orange, green, and violet. Next, add to each of these combinations an extra daub of one of the colors already present. For example, to one of the daubs of orange (red and yellow) add another daub of red, which will make it red-orange. To the other daub of orange add some yellow, which will make it yellow-orange. To one of the daubs of green (blue and yellow) add another daub of blue, which will make it blue-green.

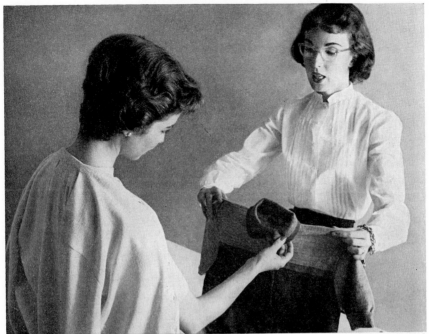

Isn't color generally the first thing you think about or notice when you are shopping for a sweater, a blouse, or a hat? If so, in your plans for decorating a room, you will first want to decide on the color that you wish to use on the walls and for rugs and fabrics.

To the other daub of green add some more yellow, which will make it yellow-green. To one of the daubs of violet (blue and red) add an extra daub of blue, which will make it blue-violet, and to the other daub of violet add some more red, which will make it red-violet.

These six new colors will be quite different from the original three in your paintbox and from the three produced in Experiment 1, but they will be clear, bright colors that are obviously related to the other six.

Experiment 3. Dampen a third sheet, and on it place separate daubs of red, yellow, and blue. Next, repeat Experiments 1 and 2. Then, to the single colors (red, yellow, and blue) and to the combinations of colors (orange, green, violet, red-orange, yellow-orange, etc.) add a small amount of any of the original three colors not present in each. For example, add a touch of green (made of yellow and blue) to the red, a touch of violet (made of blue and red) to the yellow, and a touch of orange (made of yellow and red) to the blue. Continue the experiment by adding a little blue to the orange, a little yellow to the violet, and a little red to the green. Now try adding a small amount of blue-green to the red-orange and of blue-violet to the yellow-orange. Also, add a touch of red-orange to the blue-green and of red-violet to the yellow-green. Complete the experiment by adding a little yellow-orange to the blue-violet and of yellow-green to the red-violet.

The colors that will result from these mixtures, or fusions, will be soft, grayed colors, similar to those in the middle band of the large color wheel on page 19.

Experiment 4. Dampen a fourth sheet of paper, and apply five or six sets of as nearly equal amounts as possible of the three original colors in your paintbox, letting each set of three mix, or fuse, evenly. The result will be grays, browns, tans, and blacks, similar to those at the bottom of page 30. These colors will have no brilliance and no noticeable relationship to any of the colors used in mixing them.

Theoretically, equal amounts of red, yellow, and blue, when mixed together, should produce gray or black, depending on the thickness of the paint—colors which show no trace of any of the three original colors. But actually it is very difficult for anyone to be scientifically accurate in measuring equal amounts of color with a brush. Moreover, most paints in any box, tube, or can are not completely true in color. One red will be more orange, while another will be more violet; a yellow will be more green or more orange; and a blue will be more green or more violet. For that reason, this experiment may produce some blacks and grays, but it will also produce blue-grays, beiges, tans, and browns—the result of mixtures that are not quite equal, as well as of basic colors that are not quite true.

Experiment 5. On this sheet, add a small amount of black to each of the three single colors—red, yellow, and blue. Continue the experiment by adding a touch of black to the three colors you made in the first experiment—orange, green, and violet—and the

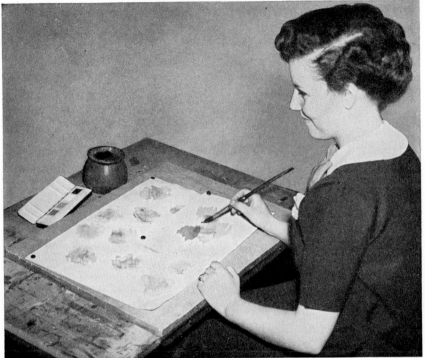

ERNEST A. KEHR

A box of water colors, a brush, a few pieces of drawing paper, and some water are all you need to do the experiments on pages 4–7 and thereby discover for yourself what makes up the content of different colors.

six colors you made in the second experiment. You will find that each of these twelve colors will be slightly darkened and grayed, or softened, in much the same way they were when you used all three colors together in uneven amounts in Experiment 3. This time, however, they will be like the dark colors of the inner circle of the large color wheel on page 19 but slightly duller.

Experiment 6. On this last sheet repeat Experiment 3, and to each of the colors add a small amount of water. You will see that the water makes the colors lighter, so that they look like the colors in the outside circle of colors of the large color wheel on page 19.

Now look over all the experiments. You will note that in Experiment 1, in addition to the three colors—red, yellow, and blue—with which you started, you now have three new colors—orange, green, and violet. These six colors are shown in the small color wheel at the top of page 19.

In Experiment 2 you created six more colors, each one of which would fall halfway between the colors in the small color wheel if those six were separated.

In Experiments 3, 5, and 6 you found three ways of creating the soft, grayed colors that appear in the large color wheel on page 19.

In Experiment 4 you discovered that by combining bright, clear colors you can produce colors that have no brilliance at all, such as tans, browns, grays, and blacks.

Having seen just how colors can be made, you are now ready to study more about color as it is organized for everyday use.

Colors are classified according to their content.

Colors, first of all, are classified according to their content. In your experiments with paint you began with three colors—red, yellow, and blue. Primitive peoples found these three colors in animal, vegetable, and mineral substances. Manufacturing processes have made it possible for you to buy these three colors in a paintbox. Neither you nor primitive man could make any one of these three. But from these three colors you, like them, are able to mix every other color in the world, as your experiments showed. The way a color is made determines its classification into one of the following groups.

Primary colors—red, yellow, and blue—are the three basic colors which cannot be made by mixing any other colors together. Yet from these three primary colors all of the thousands of other colors that exist in the world are made.

Secondary colors—orange, green, and violet—are made by mixing equal parts of any *two* of the primary colors together. For example: Equal parts of red and yellow make orange; equal parts of blue and yellow make green; equal parts of red and blue make violet. (Review Experiment 1.)

Intermediate colors—yellow-orange, yellow-green, blue-green, blue-violet, red-violet, and red-orange—are all made by mixing one *secondary* color with one of the *primary* colors which is already contained in the secondary. For example, violet, which is made of blue and red, becomes blue-violet when blue is added. Green becomes yellow-green when yellow is added. (Review Experiment 2.)

Neutralized colors are soft, grayed colors like those shown in the large color wheel on page 19. They are made by adding a touch of black to any clear color or by adding the primary color or colors not present in the clear color. (Review Experiments 3 and 5.) For example: A bright green, which contains yellow and blue, can be neutralized by adding a small amount of black or of red, the one primary not present in green; blue can be neutralized by adding a small amount of black or of orange, which is made up of yellow and red, the two primaries not present in blue.

Neutrals are made by mixing equal amounts of all three primary colors together so that it is impossible to identify any one color as dominant. (Review Experiment 4.) Technically, there are only three absolute neutrals—black, gray in all gradations from dark to light, and white. But in common usage, a neutral is any color which has been neutralized to a point where it is difficult to determine its color content. For that reason, some neutralized colors are used as neutrals because they also serve as an excellent background, or foil, for other colors. Beige, tan, ivory, brown, and cream are examples of neutralized colors which act as neutrals.

The color wheel is a convenient organization of color.

The color wheel is a man-made arrangement of colors which simplifies the study and use of color. Its inspiration can be traced easily and obviously to the rainbow. The rainbow, however, is created by light, which has far greater purity—and therefore intensity—than the color wheel, which is made of pigment, or paint—an impure substance by comparison. The color wheel has kept the same arrangement of colors as the rainbow, but its range of colors is narrower. In fact, the usual color wheel is made up of just twelve separate and distinct colors, whereas the countless colors of the rainbow fuse imperceptibly into each other.

Colors are arranged on the color wheel in such a way that the three primaries form an equilateral triangle, which divides the circle into three parts. The secondary colors are placed equidistant from each primary; they also form an equilateral triangle. The six intermediate colors are placed between the primaries and second-aries, forming a hexagon. This arrangement of colors is always main-tained, regardless of whether the color wheel is composed of many more colors than these twelve or whether it is composed of bright or dull colors, dark or light colors.

The small color wheel on page 19 is made up of six colors—three primaries and three secondaries. All of these colors are strong, clear, true, or pure colors.

The large color wheel on page 19 is made up of the primary, secondary, and intermediate colors—each of which has been grayed, or neutralized. (See Experiments 3 and 5.)

It is possible to use these color wheels for planning color schemes, which are considered in detail in Chapter 2, "Color as You Use It." While you are reading the next chapter, you will find it helpful to turn again and again to these color wheels to help you visualize statements and analyze color schemes from the point of view of their placement.

Colors are either warm or cool.

Despite the fact that scientists tell us that the average person can distinguish thousands of colors, it is possible to classify them into just two groups—warm and cool colors.

Warm colors are colors that contain a predominance of red or yellow. The reason for this is that red and yellow are the colors of the sun and of fire—the source of all the natural heat in the universe. Therefore, any color that contains a dominance of red or yellow is a warm color.

To clarify this, refer back to the colors you made in Experiments 1 and 2. Now turn to the large color wheel on page 19 and, moving clockwise, review the color content of all the colors from red-violet to yellow-green. You will find that these colors and all the colors between them have a dominance of yellow or red. They are therefore called warm colors.

All warm colors have certain distinguishing qualities. They are stimulating and exciting, and objects in warm colors appear to be larger and closer than they really are. Check this by glancing quickly over your school auditorium, over the bleachers at a football game, or over the landscape as you ride by. You will notice that all the red sweaters, the yellow and orange bows, the red barns, and the yellow flowers seem to enlarge and to come toward you. The hot yellow summer sun seems to be just a short distance from the earth even at noonday, and in the evening it seems to be setting just behind the nearest hill. When you first see a bonfire at night in the distance it may seem fairly close and large. But as you drive toward it, you find that the fire is smaller and the distance greater than you estimated. The red and yellow of the flames completely fool you by advancing toward you and seeming to increase in size.

Cool colors all have a predominance of blue. Blue is the color of water, sky, ice, snow, and distant haze—the elements from which we get all our cold. Therefore, any color that contains more blue than any other color is a cool color.

Refer back to the experiments and check the colors you made by mixing blue with other colors. Now turn to the color wheel and, moving clockwise, note the colors from blue-green around to blue-violet. All these colors have a dominance of blue and are therefore considered cool colors.

All cool colors have certain distinguishing qualities. They are calm and restful, and objects in cool colors appear to be smaller and farther away than they actually are. Mountains surrounded by a blue-violet haze appear miles and miles away and seem like large hills. As you look across a football field, a girl in a soft blue dress seems farther away and smaller than her companion in a red dress.

The two colors in between these two groups of obviously cool and obviously warm colors are violet and green. These two colors are made up of equal quantities of warm and cool colors. Violet is made up of red and blue, and green is composed of yellow and blue. A true green and a true violet can, therefore, be made to look cool or warm according to the colors they are near.

**All colors have three qualities—
hue, value, and intensity.**

After experimenting with color and analyzing it according to warmth and coolness, you are ready to consider color according to its three qualities—hue, value, and intensity.

Hue is the name of a color. It is virtually synonymous with the word "color," as the word "color" is commonly used, but the hue name is more accurate than the color name. For example, when the hue of the sky is blue or violet-blue, the color might be called "azure," a far less accurate name. The hue of a fire might be yellow, red-orange, red, or orange, but its color might be called "flame." The hue of the sun is yellow, but the color, or the popular name, might be gold. It is by the hue, or the accurate name, of a color, that we identify it on the color wheel. It is by the hue that we know the content of a color and thereby can classify it as either cool or warm.

In a two-word color name, such as green-blue, blue is the dominant hue, whereas green is simply an adjective describing the type of blue—an adjective which places the blue more accurately on the color wheel. Blue-violet is violet with a blue tinge. Its place on the color wheel is a little to the right of violet, in the section between violet and blue.

Because colors are so attractive and important to us, writers, advertisers, and manufacturers have given various names to hues for variety and interest. In consequence, the market is full of merchandise with such imaginative and fantastic names as "luggage" and "elephant's breath." Their accurate color-wheel names, or hues, would probably be "grayed light orange" and "grayed dark violet."

As a rule, these new intriguing names are not at all uniformly used and can be most confusing to anyone who accepts them as even approximate color indicators. Actually, they are only used to create interest and to make merchandise more appealing.

Value is the amount of light or dark in a color. Values of a color may vary from almost white—the lightest value—to almost black—the darkest value. The amount of white or black in a color determines its value.

Light colors, or light values, are called "tints." Pink, which is a light value of red, is a tint.

Dark colors, or dark values, are called "shades." Maroon, which is a dark value of red, is a shade. A color that has a value halfway between a tint and a shade, or between a light and a dark value, is called a "middle value," or a "normal value," of a color.

An open street that allows the sunlight to come in looks wider than a street hemmed in by tall buildings. Likewise in a room, light values give a feeling of space, while dark values close in.

13

The quick way to lighten a color, or make a tint of it, is to add white or water to it. The quick way to darken a color, or make it a shade, is to add black to it. (See Experiments 5 and 6.)

Dark values, like warm colors, have an advancing quality. A dark thundercloud seems to be low in the sky. A white cloud seems to float high. A wide street lined with high buildings that shut out light looks narrow; streets of the same width look much wider out in the suburbs where the low houses do not shut out sunlight. In a forest, where dark tree trunks and dark foliage press in closely, the world seems small and cozy. Out on the desert or plain, where the sky meets the horizon in the hazy distance, the world seems very large.

Intensity is the brightness or dullness, strength or weakness, of a color. The word "chroma" is sometimes used as a synonym for intensity. Many a bathing suit begins the summer a strong, intense blue, but after daily dips in the lake and daily sunbaths on the beach, it ends the season a very soft, dull, grayed blue. The yellow of a dandelion is brilliant, a color of high intensity. The yellow of a field of ripe wheat is a dull, mellow, soft yellow—a color of weak intensity. The colors of hummingbirds and flowers are bright—that is, they are intense. The colors of elephants, earth, and mountains are soft and grayed. Thus, in nature we find, as a rule, a rather simple formula for the pleasing use of intense and grayed colors: The larger the area, the lower or grayer is the intensity of its color, and the smaller the area, the higher or more brilliant is the intensity of its color.

So, as we observe color in nature, we usually find a neat balance between warm and cool hues, between dark and light values, and between strong and weak intensities. How important this balance is to our normal feeling of well-being can only be judged when we think what the world would be like if these balances were upset to any great degree.

Imagine a world in which for twelve months of the year there was nothing but blue-white ice and snow against a cold blue sky. Such a place exists, but no one lives there. Byrd and his men were glad to leave Little America after a few short weeks. Imagine a world of hot yellow sunshine and yellow sand unrelieved by a single oasis. Men and beasts die quickly when lost on the desert. Imagine a world of continuous darkness or a world where the sun never dimmed. Or imagine a world in which a dull blue sun was set in a dazzling yellow sky, where elephants were the color of hummingbirds or hummingbirds the color of elephants. Such a world would be a nightmare—utterly maddening and impossible.

Yet sometimes we forget these natural balances of color to which we are accustomed in nature, and we plan color schemes for our homes which distort this natural order past the pleasingly novel point. When such a color scheme is used, a room upsets us just as would a violent distortion in the world of nature. No wonder it is necessary for us, as a result, to study carefully the natural world of color before we plan color schemes for our smaller world—our rooms and our homes.

The way in which the natural laws of color have been accepted and used as the basis of the rules of good decorating will be taken up in the next chapters.

CHECKING YOUR KNOWLEDGE . . .

1. Name the general classifications of color according to color content.
2. Name the primary colors.
3. Name the secondary colors, and tell how to make them.
4. Name the intermediate colors, and tell how to make them.
5. How are colors organized for use and study?
6. What are the two big classifications of all colors?
7. What are the three qualities of all colors?
8. What is a light color called? A dark color?
9. What word do we use to describe the brightness or dullness of a color?
10. What colors advance? What values close in?
11. What colors recede? What values recede?

USING YOUR KNOWLEDGE . . .

1. Ask the head of a commercial cafeteria how he uses color to sell food.
2. Select two stores—one that is obviously prospering and one that is not—and analyze the use of color in walls, merchandise, and displays.

3. Put up two different sets of instructions on a bulletin board in a class-room. Mount one on a large red mat and the other on a neutral mat. Check to find out which one is read and followed by the greatest number of students.

4. Make a list of brilliantly colored small objects in nature and a second list of large objects of grayed colors in nature. Balance each with a list of similar length of small objects of intense color that would be attractive in a room, and another of large objects of grayed color that would be appropriate for a room.

5. Find a piece of wallpaper that has both light and dark colors in it. Have someone in the class photograph it so you can display the wallpaper and the black-and-white (value) reproduction of it together, on your bulletin board.

6. Select at random five objects of different colors, such as a scarf, a piece of colored paper, a sample of upholstery fabric, a colored pencil, and the wall of your classroom. Find pieces of gray paper that are the same values as each of these. Check by half closing your eyes and looking at the two together. They should look exactly alike.

CHAPTER 2: Color as You Use It

To use colors well and to combine them successfully in rooms, we must first of all encourage our natural liking for them—a liking that is ingrained in almost every one of us. From the time we are very small, most of us are attracted by colors—bright colors and clear colors, plain colors and patterned colors. When we were children, we reached for bright red blocks, we enjoyed sitting on the soft green grass, and we gazed in wonder at a Christmas tree patterned with colored lights and ornaments. Later, we are likely to buy a bright red sweater, to patronize the drugstore with the attractive green walls, and to wear gaily patterned scarves.

As we grow up, we can train our eyes to see more subtle colors and to appreciate more delicate beauties. Such beauties as the softly glowing colors of a sunset on a winter landscape and the delicate grayed colors of a summer afterglow are appreciated by us only as we are trained to look for color more carefully. So, begin at once to try looking at color with more observant eyes.

The moment you begin to look at color more carefully, you will also begin to see fascinating combinations of colors—combinations which fit into one or another of the color schemes we will study in this chapter. Thus you will find in nature the inspiration for the whole man-made color system—a system you will use in decorating your own room.

We also find, as we analyze color more carefully, that it exists on patterned as well as plain surfaces. Thus we must not only know color schemes, but we must know how to use them in terms of patterned as well as plain surfaces.

17

Chart 1: Working Analysis of the Two Color Wheels

(On opposite page)

COLOR WHEEL OF INTENSITIES

(A color wheel composed of the primary and secondary colors
in full intensity)

Primaries

The three primary colors—red, yellow, and blue—are the basic colors
from which all other hues and neutrals (except white) are made.

Secondaries

The three secondary colors—orange, green, and violet—are made by mixing equal amounts of primaries in groups of two—red and yellow, yellow
and blue, and blue and red. (See Experiment 1 in Chapter 1.)

COLOR WHEEL OF NEUTRALIZED, OR GRAYED, COLORS

(A color wheel composed of shades, middle values, and tints)

Shades

The colors which compose the inner circle are the dark values (or shades)
of the primary, secondary, and intermediate colors which have been neutralized, or grayed. (See Experiment 5 in Chapter 1.)

Middle Values

The colors which compose the middle circle are the middle, or normal,
values of the primary, secondary, and intermediate colors, which have
been neutralized, or grayed. They are halfway between the shades and
the tints in value. (See Experiment 3 in Chapter 1.)

Tints

The colors which compose the outside circle are the light values (or
tints) of the primary, secondary, and intermediate colors which have
been neutralized, or grayed. (See Experiment 6 in Chapter 1.)

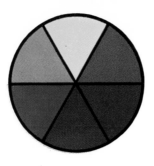

Color wheel of intensities

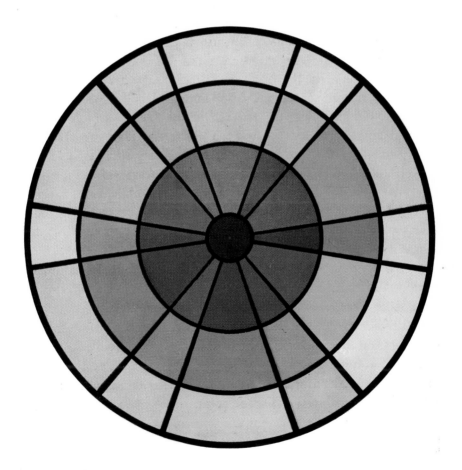

Color wheel of grayed, or neutralized, colors

**Color use in nature suggests standards
for color use in homes.**

As mentioned in Chapter 1, there are certain rather obvious standards of color use in the world around us. By analyzing these, we find a set of principles to follow in the use of color in our own rooms. The more you train yourself to see these standard uses and balances of color, the more natural it will seem to you to follow the principles behind them, which have become the basis of good decorating. These principles will help you to create color schemes that are completely satisfying and pleasing. The facts brought out in Chapter 1 indicate the following standards of color use.

Color intensities should vary inversely with the size of the area. In other words, the larger the area, the duller the color must be; the smaller the area, the brighter the color may be. This standard of good color usage is seldom varied in nature, and good decorating in homes should follow the same standard. Unless a room is most unusual architecturally, the walls, ceiling, and floor are the large areas, and—like the sky, water, and earth—they should be in soft, grayed colors. Sofas and beds, the large pieces of furniture—like the mountains and the elephants, the large objects in nature— should be in soft, grayed colors. Lamps, pictures, vases, small chairs, benches, and other small-area objects—like the hummingbirds and butterflies—can be in bright, or accent, colors.

One color should be established as a dominant. In nature we usually find that one color has been used again and again until it dominates a scene. Sometimes it is the blue of the sky; sometimes it is the blue of the water; sometimes it is the green of the foliage, the grass, or the fields. In the fall it is often the gold of ripening grain and autumn leaves. But whatever it is, we find, as a rule, that in nature one color is used to establish a background against which other colors are played as accent notes.

Some people hesitate, however, to follow this principle of repeating one color until it dominates a room. The reason for this hesitation is that they think of color in terms of intense accent colors, which of course should not be used in large quantities. They do not realize that any color can be soft, muted, or grayed (see

COURTESY ARMSTRONG CORK COMPANY

COURTESY MAINE DEVELOPMENT COMMISSION

A small room can be given the same spaciousness found in nature if the walls and ceiling are done in light-value colors. Note the similarity of values in both settings, with dark at the bottom and light at the top.

21

large color wheel on page 19) so that it is ideally suited to large-area use. They also forget that in nature no one value, hue, or intensity of a color establishes the dominant. The color of the sky, water, earth, or foliage is a blend of many shades and tints of one color, as well as of many closely blended colors. For example, the sea is a constantly changing blend of dark and light blues, of green-blues, true blues, and violet-blues, of bright and dull blues. Yet the effect is of blue water. The same variety on a smaller scale can be used in a room in establishing a dominant color.

Most decorators agree that if 60 percent or more of the room surfaces are done in one color, allowing the same variety of that color as is found in nature, a dominant color will be established.

The use of values in a room can be as varied as it is in nature. On sunshiny days the sky, from the zenith to the horizon, is the lightest value in the outdoor world of nature. Everything else—ground, foliage, and sea—is darker. In the forest dark ground, trees, and foliage are all around us. The sunlight shows only as shafts of light through the foliage. On days of scattered showers the sky may have black thunderclouds overhead, but otherwise the range of values remains the same as on a clear day. On dull days sky, ground, and foliage blend into one soft middle value. On stormy days the sky is so dark that foliage and earth look light by comparison.

These different arrangements of values in nature find their counterpart in good decorating.

The bright, sunny day suggests a room of strong value contrasts—that is, a room in which the ceiling and walls are in the same hue and equally light, and the floor and furnishings supply the dark, contrasting values. Or, following the pattern of the forest on a bright day, a room might have dark walls and floor and light ceiling, woodwork, and draperies. A day of scattered showers suggests a room with a dark ceiling, a dark floor, and light walls which furnish a dramatic background for both dark and light furnishings. A dull day suggests a room of closely knit values where ceiling, walls, floor, and furnishings all hold closely to middle values. A stormy day suggests dark walls and ceiling with light woodwork, light floors, and light draperies and upholstery.

An analogous color scheme has been selected to decorate this room. Blue-green, the dominant, is used in different values and intensities for slipcovers, walls, and rug. Against this blue-green dominant, yellow-green and yellow (used in draperies and pillows) make a pleasing accent, and the neutral of the wood color acts as a relief, or foil, for the color scheme.

Rooms which are not so much lived-in, such as bedrooms, dinettes, and powder rooms, might be done in a dramatic combination of values. Living rooms, dining rooms, kitchens, in which we spend longer hours, might better be done in a more conservative arrangement of values. This suggestion is counter to the trend in the last few years toward the use of very dark walls in the living rooms of the house, a revival of the style of the Directoire and Empire periods in France. At that time, however, the woodwork, which was done in off-white, was heavy and beautifully designed. The ceilings were very high, and the French windows—of which there were many—went to the floor. Nowadays most homes have low ceilings, very little woodwork, and until recently, fewer windows. As a result, dark walls are oppressive unless abundantly relieved by light draperies, light ceilings, and light upholstery—plus the use of many light-matted pictures for dramatic contrast.

There are four sources from which we obtain color schemes.

Sometimes, when we need a beautiful color scheme, we forget the sources from which we can obtain ready-made ones or, what is even worse, we try to be original when we have no special talent or training to help us. Actually, there are four sources of ready-made color schemes. The first is in the world of nature, as was pointed out in Chapter 1 and earlier in this chapter. The second source is in works of art, such as paintings, tapestries, pottery, china, or handmade rugs. (See Chapter 4, pages 76–78.) The third source is in manufactured products, such as a fabric, a wallpaper, or carpeting. And the last source is the color wheel itself. A study of the color wheel will help you to see and use the color schemes in the other three sources. For example, in nature we find blue and green used together constantly in sky and foliage and in blue lakes nestled among green hills. This color scheme inspired Gainsborough to paint the "Blue Boy" about two hundred years ago. Yet we did not see or use these colors as a color scheme until modern designers began talking about analogous color harmonies in fabrics and interiors just a few years ago. A knowledge of the way the color wheel can be used to formulate color schemes may help you to discover

The paintings of great artists are a source of beautiful color schemes which may be used in the decorating of rooms.

other combinations of colors that are equally beautiful, yet not continually used.

Related color schemes use colors that are close together on the color wheel.

Color schemes can be classified according to their position on the color wheel. First, there are the related color schemes, made up of one or more closely related colors which are adjacent or near each other on the spectrum, or color wheel. Within this group there are two types of schemes: (1) the monochromatic and (2) the analogous.

A *monochromatic color scheme,* or one-color harmony, is a color scheme built around different values and intensities of just one color and a neutral.

A specific example of this scheme can be found in nature. In a forest, for instance, there are many different greens in the leaves, ferns, and grasses, and the neutral browns of the tree trunks serve as a relief, or foil, for the color. Another monochromatic scheme is shown in a marine scene in which many different shades, tints, and intensities of blue sky and water are set off by the neutral grays and whites of clouds and whitecaps. Each of these color schemes uses just one color plus a neutral, yet neither is monotonous.

When used in a room, the one-color related color scheme produces a feeling of complete unity. If the colors are grayed and softened, the room is quieting and relaxing. If the colors are strong, the room is dramatic.

Sometimes it is interesting to create a monochromatic color scheme by using the neutral as the dominant and using the color, in all its strength and intensity, as the accent against the neutral background. A gray room in which brilliant green has been used as an accent is a good example. Such a room, because of the gray dominant, is very quiet; yet the green gives it considerable drama. It is interesting to know that neutrals may be added to any color scheme; but in the monochromatic color scheme they are especially important. (For specific examples of monochromatic schemes, see Chart 2 in this chapter and Chart 6 in Chapter 3.)

An analogous color scheme is made up of closely related colors lying side by side in a small section of the color wheel. This type of scheme is especially effective when it is composed of related colors that have one color in common and that lie between one primary and one secondary or, if more colors are desired, between two primaries. For example, one very popular analogous color scheme which was mentioned before is made up of blue and green. If more colors are desired, this scheme can be expanded without taking it out of the analogous color scheme classification. It can include yellow-green and blue-green, as well as blue and green. All these colors contain blue and so are related colors. They also all lie between the two primaries, blue and yellow.

There are, of course, many obvious examples of the analogous color scheme in nature. The yellow, yellow-orange, and orange colors of an autumn scene form one we all know well. The blue, blue-violet, and violet of an evening sunset is another scheme we see frequently. Locate each of them on the color wheel on page 19. Note that each scheme is composed of related colors that appear in just one section of the color wheel.

An analogous color scheme has flexibility that is especially good in a room shared by girls of different temperaments. In this room two girls have agreed on a wallpaper as the source of an analogous color scheme, but each has applied the colors and decorated her corner in a different way.

If you want to work out an analogous color scheme for your own room, begin by selecting your favorite color. Select the other colors by turning to the color wheel and choosing those colors that not only are close to your favorite color but also contain some of it in their make-up. Check to be sure that all the colors of the scheme lie between one primary and one secondary or between two primaries. If your favorite color is a primary, do not take colors lying on both sides of it because they often are difficult to harmonize. For instance, if red is your favorite color, the other colors of the scheme should be selected from those colors which lie on one side or the other of red—not both sides. (For examples of good analogous color schemes, turn to Chart 2 in this chapter, Chart 7 in Chapter 3, and Charts 8 and 9 in Chapter 4.) Information about applying this type of color scheme to your own bedroom is given in Chapter 3.

**Contrasting color schemes are composed
of unrelated colors.**

The second group of color schemes is made up of contrasting, or unrelated, colors. These color schemes are very rich and satisfying to the eye and are particularly effective in large rooms where a variety of colors can be used.

The fact that the eye seems to desire this wider variety of color whenever color is used in its intense form can be checked by performing an experiment. Turn to the plate on page 30 and stare at the exact center of the intense red square in the upper part of the page. Gradually your eyes will begin to feel stiff and drawn. But don't move them! Continue to look straight at the center. Finally, when your eyes are so tired that they begin to water, cover the red square with your hand and stare at the white outlined square at the bottom of the page. You will find that you will not see the white square. Instead, for several seconds you will see a green square the exact size of the red one. Now look at the color wheel on page 19 and note that green appears directly opposite red. Next turn to Experiment 1 in Chapter 1 and note that green is made up of yellow and blue, the two remaining primary colors.

This optical illusion, or "afterimage," is caused by the physical reaction of the retina of the eye to the strain of intense color. It demands rest. Grayed colors never produce afterimages because they soothe and satisfy, but intense colors weary the eyes. You looked at red so long that you saw green. The reason you saw green after looking at red is that the retina of your eye was resting itself from red by seeing green, the color produced by the remaining two primaries of the spectrum—blue and yellow. The muscles of your body react in a somewhat similar way. For example, when you bend forward so long that your back aches, you automatically rest yourself by bending back the other way as far as you can. You bend backward because doing so rests your muscles more quickly than merely standing up straight.

The retina reacts in much the same way by refusing to see the white square which, in terms of light, includes red as well as blue and yellow in its content. Seeing white would be the visual equivalent of standing straight because, visually, white is the even blend of all the colors of the spectrum, including red. Instead of seeing white, the eye saw green, which contains the balance of the spectrum primaries, yellow and blue, but no red. Thus, seeing green is seeing the other extreme of the spectrum in which there is no red. Seeing green is therefore similar to bending way back to rest muscles which were overtired from bending forward.

Here, then, is an interesting illustration of the contrasting color scheme and the reason why the combining of opposites in intensities is satisfying to the eye as well as pleasing artistically. Here is a warning against the use of bright colors for large areas. And here also is a warning to be very sure that the colors used in related color schemes are soft enough to soothe the eye so that the presence of the opposite, or unrelated, colors will not be required to make the color scheme comfortable and attractive.

Within the contrasting color scheme classification there are the following types of color schemes: (1) the complementary color scheme, (2) the split complementary color scheme, and (3) the triad color scheme.

The complementary color scheme is a two-color harmony composed of unrelated colors which are directly opposite each other on the color wheel. When mixed together, these two colors form a neutral because they complement or balance each other. (Re-

For directions on how to use the red and white squares in an experiment, see pages 28 and 29.

Neutralized colors   Neutrals

The pink and green of the chintz curtain fabric are the source of a complementary scheme for this room. The background color of the fabric in various values is used for the rug, walls, and day bed. The green of the design in the fabric furnishes the accent.

view Experiment 4 in Chapter 1.) Together they represent all the primaries of the spectrum, or color wheel.

An example of this scheme in its intense form is the red-green experiment you have just completed. The red, a primary with which you began, was complemented or balanced when your eye automatically furnished the secondary color green, which is made up of blue and yellow—the two remaining primaries that complete the color wheel. If you had started with a secondary color, such as orange, made up of yellow and red, the complementary, opposite, or completing color would be blue. If you had started with the primary color yellow, the complementary, opposite, or completing color would be the secondary color violet, made up of the remaining primaries of the spectrum—blue and red.

In applying complementary color schemes to rooms, you will of course individualize and vary your interpretation of the color scheme. For instance, you may use a yellow-green with a red-violet, a yellow-orange with a blue-violet, or a blue-green with a red-orange. All three of these color combinations preserve the same relationship on the color wheel as did the original red and green scheme. They will, however, have more individuality because they are less frequently seen. (Turn to Chart 2 in this chapter and Charts 10 and 11 in Chapter 5 for examples of other specific complementary color schemes for rooms.)

The split complementary color scheme is a three-color form of the contrasting color scheme. It is formed by choosing a dominant color and combining it with the closest color on each side of its complement. In other words, the complement is split so that the scheme becomes a three-color scheme instead of a two-color scheme. This type of scheme, however, should not be tried until one has had considerable experience with color because it is a difficult scheme to harmonize. To test your academic knowledge of this type of color scheme, find a split complementary color scheme on the color wheel on page 19.

The triad color scheme is the third form of contrasting color scheme. To form a triad, begin with just one color, as in the other schemes. If that color is a primary, such as blue, it is combined with the two remaining primaries—yellow and red—to form a triad, or three-color scheme. If the color selected is a secondary color, such as green, it is combined with the two remaining secondaries—orange and violet. Of these three colors, one must be chosen as the dominant and must be used in varying values and intensities over 60 percent of the surface of the room. A second of the three colors may be chosen as the accent and should be used in its intense form in the small-area objects in the room. The third color should be used in a lesser intensity as a secondary accent.

To help you visualize this scheme in nature, try to recall what the country looks like in August—a soft blue sky overhead, a golden wheat field in the foreground, and a red barn in the distance as a note of accent. This scene is a perfect example of a triad color scheme of red, yellow, and blue. In using a triad color scheme for a room, which of the three colors you choose for the dominant depends on two considerations: The first is a matter of your personal preference; the second depends on whether you want a warm or a cool room. If you select one of the warm colors for the dominant, blue becomes the natural accent, and the second warm color, in more grayed form, becomes a secondary accent. If you select the cool color as the dominant, you must then choose one of the warm colors for the accent and use the remaining color in a grayed form for the secondary accent.

Another example of the triad color scheme in nature can be seen on many a summer evening. The green of foliage and grass, the violet haze of distant hills or buildings, and a skyline ablaze with the orange of the setting sun form a triad color scheme of green, violet, and orange. If this color scheme were used in a room, either green or violet might be selected as a dominant, depending upon circumstances or preference. The color not used as a dominant becomes the secondary accent, and the brilliant orange is of course a natural choice for the main accent.

In each illustration you will notice that the two colors which you see in quantity are soft and mellow, and only the accent is strong and bright. This relationship is very important. It is this dominance of soft, muted color that saves this type of scheme from being garish and crude. (Turn to Chart 2 in this chapter and Chart 11 in Chapter 5 for specific applications of the triad color scheme.)

Chart 2: Sample Color Schemes

RELATED COLOR SCHEMES

Monochromatic (One-color) Harmonies

GREEN DOMINANT: Green in all shades, tints, and low intensities, with intense green as an accent and combined with brown, beige, and cream for relief.

GRAY DOMINANT: Gray in light, middle, and dark values, accented by one intense color, such as red-orange.

Analogous (Adjacent) Color Harmonies

BLUE DOMINANT: Blue, blue-green, green-blue, and green in different values and low intensities, with intense green as accent.

GREEN DOMINANT: Green, yellow-green, green-yellow, and a grayed yellow in different values and low intensities, with intense yellow as accent.

CONTRASTING COLOR SCHEMES

Complementary

BLUE DOMINANT: Blue in all shades, tints, and low intensities, with intense orange as accent.

VIOLET DOMINANT: Violet in all shades, tints, and low intensities, with intense yellow as accent.

Triad

GREEN DOMINANT: Green in all shades, tints, and low intensities, with violet in several shades, tints, and middle intensities as secondary accent, and with orange in strong intensity as primary accent.

RED DOMINANT: Red in all shades, tints, and middle intensities, with blue in all shades, tints, and middle intensities as secondary accent, and yellow in strong intensity as primary accent.

A favorite picture was used as the source of the red, yellow, and blue triad color scheme for this room. Since no other pattern is used in fabrics or walls, the picture also becomes the climax of the scheme.

Colors are affected by their surrounding colors.

Up to this point, for clarity, we have talked about colors as if each were in an airtight compartment, completely separated from every other color. Now we are ready to consider the effect of colors on each other.

Colors, like people, do not stand alone. You doubtless have noticed that people act quite differently in different situations and with different people. Colors, like people, change in different situations. These changes fall into three classifications—change of hue, change of value, and change of intensity.

Change of hue is the most surprising change that color makes when associated with other colors. Have you ever had the experience of having someone say, "That is a keen blue sweater you have on!" when you had chosen it because it was green? You may have thought the one who said it was color-blind, but if you had glanced around, you might have found that your sweater did look blue because you were standing beside another girl who was wearing an intense green sweater. An intense green will force a soft blue-green to take on a more bluish cast.

Soft colors, or those of low intensity, are more easily influenced by other colors; but even bright colors, or those of high intensity, are affected by the colors with which they are combined. Experiment with pieces of colored paper or fabric to see the change that takes place in one color when placed beside another.

Most colors change considerably under artificial light, whether it is incandescent or fluorescent lighting. For this reason, be sure to try colors for rooms in artificial light as well as daylight before deciding on them. Only in this way can you be sure that they will be attractive at all times.

Change of value is another change that may be produced by combining one color with another. This effect of one value on another can be seen in people constantly. For instance, a girl who looks quite sun-tanned as she stands next to a friend who is a fair-skinned blonde will look almost delicately fair when she stands next to a deeply tanned lifeguard. In the same way, a color that is quite dark can be made to look several degrees lighter if it is placed beside black. A color that is quite light can be made to look darker if it is placed beside an even lighter tint.

When you are selecting the value of each color for a room scheme, be sure to try it in the exact place where it is to be used. It will be strongly affected by the values of the colors surrounding it.

Change of intensity is a startling change that occurs when color is used in quantity. Here again, colors are like people. Girls and boys who are quiet in adult groups may become excited when they are in a crowd of others their own age. They laugh louder and talk louder. They seem to stimulate each other. Colors used over large areas, especially on the walls of a room which reflect back and forth on each other, increase in intensity in the same way. It is necessary to keep this fact in mind in selecting color for any large area or object. If you select a color that is lighter in value and lower in intensity than you really want, it will increase to the value and intensity you want when it is used in quantity.

Thus, in dealing with color, you must keep in mind that color, like people, changes in appearance under different circumstances. Only in this way can you save yourself costly mistakes.

Colored surfaces are both plain and patterned.

Tonight as you go home, look at the colors around you with an analytical eye. You will find that the colors you see divide into stimulating patterned surfaces and quieting plain ones. If you live in the country, you will probably see large, wide areas of plain color in sky, fields, or rolling hills. These areas of plain color are one of the reasons why people can relax in the country. If you live in the city, you will be constantly seeing patterns of many different kinds. The streets are lined with the patterns formed by houses, signs, people, and traffic. For this reason, life in the city is stimulating but tiring.

Plain surfaces in the very same color will differ from each other in appearance according to the texture or character of the surface. For instance, the yellow of a polished stone will look very different from the same yellow of sand or of a field of ripening wheat. Because the surface texture of the stone is smooth, it reflects light, whereas the other surfaces are rough and absorb light. In man-

Girls may use color schemes for their bedrooms that complement their own coloring. This red-haired girl selected a green monochromatic scheme. The green, in various values and intensities, flatters her hair and complexion, and the neutral of the blond wood repeats the golden highlights of her hair.

For this boy's room a monochromatic scheme has been used. The neutral (brown) has been established as the dominant and the red-orange is used for the accent. The window is framed by a wooden cornice covered with a patterned fabric.

made products the same differences exist between objects that seem to be the same color. Colored fabrics with a smooth surface, like taffeta and sateen, reflect light, which makes their colors appear brighter. Colored fabrics with nubby, rough-textured surfaces have tiny shadows, which make their colors appear duller. Even wallpapers have both smooth and rough surfaces. In all cases, the smooth surfaces appear lighter than the rough surfaces, even though the color values used for both are identical.

Patterned surfaces in color take one of three forms: realistic, conventionalized, or abstract. (See illustrations on opposite page.)

1) Realistic, or naturalistic, pattern is the most familiar form of pattern. It is the picture type of pattern made up of representations of recognizable objects copied from the world around us. A house, a barn, trees, animals, or people all form patterns against the landscape. A representation of any of these could be used as a decoration, either singly or in a repetitive design. Used singly, as a picture, one of these could decorate a wall or an object, such as a box or a book jacket. The same picture, repeated, would form a realistic pattern that could be used for a drapery fabric or wallpaper.

2) Conventionalized pattern is a stylized pattern originally inspired by natural or real forms. In such a pattern realism has been sacrificed for more effective arrangement and decoration. Many people think they see conventionalized patterns in the world of nature. In the shapes of clouds, of mountains, and of rocks, they see animals, faces, and air castles. In the art world, artists create conventionalized patterns by eliminating or varying details of realistic objects so they will fit the space to be decorated or so they will work into a repetitive design more effectively. Conventionalized designs can be used upside down or right side up equally well because they have ceased to be a realistic representation.

3) Abstract patterns include all nonobjective or nonrepresentational designs. There is a wide difference of opinion as to the different types of design that fall into this classification, but the following two are generally considered basic.

a. The geometric pattern, which is an exact type of pattern, is the best known. In nature this pattern is found in such forms as

Kinds of Design

COURTESY *The New York Times*

REALISTIC

COURTESY W. H. S. LLOYD CO., INC.

CONVENTIONALIZED

COURTESY *Interiors*

ABSTRACT (GEOMETRIC)

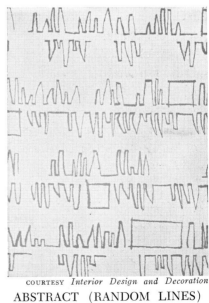

COURTESY *Interior Design and Decoration*

ABSTRACT (RANDOM LINES)

For detailed descriptions of the kinds of design, see page 40.

snow crystals and rock crystals, on the shells of turtles, and on the skins of reptiles. In man-made products we find this type of design in registers, radiator meshes, tile patterns, and patchwork quilts. Plaids, stripes, checks, circular and diamond shapes also fall into this category.

b. Random lines and free forms, which have no definite shape, form a second type of abstract pattern. In the world of nature this type of pattern is found in cloud formations, the markings on the zebra, the spotted cow, or the mottled cat. This type of pattern is becoming very popular in modern design and is being used for fabrics, wallpapers, and carpeting.

Pattern use in nature suggests standards for pattern use in rooms.

In deciding how much pattern to use in a room and how it can be used in the most effective way, we must recognize another precedent that has been established by nature—the sparing use of pattern. For example, the blue of the water is only occasionally broken by whitecaps, but it frequently has an interesting surface effect produced by ripples and small waves. The sand of the desert stretches out as far as the eye can see almost unpatterned, except by an occasional oasis, but it also has a rough-textured effect blown into its surface by the wind. The blue sky is filled only occasionally with clouds. Most large animals, such as the elephant, the seal, and the bear, are unpatterned. Imagine the world if all this were reversed—if the water were covered with whitecaps, if the sky were constantly cloud-filled, if the animals were all patterned like zebras!

Actually, it is the large areas of plain color in the outdoors which give us a feeling of rest and relaxation. How much more do we need these large plain surfaces in the infinitely smaller spaces of our own rooms to which we retreat for rest and refuge.

Even large rooms look small if the walls are covered with strong patterns, just as a room of similar size seems crowded when active children are shouting and jumping around in it. Patterns composed of strong colors demand our attention like shouting children. They will not allow us to forget them for one moment. Because of this fact, in times of strenuous living, such as we have

The patterned surfaces and the clutter of accessories in the room above create an old-fashioned "busy" atmosphere as compared with the simplicity of plain surfaces and a few well-chosen accessories in the room below.

today, there is a very definite trend toward the decorating of our rooms in plain color—often enhanced by the rise of interestingly textured surfaces. We seem to be copying the quiet of nature in our homes rather than following the more hectic man-made city world. Realistic patterns, especially, are being used less and less.

Homes furnished in modern style almost never incorporate realistic patterns in the decorating scheme; and even homes furnished in traditional style use it sparingly. It is true, however, that realistic scenic murals are becoming popular because they seem to increase the size of a room by apparently destroying the flat wall they decorate and extending the limits of the room indefinitely.

Pattern of any kind is not necessary to room decoration. Many beautiful rooms use plain or textured surfaces entirely. However, most people like to use some pattern, and so a safe plan to follow in order to avoid its overuse is to keep patterned surfaces to 30 percent or less of the total room surface. If the room is very small, even a smaller proportion of patterned area is advisable.

If a patterned rug is used, a large share of the pattern allowance for the whole room has been used. If a room has a patterned wallpaper on all four walls from floor to ceiling, more than all of the pattern allowance has been used, and it will be necessary to use a plain rug and plain fabrics for draperies, upholstery, and bedspread.

**Patterned surfaces should be contrasted
with plain surfaces for effectiveness.**

Any pattern will show off best if it is contrasted with, or set off from, other patterns in the room by plain surfaces. In addition, if two or more patterns are used in one room, it is best to use different types of pattern.

Separating patterned areas with plain areas is a plan that is safe to follow because it isolates each pattern from every other pattern. A picture looks best on a plain wall. If it is matted widely with a plain mat, however, it can be used on a patterned wall because the mat isolates it from the pattern of the wall. A patterned drapery looks best against a plain wall. A chair covered in a patterned upholstery looks best when standing on a plain carpet. These are obvious situations.

Chart 3: The Use of Pattern in a Room

KEY: P, plain; R, realistic; G, geometric, abstract, or conventionalized; and S, stripe.

Room*	Floor covering	Walls	Ceiling	Draperies	Upholstery	Wall decoration
1	Realistic	P	P	P, S, or G	P, S, or G	Mirrors Pictures
2	Plain	P	S	P, R, or matching S	P or R	Pictures Mirrors
	Plain	P	P	P, S, R, or G	P, S, R, or G	Pictures Mirrors
	Plain	G	P	P	S, P, R	Matted pictures Mirrors
	Plain	S	P	P	P, G, or R	Mirrors Matted pictures
	Plain	R	P	P	P or S	Mirrors
	Plain	P	R	P	P, S, or G	Mirrors Pictures
3	Geometric	P	P	P, R, or S	R, P, or S	Pictures Mirrors

* Because there is a plain rug in Room 2, it may be decorated in six different ways. Rooms 1 and 3, with patterned rugs, are more limited as to decorating possibilities.

Some of the less obvious situations where this rule should be applied are as follows: Plain paper should be used in a hall if patterned wallpaper is used in several of the rooms opening from it. Plain draperies should be used when the window looks out on a beautiful scene. Reserve your elaborate frames for mirrors and your strongly patterned draperies for less important views. Stand your delicately patterned objects of art on a plain table top, a plain leather mat, or a teakwood stand. Figured mats detract from their beauty. Plain linen is best with patterned china; plain lamp shades are best with patterned lamp bases; and plain pillows should be used on patterned sofas, unless they are made in the same material as the upholstery fabric.

Combining patterns of different types in the same room is another plan of good pattern usage. One realistic, one conventionalized, and one abstract pattern can be used in the same room, provided they are separated from each other by plain areas. Modern free form pattern is an exception to this rule. It does not combine well with realistic pattern because it is so very distinctive. However, all other types of patterns may be combined, but it is unwise to combine two patterns of the same classification in the same room. For instance, two realistic patterns used in the same room of average size will detract from each other in coloring, drawing, and scale of design. If the room is large, it is possible to use two designs of the same type, provided they are widely separated.

However, the trend in all good decorating is toward simplicity and fewer, if any, patterns. As a result, it is possible to show off beautiful pictures and objects of art of personal importance to far greater advantage than it was in the days when rugs, wallpapers, and fabrics were almost all patterned.

CHECKING YOUR KNOWLEDGE . . .

1. What three standards of color usage in home furnishings have been adapted from the use of color in the world of nature?
2. Where can we find help in creating color schemes for our rooms?
3. What are the two related color schemes?
4. Plan two different analogous color schemes in which blue is the dominant color.

COURTESY MARSHALL FIELD & CO.

Pattern is most effective in a room when it is used sparingly and when it is contrasted with plain areas.

5. What are the three contrasting color schemes?

6. Why do you see an afterimage when you look at an intense color a long time?

7. What color is the complement of (a) red, (b) yellow, and (c) blue?

8. Name two colors that could be combined with green to form a triad color scheme.

9. In what three ways do colors change because of their effect on each other?

10. In what ways must we guard against having these changes upset the use of color in a room?

11. What are the different types of pattern?

12. Is it necessary to use pattern in a room? How much can be used?

USING YOUR KNOWLEDGE . . .

1. Each day for a week look for a beautiful color combination and jot down its colors. Then locate it on the color wheel and decide which of the various color schemes it represents.

2. Visit an art gallery or look through the files of your library for reproductions of famous paintings, and analyze the color schemes used in two or three of them.

3. Describe two rooms you have seen in pictures or in reality that especially appealed to you. What type of color scheme was used?

4. Discuss in class the possibility of decorating the homemaking center in your school according to a color scheme selected from nature. List all the room areas and furnishings under the headings "Large-area Colors" and "Small-area Colors." Bring swatches of material to class to show colors you would like to use for each.

5. Select a pattern of china which appeals to you, and plan a dining room around it in a contrasting color scheme.

6. Select one room in your home for a pattern analysis. In the light of what you have learned, plan the minimum changes necessary to separate all patterns from one another.

CHAPTER 3: Color in Your
. Own Room

So far we have considered color as we see it in the world around us and have suggested the principles that underlie its application in decorating and furnishing a home. In this chapter we want to help you plan a color scheme that can be carried out in your own room.

Because it is your own room, we are going to suggest decorating it according to your own coloring, so you will have a flattering background. Also, because most girls have small bedrooms, we will suggest the use of a very closely knit color scheme—the monochromatic scheme—which, because of its simplicity, makes a room seem larger. We will explain how to use this type of scheme most effectively, and we will also suggest how to apply it with the least expense.

Girls who have a medium-sized or large room may want to use an analogous color scheme. So, some suggestions on how to use this scheme in a bedroom are also given.

Of course the greatest single expense in any decorating job is the labor. For that reason, more and more people are learning to do their own painting and papering. The time is past when a lack of money to hire professional help is considered a valid excuse for not redecorating. We now do our own decorating, just as we wash windows or cut grass when we lack money to hire someone to do it for us.

Actually, redecorating a room can be a fascinating project that will interest every member of the family if you present it well. So, after you have studied your room and made your plans, tell the family about them some night at dinner. If you make them sound attractive, you may have several offers of help. Stripping off old paper, painting with a wide brush, or cutting out and pasting on wallpaper motifs are jobs that your sister and brother, your father and mother can all enjoy. When these background projects are completed, the remodeling of furniture and the making of rugs, slip- covers, and bedspreads are doubly interesting.

**Bedroom color schemes may be selected
to suit your complexion.**

Because bedrooms are such personal rooms, it is possible to choose colors that reflect your personality. Here is one room where you can use the colors that make the best background for your complexion and coloring.

Blondes, with their light skin and fair hair, can use any soft, grayed, dark color or any light, clear color, with the exception of yellow. Yellow is too close in hue to the hair color of a blonde to make a good background for her. But dark colors act as a foil to set off a blonde's light coloring; and light, clear colors heighten her fragile quality.

Plain, unpatterned surfaces are the most effective backgrounds for blondes. Patterned surfaces with strong contrasting colors make a blonde's skin, hair, brows, and lashes fuse into one light color and value, utterly lacking in accent. In order to prove this, drape pieces of fabrics in plain colors and some in patterned colors around a blonde in your class. You will see at once that plain, soft, very light or dark colors add importance and sparkle to her coloring, whereas patterns in strong, contrasting colors make her look dull and lifeless.

Brunettes, with their dark hair, eyebrows, and lashes, can use any plain colors, as well as patterns in strong color contrasts. The Irish type of brunette, with very light, clear skin tones, can use the clear, more intense colors—especially red-violet and blue-green

—as well as colors in light or dark values. Brunettes with olive skin would be wiser to use more grayed colors, so that their olive skin will not be made to look sallow by contrast.

Plaids and checks in strong colors were made for brunettes. A strong red or a strong green sets off their dark hair to perfection.

The experiment you tried with fabrics draped on blondes should be repeated with some of the brunettes in the class. You will see that the light, soft colors that did so much for the blondes will make the brunettes look washed-out and faded, whereas strong colors are a vibrant complement to their natural coloring.

Red-haired girls can use any colors except the bluish reds. All natural red hair, even if it is dark, has a great deal of yellow and red in it, which makes it a natural enemy of the bluish reds. Such colors as fuchsia or cerise, for instance, bring out the carroty color in red hair. Every other color—especially blue-green, brown, and green—enhances red hair and shows off its beauty.

The lighter the red hair is in value, the closer the complexion tones approach that of the blonde and the more nearly the red-haired girl should follow the rules of color and pattern that apply to blondes.

Medium-brown-haired girls can use any colors, provided they are softened or grayed. The girls who fall into this large group of in-betweens—the girls who are neither blonde nor brunette—are especially fortunate. For them, there are no limitations in the selection of the hue. The whole world of color is open wide. The only thing they must watch is to use softened or grayed colors in direct ratio to the degree of softness of their own coloring. Thus, grayed, muted colors will set off the soft, muted coloring of skin and hair, whereas strong colors will overpower it.

Color schemes must be interpreted and adapted for interior decorating use.

Once a color scheme is selected, the next step is to interpret it and adapt it for use in decorating. Up to this point we have spoken of schemes simply as a combination of colors that look well together.

The 60 percent dominant in this room is achieved by using the same color in different values for the rug, three dark walls, two picture mats, the slipcover on the chair, two pillows, the lamps, and as an accent in the fabric for the bedspread and drapery.

There has been no indication of how they can be used in a room. First, we must decide which of the colors is to be the dominant and which the accent or accents. Then the colors must be grayed or intensified according to their use in the scheme.

Choosing the dominant color is the first step in applying a color scheme to a room. (See page 20.) In your own bedroom you are free to select your favorite color for the dominant, because such considerations as practicality and the preferences of the rest of the family are not important here. If you want a white bedroom or a blue one and are willing to do the work to keep it white or blue, the privilege is yours. The fact that your brother or your father may consider the dominant you select a "sissy" color proves rather than disproves the correctness of your choice of it for your own room— a girl's room.

After the dominant is selected, it must be grayed for use on the large areas of the room. Colors that look well in small quantities usually are far too intense for use as the dominant unless they have been considerably softened.

Selecting the accent is the second step in interpreting and adapting a color scheme for use in a room. If a monochromatic scheme is being used, the most intense form of the dominant hue automatically becomes the accent. If a two-color scheme, such as a complementary scheme, is being used, the accent is also dictated because it is the only remaining color after the dominant has been chosen. In schemes of more than two colors, such as the triad or analogous, the accent can be selected according to preference. Any remaining colors become secondary accents. The primary accent is used in full intensity, whereas the secondary accents are used in a slightly more grayed form. They should, however, be more intense than the dominant, which must be grayed a great deal.

The distribution of colors in a room must follow decorating principles.

Once you have chosen the dominant color which is to be the basis of the color scheme, you must decide where and how you will use it to achieve dominance. You will remember that if 60 percent of the total room surface—floor, walls, ceiling, upholstery, draperies, or spreads—is in any one color, even though in different tints and shades, the dominance of the color is assured. The problem is, therefore, to decide just how and where to obtain that coverage.

The first step in solving that problem is to take an inventory of the surfaces. Which ones can be most inexpensively changed? Which ones can be most easily changed?

Floors are one place where the dominant color can be used without too great expense if ingenuity is applied. If the floor is of wood that is in bad condition or covered with linoleum that is worn, it might be painted with a shade of the dominant color and stenciled or spattered with a lighter value (tint) of the same color; or, if you wish to add space to the room, you may paint the floor in a light value of the dominant color and decorate it with a darker shade.

If the floor is in such good condition that it should not be painted, the dominant color must be established by the rugs. Braided or hooked rugs, made of materials from the scrap bag and dyed a deep shade of the dominant color, are one possibility. (See page 253 in Chapter 12.) The type of design used for the rug is determined by the tone of the room. If the room is quaint and dainty, a hooked rug with a floral design is the best selection. If the room is modern in its simplicity, either a braided or a hooked rug can be used, but it must be plain or be decorated only with bandings or a simple geometric design.

Walls are a second large area that should be carefully considered in the plan to establish the dominant color in the room. If the paint or paper on the wall is still in good condition, its color should be accepted as the dominant color of the scheme. If walls are not in good condition or are to be redone anyway, there are two ways of treating them.

1) When walls are already painted in a neutral or a grayed color, interest can be added by applying cut-out wallpaper motifs of the dominant color in various values. These motifs can be added in several ways. The most common way is to scatter them over one or two important walls. If the room is large enough, the motifs can be used on all four walls. A more unusual method would be to use motifs on a dado that has been created by pasting a wallpaper band-

Chart 4: Wallpaper Requirements According to Room Measurements *

Floor size of room	Number of rolls required for walls of rooms			Number of rolls for ceiling
	with 8-foot ceiling	with 9-foot ceiling	with 10-foot ceiling	
8 × 10	9	10	11	3
10 × 10	10	11	13	4
10 × 12	11	12	14	4
10 × 14	12	14	15	5
12 × 12	12	14	15	5
12 × 14	13	15	16	6
12 × 16	14	16	17	7
12 × 18	15	17	18	8
12 × 20	16	18	20	8
14 × 14	14	16	17	6
14 × 16	15	17	19	7
14 × 18	16	18	20	8
14 × 20	17	19	21	9
14 × 22	18	20	22	10

* For every three ordinary-sized doors or windows, deduct two single rolls from the number of rolls required for the walls of the room.

Chart 5: Paint Quantities

Coating material	Character of surface	Surface covered by 1 gallon (in square feet)		
		One coat	Two coats	Three coats
Oil paint (gloss)	Smooth wood or wallboard	600	325	225
	Plaster	450	250	175
	Smooth cement	350	200	150
Oil paint (flat)	Smooth wood or wallboard	500	275	200
	Plaster	400	225	160
	Smooth cement	300	175	125
Enamel paint	Smooth painted with undercoats	500	250	
Interior finishing varnish	Smooth wood	450	250	175
Shellac	Smooth wood	600	300	
Cold-water paint (5 pounds)	Smooth	300		
Calcimine powder (5 pounds)	Plaster	400		

When walls are painted in a neutral or a grayed color, additional color interest can be supplied by applying wallpaper borders or cut-out wallpaper motifs.

ing or nailing a wooden molding on the walls of the room about 30 inches above the floor. Motifs can also be used to decorate a wall above a plain painted dado.

2) When walls are covered with a dull, colorless paper, it is possible—provided the laws of the community permit—to paper over the original paper or to paint over the paper with water-based or oil paint. Water-based paint is very inexpensive and relatively easy for the amateur to apply. The handicap is that, as a rule, it cannot be washed when soiled. Oil paint, however, which is more expensive and more difficult to apply, can be washed. (See Charts 4 and 5.)

Ceilings are another large area where the dominant color might be used. If a ceiling is over 8 feet high, it can be done in a dark shade for a smart and dramatic effect. If a ceiling is lower than

A bedspread that repeats the color of the rug, the ceiling, and the bed niche will help to establish the dominant color. The use of a plain spread will also help to decrease the apparent size of the bed and allow for the use of a pattern in the draperies and slipcovers.

8 feet, it should not be further lowered by covering it with a dark color. Of course a ceiling cannot be emphasized in this way if it is cut in with gables. It must be a relatively unbroken rectangle. If the walls and floor covering are plain, further interest can be added to the ceiling by the application of cut-out wallpaper motifs.

Bedspreads, which cover a relatively large area in bedrooms, should, as a rule, be in a plain fabric of the dominant color in the room. A figured spread increases the apparent size of the bed and thus decreases the apparent size of the room. It demands attention and dominates the room. It demands that everything else in the room be plain. If, by any chance, you happen to have a really beautiful patchwork, woven, or appliquéd quilt that is worthy of attention, use it and sacrifice pattern elsewhere.

If, on the other hand, the design of your spread is nondescript, the sacrifice of pattern elsewhere in the room is not warranted, and a plain spread would be far better.

If the dominant color is used for the walls, the bedspread can match them in value as well as in hue. If the dark value of the dominant has been used for the floor or rug color, a repetition of that color in the spread will make the bed seem small and inconspicuous. If the room is small, a light bedspread against a dark rug or floor shouts to the world: "Look at me. I'm about the biggest single object in this room. In fact, I practically cover the floor area." On the other hand, the bedspread that matches the rug says: "Don't pay much attention to me. I'm not important. Look at other things—the lamps, the pictures, the draperies. They are important." As a result, the bed is less noticeable and the entire room seems more spacious.

If your bedspread is the wrong color, you might dye it to suit your color scheme. If, for some reason, dyeing it is not feasible, you can buy material in the dominant color and make a bedspread. It may be necessary to hunt in the yard-goods departments or drapery departments before you locate a fabric in the color you wish to use. (See Chapter 11.)

Only if the room is large would it be right to use an intense color for the bedspread, and even then it might be more effective to use the dominant color in a dark value for the dust ruffle.

Colors must balance in a room.

The balancing of colors within a room demands careful thought. In a well-decorated room, colors are repeated on all sides of the room and at all levels so that each part of the room expresses the entire color scheme.

Repetition of the same colors on all sides of a room is necessary if colors are to be balanced in the room. For instance, if a flowered fabric is used for draperies at the windows—all of which are on one wall—the colors in that drapery fabric or the fabric itself should be used in some manner on the opposite side of the room. The fabric could be used for a dust ruffle on the bed, for a slipcover on a chair, for a lamp shade, or for a pillow. In this way a complete color balance is achieved.

If a strong color accent is used for the upholstery of one chair

Repetition of color on different sides of a room and at different heights can be achieved by using the same fabric for draperies, upholstery, and dust ruffles.

(COURTESY *Better Homes and Gardens*)

next to the bed, that same color must be repeated on the opposite side of the room for another seat cover, a lamp base, or a small object of art.

Repetition of the same colors at different levels in a room is also important if there is to be a balancing of colors in the room. The color which appears in the rug should be used at other levels of the room. It must be repeated at chair-seat height and then carried higher—for example, in brush fringe on the edge of the curtains, in the pictures, or on the ceiling. This method of distributing colors applies to all colors—dominant and accent alike—so that each color leads the eye around different levels of the entire room.

**A monochromatic color scheme is the
simplest scheme to apply.**

The monochromatic color scheme is, as you remember, the simplest type of color scheme and, therefore, the easiest to apply. It is especially effective in small rooms that need closely unified color to lend a feeling of space. There are, as was pointed out in Chapter 2, two possible interpretations of this type of scheme. The first, or usual one, is the use of one color in various tints and shades to form the dominant color, the use of the same color in intense form as the accent, and the use of a neutral for relief. The second interpretation is the use of a neutral as the dominant and the use of one color in its full intensity as the accent.

The use of one color for both dominant and accent produces a room that has a great deal of color unity. The first step is to establish the dominant by using the one color in grayed form for some of the large areas of the room. If you want to develop a dramatic scheme and the room has plenty of light and size, it might be interesting to use a fairly dark, yet soft, shade of the color on walls and ceiling and repeat it in a dust ruffle on the bed. By using the neutral—say, off-white—for the woodwork, throw rugs, curtains, and bedspread, lamp shades, and picture mattings, you will provide relief and lightness.

The accent in such a room could be the same color in its intense form used for the small areas, such as lamp bases, brush

Chart 6: Monochromatic Color Schemes for a Small Bedroom

A BLUE ROOM

Use a light, cool blue as the dominant color to produce the greatest possible effect of size. Accent with cool, neutral silver.

WALLS, CEILING, AND WOODWORK: Tint of soft, grayed light blue. Remove all picture moldings or paneling that would break the flat surface or attract attention. Use flat paint. Wax woodwork for protection.

FLOOR: Rag, braided, or hooked rug, of same blue as walls, with no pattern.

DRAPERIES, BEDSPREAD, AND UPHOLSTERY: Same color as walls in a glossy plain fabric, such as percale or chintz. that can be quilted to lend decorative interest.

ACCESSORIES: Use large mirror and pin-up wall lights or strip lights to extend apparent limits of room. Use silver picture frames and light fixtures for accent. Very few pictures should be used, because they accentuate walls and make a room seem smaller.

A GREEN ROOM

Use various tints and shades of green as the dominant color, intense green as accent, and white, gray, and black as neutral for relief.

WALLS AND WOODWORK: Light, soft green.

CEILING: Dark, soft green.

FLOOR: Rug or painted floor in same color as ceiling.

DRAPERIES: White percale trimmed with dark, light, and brilliant green fringe, set side by side.

BEDSPREAD: Dark green dust ruffle with white quilted top, monogrammed in light, dark, and brilliant green.

CHAIR: Upholstered in green, white, gray, and black cretonne, with white pillow, edged with dark green brush fringe.

ACCESSORIES: Brilliant green lamp base; marbleized paper (black, white, and silver) shade. Black-and-white photographs of family and friends. Mirror with black-and-silver frame.

fringe on the curtains or pillows, and pictures. (For less dramatic applications of the monochromatic color scheme, see Chart 6 on the opposite page and Chart 10 on pages 84 and 85.)

The use of a neutral for the dominant and one color in its full intensity as the accent produces a monochromatic scheme that is very quiet and smart. If a neutral, such as beige, cream, or tan, is chosen as the dominant, the walls, carpets, ceiling, and bedspread can be done in varying values of it. Using dark brown lacquer for the furniture would be a good way to unify the furniture and at the same time to add beauty to the room. Then, for the accent, use an intense color, such as flame (red-orange), on one upholstered chair and repeat it in the base of a lamp, for book ends, as the cording on a lamp shade, or as edging on a pillow.

An analogous color scheme allows variety in hues.

If your room is large, you may want greater variety of color than is possible with a monochromatic scheme. An analogous color scheme allows this and yet retains much of the unifying effect of a monochromatic scheme because it includes only colors that are closely placed on the color wheel and therefore closely related. For example, if green is the dominant color, you may form an analogous color scheme by using blue-green and blue or yellow-green and yellow. Your choice will depend on whether you prefer a cool scheme or a warm one.

Because analogous schemes have more variety of hue than monochromatic schemes, they have greater possibility of color interest. But because of this greater variety, more care must be taken in selecting and combining the colors. (For detailed analogous color schemes, turn to Chart 7 in this chapter and Charts 8 and 9 in Chapter 4.)

Look over your room at home this evening. It may be that some of the ideas in this chapter can be applied immediately to improve it. Do not wait until you have lost your enthusiasm. The sooner you begin using your knowledge, the better. Even small changes may make surprisingly large improvements.

Chart 7: Analogous Color Schemes for a Bedroom

A YELLOW-GREEN, GREEN, BLUE-GREEN, AND BLUE HARMONY

Use green as the dominant with yellow-green as the accent.

WALLS AND WOODWORK: A light tint of soft, grayed blue.

DRAPERIES, CEILING, AND RUG: Middle value of soft, grayed green.

UPHOLSTERED CHAIR OR CHAISE LONGUE AND CORNICE AROUND WINDOWS: Cretonne in floral design of blues, greens, and off-white with green background.

BEDSPREAD: Dust ruffle in middle value of green with quilted top in light tint of blue.

ACCESSORIES: Lamp with yellow-green base and off-white shade. Small pillow on bed, wastebasket, and small objects of art in yellow-green.

A RED, RED-VIOLET, VIOLET, AND BLUE-VIOLET HARMONY

Use dusty rose (light grayed red) as the dominant with blue-violet as the accent.

WALLS: Dusty rose in light tint.

CEILING, WOODWORK, AND DRAPERIES: Ivory, with edging of plum (red-violet) fringe on draperies.

RUG: Hooked or braided in middle value of rose.

BEDSPREAD: Plum dust ruffle with ivory top and initials in dusty rose, plum, and violet.

CHAISE LONGUE, CORNICE, AND PILLOW ON BED: Chintz or cretonne in floral design of dusty rose, plum, and violet with cream background.

DESK CHAIR AND ACCESSORIES: Seat of chair, book ends, wastebasket, lamp base—all in blue-violet.

CHECKING YOUR KNOWLEDGE . . .

On a piece of paper write the numbers from 1 to 6. After each number write the word or words from those in parentheses that make a correct statement.

1. Brunettes (should) (should not) use strong, contrasting colors in their clothes or rooms because they (have) (have not) strong contrasts in their skin and hair.
2. Bluish reds in any intensity (are) (are not) flattering to a red-haired girl.
3. A brunette (can) (cannot) use vivid colors in clothes and room schemes because they (overpower) (enhance) her own coloring.
4. A brown-haired girl (must) (must not) use grayed color to enhance her soft coloring.
5. A room (should) (should not) have 60 percent of its color area in one hue.
6. A monochromatic scheme (needs) (does not need) a neutral for relief.

USING YOUR KNOWLEDGE . . .

1. A good class project would be to buy one-yard pieces of plain-colored cotton material in at least two values of each of the six spectrum colors. Make them into large collars by cutting a center hole large enough for the head to pass through. Try these on each girl and note the effect of each on complexion and hair colors. Using this knowledge, plan two color schemes for two girls in the class.
2. Plan several inexpensive methods by which you might make your favorite color the dominant color in your room.
3. Using your favorite color, plan a monochromatic color scheme. Get samples of inexpensive materials and wallpapers that could be used to carry it out. Estimate the cost of these steps in the redecorating.
4. Make a specific list of all the jobs involved in carrying out the color scheme you planned in Number 3. Decide which ones you can do alone and with which ones you will need help from members of your family.
5. Clip three color photographs which show (*a*) a room decorated in a monochromatic scheme; (*b*) a room decorated in an analogous scheme; and (*c*) a costume which would suggest a monochromatic or an analogous color scheme that could be adapted for a girl's bedroom.

CHAPTER 4: Color in an Apartment

When carefully used, color can completely transform a small apartment. Most single girls, furnishing an apartment of their own, and most young couples, just starting to keep house, are forced by circumstances to accept small, cramped quarters that are below the standards set by the homes of their parents. For them, the effect of a closely knit, or closely related, color scheme becomes tremendously important. By the use of an analogous color scheme, they can not only increase the apparent size of an apartment, but they can change its drab, characterless appearance into a gay, charming one. By the proper use of color, they can establish homes that are distinctive and charming, instead of living in a grim environment just to get by until a better day comes along.

Magazines and newspapers are full of stories of this type of transformation. The Cinderella story of the small orange pumpkin that changed into a glamorous coach is easily matched by the articles about Quonset huts, barracks apartments, remodeled attic apartments, and walk-up flats that have been changed into charming homes by the application of closely correlated colors, plus the energy and ingenuity of the occupants. Go to the library and check back in the *Readers' Guide* for magazine articles about such apartments. Look through the files of newspapers for others. If any of the apartments described are nearby, perhaps you can arrange to inspect one and thus get firsthand information as to how the transformation was accomplished.

In this chapter we will take up the ways in which color can play an important part in increasing or decreasing the apparent size

The use of a monochromatic color scheme with one light value (tint) for walls, woodwork, ceiling, folding doors, and upholstery, set off by darker values (shades) of the same color in linoleum, patterns in curtains, and accents of room, increases the apparent size of this multiple-function room.

of rooms, in blotting out architectural errors, as well as in adding individualized charm. We will discuss the way in which related color schemes can be adapted from different sources and how they can be varied to fit different situations. We will show that color is a practical as well as a decorative medium which can be used effectively, regardless of a limited budget.

Rooms look larger when painted with cool hues, light values, and in related color schemes.

There are three ways that color can be used to make rooms look larger: (1) by the use of cool hues; (2) by the use of light values; and (3) by the use of a closely related color scheme.

The use of cool hues is the easiest way to increase the apparent size of a room. Since cool hues appear to recede, walls painted with them also seem to recede. Consequently, a room in blues and blue-

Chart 8: Analogous Color Scheme for a Small Apartment

A GREEN AND YELLOW HARMONY
Use green as the dominant and yellow as the accent.

Living Room and Dinette
Treat identically to increase the apparent size of both rooms.

WALLS, CEILING, AND WOODWORK: Light grayed green for all three.

CARPET: Plain; in middle value of green.

DRAPERIES: Soft yellow, trimmed with the same green as in the carpet.

DINETTE CHAIR SEATS (one to be used as a desk chair): Yellow leatherette.

HOST AND HOSTESS CHAIRS (to be used in both rooms as needed): Cretonne in yellow, yellow-green, green, and off-white, corded in the same green as in the carpet.

LOUNGE CHAIR: Stripe in different values of green and yellow, and off-white.

STUDIO COUCH WITH BOLSTER PILLOWS: Same green as carpet, with smaller pillows in cretonne used on host and hostess chairs.

ACCESSORIES: Lamps with brass bases and off-white shades. Mirror with gold frame hung over table in dinette. Screen covered in same cretonne as used on host and hostess chairs.

Kitchenette and Bathroom
If the kitchenette is not separated from the dinette by a door, it should be painted the same color as the dinette. If it is separated by a door, it, like the bathroom, may be treated more dramatically.

WALLS: Chalk-white to match plumbing fixtures.

CEILING: Dark green.

SMALL RUGS: Dark green.

TOWELS: White for general use; green for guests.

greens will look larger than one in warm hues, which seem to advance.

The use of light values is a second way to make the walls of a small room seem to recede, thereby giving the effect of added space. When the walls of a room are painted in a tint of blue, blue-green, or blue-violet, or in off-white, the room will look much larger than it really is.

The use of closely related color schemes is a third way to make a room seem larger than it is. A room that is decorated in a monochromatic or analogous color scheme looks considerably larger than the same room done in a contrasting color scheme. To visualize this more clearly, translate it into terms of clothes. A short girl wearing a dark blue skirt, a lighter blue or green sweater, and a dark blue beret will look much taller than her actual height in inches. If she wore a bright red sweater, a many-colored scarf on her head, and the same blue skirt, the variety of colors would make her look even shorter than her actual height.

Thus, if the same colors are used in all the rooms of an apartment, the whole apartment and each of the rooms will look larger. Each room will blend into the next, and there will be no sharp lines of contrast. (For a detailed color scheme of this closely unified type for an apartment, see Chart 8.)

Rooms look larger when background areas are unified in color.

The use of one unifying color for the large background areas in a room or apartment is an effective means of increasing its apparent size. The repetition of one color on floor and walls or on walls and ceiling gives an effect of spaciousness.

The unifying of color for walls and ceiling is especially effective in a room with a ceiling broken by gables or dormers. By painting the walls and the ceiling all one color, the problem of where to stop the wall color and begin the ceiling color is avoided. The uneven line where ceiling and walls meet would, in this way, be completely eliminated. Consequently, the size of the room and its height will appear to be materially increased.

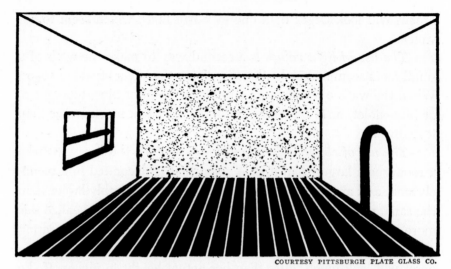

A room will appear much larger when the walls and ceiling are in light colors than the same room (*opposite*) with dark walls and ceiling.

The unifying of color for walls and woodwork is another method of increasing the apparent size of a room. If the walls are papered, the woodwork should be painted the background color of the wallpaper so that there is as little break as possible in the unity of color in the room. If the walls are painted, the same color that is used for the walls should be used for the woodwork.

The unifying of color for walls and draperies is still another possible method of increasing the apparent size of a room. The fact that the color of the draperies matches the color of the wall will make the break between the wall and the windows less noticeable—especially when the draperies are drawn at night. This is important. If the walls are covered with a patterned wallpaper, the draperies should match the background color of the wallpaper so they will not demand attention and thus break the unity of the scheme. Occasionally it is possible to buy drapery fabric and wallpaper in the same pattern so that when the draperies are drawn no break is noticeable between draperies and walls and the window walls of the room are completely unified.

The unifying of color for rug and large pieces of furniture will make the room seem to be larger than it actually is. If the sofa,

Note that even the floor space in this room looks smaller than the one in the room opposite, even though it has been given the same treatment.

studio couch, or large upholstered chairs in the living room are covered with a fabric in a color that matches the rug in hue and value, the room will seem materially larger than it would if these pieces were covered in a fabric of a color contrasting with that of the rug. In a bedroom, if the color of the bedspread matches or blends with that of the rug, the room will look much larger. If the bedspread is in a lighter color than that of the rug, the walls might be done in the same light color, and the darker color of the rug could be used for the dust ruffle on the bed. Unity will be achieved in both cases, but it is well to remember that a bed in a dark color will usually seem smaller and therefore make the room seem larger.

Rooms look larger when background areas are plain.

The apparent size of rooms can be increased by the use of plain rather than patterned surfaces. Patterned surfaces fill space and make a room seem smaller, whereas plain surfaces increase the effect of space.

Plain walls appear to recede, just as a cloudless sky seems to fade into the distance. Therefore, if a feeling of space is desired, the walls should be kept plain. The use of patterned wallpaper

Bold-patterned fabrics make furniture seem to advance and fill a room. Plain fabrics seem to decrease the size of furniture, especially when the walls against which the furniture is placed are plain.

should be avoided. No more than one or two good pictures should be used, and all side brackets, center light fixtures, and moldings should be removed, because these act as patterns and attract attention.

Mirrors on a wall, however, are a help rather than a hindrance in creating a feeling of space, because they present no new pattern and reflect more of the same room.

Plain rugs will increase the apparent size of a floor, just as an expanse of well-kept lawn seems to increase the size of a small yard. Any banding, or border, on a figured rug will decrease the apparent size of the room. Any pattern in rugs or carpeting, even when the carpeting extends from wall to wall, makes the room look smaller. (See drawings on page 245.)

Plain upholstery has the same effect on furniture as plain-colored clothes have on people. Large-patterned fabrics have an advancing quality, and therefore when used in a dress they make a girl seem much larger than she would appear in a dress of plain-colored fabric. Bold-patterned upholstery on furniture makes it seem to advance and fill the room; but plain upholstery, which fades into the background of plain or patterned walls, will seem to decrease the size of the furniture and, therefore, to increase the size of the room.

It is only in a really large room that it is possible to use a dramatically figured material on large furniture. In a small room it would dominate everything and seem to shout, "I am this big, and this poor room is really very small by comparison."

Plain bedspreads will increase the apparent size of a bedroom by decreasing the apparent size of the bed. A double bed, in even a medium-sized room, will seem to fill the room unless it is covered with a plain spread.

**Rooms look smaller when painted in warm,
dark hues or in contrasting colors.**

It is hard to believe that reducing the apparent size of a room would ever be necessary or even desirable. There are times, however, when we do want to draw the walls of a room in around us to achieve an effect of cozy snugness. This, too, can be done by the proper use of color.

The use of warm, dark hues is the easiest way to decrease the apparent size of a room. When you are driving along a country road at night, the broad, far-stretching fields are blotted out, and the lights of the car show, instead, a small tunnel, just large enough for the car to pass through.

Dark walls and low lights in a room produce the same effect. If, in addition to being dark, the color used on the walls is also a warm color, the size of the room will be diminished even more because the warm color will, in itself, seem to advance.

The use of contrasting colors is another method of making a room seem smaller. For example, in reality a bookcase cuts off just 10 inches of floor space, but when it is filled with a variety of brightly colored books it will reduce the apparent size of a room far more than the 10-inch width of the bookcase.

Woodwork that is painted to contrast with the walls in color and value will also cut down the apparent size of the room. Deep maroon walls with chalk-white or cream woodwork will seem to decrease the room size greatly.

Larger apartments permit variation in the application of a color scheme.

In these days when small apartments are as standard as crowded trains, a good-sized apartment is an unusual luxury. But even an apartment with several rooms can be made to look more spacious when one very closely related color scheme is used throughout. The application, however, of that one color scheme can be varied. For example, in a blue and green color scheme, if blue is the dominant and green is the accent in the living room, this can be reversed in the bedroom. Green may be used as the dominant, and blue may be used as the accent. Thus, variety is added without upsetting the unity of color in the apartment.

If blue carpeting is used to help establish the dominant in the living room, it could also be used in the bedroom but as a part of the accent color. Sufficient green would have to be used in walls, ceiling, and bedspreads to establish the 60 percent dominance of

Chart 9: Analogous Color Scheme for a Large Apartment

A BLUE AND GREEN HARMONY

(In a large apartment the dominant and accent colors used in the living room, dinette, and kitchen may be reversed in the bedroom for variety.)

Living Room, Dinette, and Kitchen

Use blue as the dominant with green as the accent.

WALLS: Light grayed blue.

CARPETING AND LOUNGE CHAIR: Middle value of grayed blue.

CEILING, DRAPERIES, LAMP SHADES, PICTURE MATS: Off-white with brush fringe on edge of draperies and lamp shade in same color as carpet.

SOFA AND SCREEN: Cretonne cover in blue, green, gray, and strong green.

OCCASIONAL CHAIRS (TWO): Strong green.

DINETTE CHAIRS: Stripes in strong green, blue, and off-white.

Bedroom

Use green as the dominant with blue as the accent.

WALLS, CEILING, AND WOODWORK: Light grayed green.

CARPETING: Same as in living room (middle value of grayed blue).

DRAPERIES: Same cretonne as used on living-room sofa.

UPHOLSTERED CHAIR: Blue velveteen to match color of carpeting.

BEDSPREAD: Dust ruffle of green; white top.

VENETIAN BLINDS: Off-white with blue tapes.

LAMP: Blue base with shade in same cretonne used for draperies.

Bathroom

Use green as the dominant with blue as the accent.

WALLS AND CEILING: Same as in bedroom (light grayed green).

RUG AND GUEST TOWELS: Middle value of grayed blue to match carpet in bedroom.

BATH TOWELS, CURTAINS, SHOWER CURTAIN: White.

green. The blue of the carpeting would then have to be repeated, in stronger intensity, in a chair, a lamp base, and a few other articles to make it the accent color of the bedroom. (For a more detailed analysis of this type of variation, see Chart 9.)

Color schemes can be adapted from works of art, from fabrics, and from wallpaper.

As a rule, most people start selecting colors for their homes to harmonize with a treasure they have bought or a gift they especially like. In the case of a bride and groom, it may be a picture of a favorite haunt of their dating days. It may be a map of the place they met. It may be a vase, a tray, or a lamp they bought together as a "first" for the home they were establishing. It might be a wedding gift.

A business girl establishing her own apartment may also begin a color scheme with a treasure she wishes to use as the climax of the room. It may be a small rug, a beautiful leather folder, a piece of weaving, or a lamp base which she has picked up while away on a trip. It may be something of beauty which she has bought in memory of some special occasion during a trip. Any of these would be a perfect start for the color scheme of an apartment, and a smart traveler is constantly on the watch for such objects. A decorating goal of this sort will often save a tourist from being "taken in" by the usual motley selection of souvenirs which are nothing but a problem in a home.

Paintings are an excellent source of beautiful color schemes, as well as a charming climax to a decorating scheme. Fortunately, most places that are visited by tourists have at least one collection of reproductions which, when framed, are appropriate for rooms in a home. For those who want to spend more money, good paintings are available. People who are not sure of their own taste can undoubtedly find someone among their friends who has studied art and can check their selections.

The art room of a public library also contains files of reproductions of famous paintings. Magazines frequently publish reproductions and also sell reprints of pictures used to illustrate articles on art. The *Readers' Guide* in the library will be helpful in locating these articles in magazines.

Art institutes and art departments of stores also have pictures which can be studied or purchased for a small amount of money. Sometimes club groups buy a group of original paintings and rent them out to members for a year at a time.

Reproductions and originals frequently are loaned to classes for study. Search your community for some source that will supply you with good art which you can have for studying as a class and from which you can adapt color schemes.

Fabrics, another excellent source of color schemes, have both a decorative use and a practical use. They may climax the scheme as draperies or slipcovers. They can be used to make pillows or to cover a screen.

It is important to realize, however, before the selection of a fabric is made, that a color scheme which is dramatic or strong in color might become tiresome when used over a long period of time. Therefore, a fabric in which more subtle color is used will give greater satisfaction as the basis of a color scheme for a whole apartment.

Wallpaper is another source of a ready-made palette of color. Schemes from this source are especially useful in an apartment with a separate dinette which can be either partially or entirely papered.

If the wallpaper cannot be used for the walls, it might be used as a climax to cover a screen and to show the source of the color scheme.

If the pattern of the wallpaper has no up and down, or line of growth, it can be used on the ceiling of the dinette, provided the ceiling is 8 or more feet high. Wallpaper can also be used behind the glass of French doors or cupboard doors to make them opaque or on a wooden window cornice to add a decorative note to a window which is curtained in a plain casement cloth.

Once a choice of painting, fabric, or wallpaper has been made, its color scheme will act as a palette from which to choose the colors for the room in which it is used. Each color used in the room should be taken from that scheme in order to be sure that it will harmonize and blend with all the other colors. The harmony of the color

COURTESY BIGELOW-SANFORD CARPET CO.

Patterned wallpaper, used as an accent on one wall of a room, may serve as a palette of color for the color scheme of other furnishings in the room.

scheme has already been demonstrated in the painting, fabric, or wallpaper. However, it is well to remember that a color appearing in small areas in the ready-made scheme must be grayed and lightened when used for large areas in the room because color darkens and intensifies in proportion to the area covered.

CHECKING YOUR KNOWLEDGE . . .

On a piece of paper write the numbers from 1 to 4. After each number write the word or words from those in parentheses that make a correct statement.

1. If the color used in a room is (light) (dark) enough, it is possible to make the room look considerably larger than its actual size.

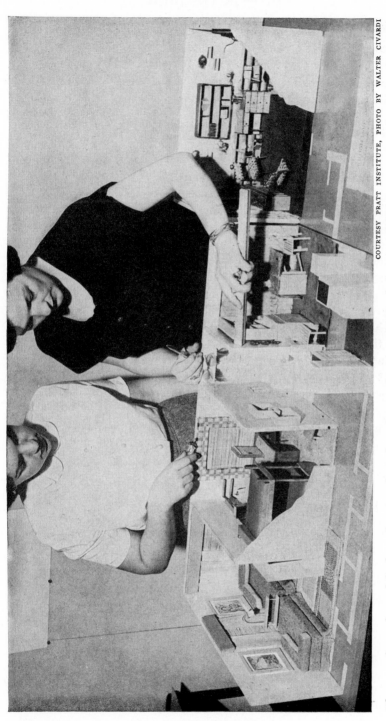

COURTESY PRATT INSTITUTE, PHOTO BY WALTER CIVARDI

The use of a scale model when planning the color scheme of an apartment or house will help you to visualize the importance of color unity between rooms.

2. If a room is small, it is wise to use (much) (very little) pattern.

3. A room will look (larger) (smaller) if the sofa is covered in a color and value that matches either the walls or the carpet.

4. If a room is small, it (is) (is not) wise to use the same color on woodwork and walls.

USING YOUR KNOWLEDGE . . .

1. Find two samples of patterned fabric and two of patterned wallpaper with analogous color schemes which contain your favorite color.

2. Make a shoe-box scale model (see photograph on page 79) of a dinette apartment or the homemaking center in your own school. Paint all the walls and woodwork your favorite color in a soft, middle value. Then show how you can add individuality by creating an accent with (a) the patterned fabric and (b) the patterned wall-paper.

3. Select a lounge in your school, your church, or a public building that has oak woodwork and tan walls. Inspect it as a class and have each member plan how she might improve it by changing the color of the ceiling, walls, woodwork, draperies, and some upholstery, using an analogous color scheme. In making your plans, consider that you have a minimum amount of money to spend for the project.

4. Use the colors in one picture as the basis for a color scheme for an apartment with a living room, a dinette, a kitchenette, and a bath-room. Use the same hues in each room, but vary the dominant in the manner suggested in Chart 9.

CHAPTER 5: Color in a House

In the preceding chapters we considered the application of color in a girl's room and in a small apartment. Now we are ready to consider how color might be applied to a whole house, where a greater number of rooms and larger rooms make a greater variety of colors possible.

It should be remembered, however, that this greater variety of colors is not necessary in a home. Sometimes people prefer the closely knit color schemes, suggested for small rooms and small apartments, regardless of the fact that they have a large home. They feel that the result is more quieting and individual than that produced by the use of greater color variety. So, those who are planning color schemes for a rather large house may use any of the suggestions in Chapters 3 and 4, as well as those in this chapter.

If your home, like most homes, needs some redecorating this season, suggest that your father and mother read this whole color section together. Parents are just as keenly interested and eager for help in planning color schemes for their homes as you are in planning a color scheme for your own room. In addition, since a great deal of money is involved in a redecorating project for a whole house, they are even more concerned about making the correct decisions.

One family, in which there were two high school students, studied this whole project of redecoration together and made a definite plan of procedure. Then, with radio accompaniment and carefully spaced refreshments to make the work more fun, they, as a family, systematically worked their way through their home. They stripped walls, papered, and painted to create a beautiful place which they were proud to show to their friends. After the project was completed, home entertaining became so popular with all the members of the family that nights for possession of the living room had to be spoken for well in advance.

At first thought, a redecorating project for a whole house is frightening in its immensity. The size of the job, however, does not seem quite so appalling once the color schemes are chosen. The selection of a unifying color is an important first step in that direction.

A color thread is a practical aid in decorating a home.

A color thread is any one color which acts as a unifying note by being used—either as an accent or as a dominant—in most of the rooms of the house. Without a color thread the colors of a house are like an unrelated group of fabrics scattered on a counter for a remnant sale. The use of a color thread in the decorating of a house has great practical as well as artistic value.

Interchangeability of furniture and furnishings is one practical advantage of establishing a color thread in a home. Any article that is done in the color selected as a color thread will look well when used anywhere in the house. For instance, suppose that green has been chosen as the color thread. If the dining-room chairs are upholstered in green, they can be brought into the living room for a card game and will at once become an integral part of the setting. An afghan made in green will blend with the colors in the room when tossed over a sofa in the living room or used on a chaise longue in a bedroom. Green blankets can be used in any of the bedrooms as part of the carefully planned color scheme. This interchangeability is important in a large house, where furnishings are apt to be switched about frequently.

Harmony among the different rooms is another virtue of a well-established color thread. A house with a lot of unrelated rooms, each singing its own color song, is like an orchestra during the tuning-up process. If, instead, each room is harmonized with the next by a color thread, the house will be like an orchestra playing a symphony. Each color will add richness and beauty to the other, the color scheme of each room will flow into the next, and, in consequence, each room will seem larger because there will be no sharp break at the doorway.

Individuality is a distinctive quality which a color thread lends to a house as a whole. If all the rooms are bound together by a color thread, there is a unified impression that creates harmony and distinction in a home. Used in this way, a color thread is something like a family trait which appears in each member yet does not rob any one member of his own personality.

Personal usability is one immediate value of a color thread to teen-age girls. Why? Because many of you may have someone— a doting grandmother, a fond aunt, or a farsighted mother—who wants to make something for your future home, such as a quilt, a needle-point chair seat, or a bedspread. Any one of these objects represents an important investment in money, time, and effort. Naturally, such a gift should be used prominently in your own home and, of course, you will want it to appear to the very best advantage.

By selecting your favorite color now and thinking of it as a color thread for your future home, you will be able to tell them just what color you would like to have them use for the gift they are making. In that way you will be sure to have things that are harmonious later on. (For detailed plans for the use of a color thread in a home, see Chart 10.)

Contrasting color schemes are effective in large rooms.

In the large rooms of a home, where there are many pieces of furniture, numerous fabrics, and quantities of accessories, the contrasting color schemes discussed in Chapter 2 can well be used. There must, of course, be the clear-cut dominance of one color; but against that dominant color as a background it is possible to use a much wider variety of colors for other things than is artistically correct in small rooms. The complementary and triad schemes can be used to give rooms a wealth of color for interest and charm.

Chart 10 gives two plans for complementary color schemes which can be used in the larger rooms of a house. Chart 11 gives plans for both complementary and triad color schemes for use in living rooms and dining rooms.

Chart 10: Color Thread to Unify a Home

A. ROSE COLOR THREAD

Hall

Use ROSE as the dominant with green as the accent. (Complementary)

WALLS: Scenic pattern in ROSE, green, and cream.
BENCH OR CHAIR: Green upholstery.
CARPETING: ROSE.

Living Room

Use ROSE as the dominant with green as the accent. (Complementary)

WALLS: Dusty ROSE.
CEILING AND WOODWORK: Off-white.
CARPETING: ROSE.
DRAPERIES AND WING CHAIR: Cretonne in green, ROSE, gold, and blue.
SOFA: Dark ROSE with violet cast.
LOUNGE CHAIR: ROSE in a slightly darker shade than the carpeting.
PAIR OF CHAIRS: Intense green.
LAMPS: Brass bases with white shades.

Dining Room

Use ROSE as the dominant with green as the accent. (Complementary)

WALLS ABOVE DADO: Floral pattern with light grayed ROSE background.
WOODWORK, CEILING, AND DADO: Dusty ROSE like living-room walls.
CARPETING: ROSE.
HOST AND HOSTESS CHAIRS: Green, ROSE, off-white, gold, and blue stripe.
DINING CHAIRS: Green seats.

Master Bedroom

Use plum as the dominant with dusty ROSE as the accent. (Monochromatic)

WALLS: Geometric figures in plum and dusty ROSE on off-white background.
CEILING AND CARPETING: Plum.
DRAPERIES: Off-white with dusty ROSE and plum fringe.
BEDSPREADS: Plum dust ruffle with off-white top.
CHAISE LONGUE: Dusty ROSE.

Girl's Room

Use blue as the dominant with ROSE as the accent. (Analogous)

WALLS, WOODWORK, AND DRAPERIES: Light grayed blue.
CEILING: ROSE and plum floral pattern on a blue background.
CARPETING: Soft, grayed blue.
BEDSPREAD: Floral cretonne dust ruffle, to match ceiling wallpaper, with light grayed blue top.
UPHOLSTERED CHAIR: ROSE.
LAMP BASE: ROSE.

Boy's Room or Den

Color thread broken to allow for masculine tone in the room. Since green appears in many other rooms, it can be used here to tie in this room with the other rooms in the home.

Chart 10: Color Thread to Unify a Home

B. GREEN COLOR THREAD

Hall

Use GREEN as the dominant with cherry red as the accent. (Complementary)

WALLS AND WOODWORK: Light grayed GREEN.
CEILING: Off-white.
CARPETING: Middle value of GREEN.
DRAPERIES: Cretonne of GREEN, gold, and red on off-white background.
BENCH: Cherry red.

Living-Dining Room

Use GREEN as the dominant with cherry red as the accent. (Complementary)

WALLS: GREEN and white jaspé stripe.
CEILING AND WOODWORK: Off-white.
CARPETING, SOFA, AND DINING-CHAIR SEATS: Middle value of GREEN.
DRAPERIES AND LAMP SHADES: Off-white.
LOUNGE CHAIR: Dark GREEN.
WING CHAIR: Cherry red.
ACCESSORIES: Small lamp bases and mirror frame in brass and gold. Other accessories and large lamp base in cherry red.

Master Bedroom

Use brown as the dominant with GREEN as the accent. (Monochromatic)

WALLS: Floral paper in brown, beige, and yellow on yellow-GREEN background for bedhead wall. Other walls in light yellow-GREEN.
CEILING, CARPETING, AND DRAPERIES: Brown.
BEDSPREAD: Yellow-GREEN dust ruffle with brown top.
CHAISE LONGUE: Yellow-GREEN.
LAMPS: Brass bases with cream shades.

Girl's Room

Use GREEN as the dominant with rose as the accent. (Complementary)

WALLS: Wallpaper with tiny rosebud design on white background.
CEILING: White.
DRAPERIES: White with GREEN cornice.
BEDSPREAD: GREEN dust ruffle with white quilted top.
RUGS AND HEADBOARD: GREEN.
CHAIR: Rose.

Boy's Room

Use same color scheme as used in master bedroom.

COURTESY MOLLA, INC.

When adjoining rooms are small, they should be decorated in identical colors, style, and spirit. In this way, each room seems larger and the effect is that of one large room.

Adjoining rooms should be closely related in color.

A very definite feeling of harmony and unity should exist between the adjoining rooms in a house. Such a feeling can be established without repetition by using the same colors in different arrangements, quantities, intensities, and values.

A *living-room, dining-room combination* with an archway between is an example of a situation in which there should be a very close and obvious color relationship between the rooms. Although each room may be large enough to have a color scheme of its own, the fact that each is so much a part of the other demands that each blend with the other. Each may retain its own individuality through the use of different wall treatments, draperies, and upholstery, but the colors should flow into each other without a break at the archway.

Chart 11 gives complementary and triad color schemes for adjoining rooms. In each example, the same colors have been used in both rooms, but the colors are used in different ways. Thus, by varying the way in which the colors are used, each room has been made distinctive without sacrificing harmony between the adjoining rooms.

In many homes—especially where there are no children—the combination living-and-dining room is gaining great favor. Sometimes it is an L-shaped room, in which the short end is furnished with a small but extendable table for either games or meals. In this way the whole room may be used at all times.

In other cases, and usually, the living-dining room is a large rectangular room, divided into living and dining areas by means of furniture groupings. The dining area, as a rule, is placed as near the door to the kitchen as possible.

In these combination rooms there should be no break at all in color or decorating scheme. Walls, rugs, draperies, and color all should be planned to accentuate the unity rather than to emphasize the dual function of the room. (See suggested color scheme for a living-dining room in Chart 10B.)

A *bedroom-bathroom combination* lends itself well to a very close color relationship. If the tiling in the bathroom is very plain, it is possible to introduce the same wallpaper used in the bedroom for the ceiling or walls of the bathroom. If the bathroom is very small, the walls might be painted in the background color of the bedroom wallpaper, and the walls, ceiling, or window cornice might be appliquéd with just one or two of the motifs from the bedroom wallpaper.

A *powder room off the hall* is often decorated without thought as to the possibilities for interesting color relationships. Women are

Chart 11: Color Schemes for Adjoining Rooms

A. COMPLEMENTARY COLOR SCHEME

Living Room

Use rust as the dominant with green as the accent.

WALLS, WOODWORK, AND DRAPERIES: Light grayed yellow-green.

CEILING, CARPET, GAME CHAIRS, LOUNGE CHAIRS: Rust.

FIREPLACE BRICK: Rust.

FIRESIDE CHAIRS (two): Dark grayed yellow-green.

SOFA: Green, brown, gold, flame, and tan design on rust background. Rust scatter pillows.

DESK CHAIR: Rust, green, and gold stripe.

Dining Room

Use green as the dominant with rust as the accent.

WALLS: Papered above dado in pattern of gold, rust, brown, and dark green on light grayed yellow-green background.

CEILING, WOODWORK, DADO, DRAPERIES, HOST CHAIRS: Light grayed yellow-green.

SIDE CHAIRS: Green and rust stripe.

RUG: Rust.

Chart 11: Color Schemes for Adjoining Rooms

B. TRIAD COLOR SCHEME

Living Room

Use blue as the dominant with red and gold as accents.

WALLS AND WOODWORK: Light grayed blue.

CEILING AND DRAW CURTAINS: Off-white.

CARPETING, SOFA, CURTAIN FRINGE: Middle value of blue.

LOUNGE CHAIRS: Rust, blue, and gold stripe.

WING CHAIR: Gold, red, blue, and green cretonne.

GAME CHAIRS: Two in gold; two in blue.

DESK CHAIR: Blue.

LAMPS: Oxblood red.

Dining Room

Use blue as the dominant with red and gold as accents.

WALLS ABOVE DADO: Floral wallpaper in blue, gold, brick red, and green on off-white background.

CEILING, DADO, and CURTAINS: Off-white.

WOODWORK: Light grayed blue.

RUG: Middle value of blue.

HOST CHAIRS: Brick red.

SIDE CHAIRS: Blue, rust, and gold stripe.

far too prone to consider fish, water lilies, and storks as the only legitimate motifs of decoration for rooms in which there is running water. Actually, a powder room on the first floor is less a bathroom and more a powder room if its decoration echoes the hall and living-room colors. It is better for a powder room to take its decorative scheme from the hall and living room it adjoins than to have it done in a totally unrelated color scheme.

Special rooms may be set off by the use of different color schemes.

There are some rooms which may well be set off from the rest of the house because of their unusual function. The use of individualized color schemes is one way of doing this, and it is quite proper artistically. Actually, any room that closes with a door can be treated without relation to the rest of the house if it seems decoratively desirable.

A *recreation room* is an obvious example of a room that may be decorated to vary from the rest of the house. Often recreation rooms are furnished with rustic, modern, or porch furniture—any of which styles of furniture permit a complete change in color treatment. If the recreation room is separated architecturally from the rest of the house—that is, if it is in the basement or over a garage—it may be done in an exotic or dramatic color scheme that has no connection with the color schemes used in the rest of the house.

A *workroom or hobby room* should be decorated according to the function of the room and the tastes of the occupant—unaffected by the influence of the rest of the family or the colors used in other rooms. A room for the photography enthusiast might be done in dark gray to supply a flattering background for exhibiting photographs. A sewing room, where light is imperative, might be done completely in off-white. Even the floor could be of marbleized white linoleum that would not show threads or clippings.

Patterned rooms should be separated by plain rooms.

The matter of using pattern in a home is one that is sometimes handled much too casually. When presented with books of wall-

A basement can be turned into a recreation room with some planning and effort on the part of all the family. A recreation room may be decorated in an entirely different tone and manner from the rooms in the rest of the house.

91

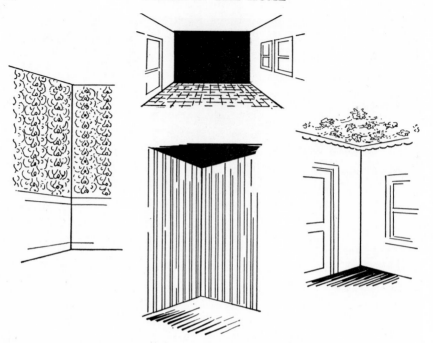

By varying the treatment of walls and ceiling in different rooms of a home, monotony can be avoided while unity can still exist by repetition of color and the maintenance of a similar scale in design.

paper, people are likely to select one pattern after another for succeeding rooms without realizing how confusing the result will be. Artistically, no two adjoining rooms should be papered in competing patterned wallpapers. The rooms on either side of a room with patterned wallpaper should have plain walls so that the pattern of the wallpaper in the room between may be given its full importance. When the patterned wall of one room is seen from the doorway of another room with a patterned wall, each suffers by the contrast.

Halls that lead to a succession of rooms, some of which have patterned walls, should have plain walls. If the downstairs hall does not open onto a room with patterned walls, it can be papered in a fairly bold pattern. It is wise, however, to end that pattern at the stair well and to keep the upper hall in the plain background color of the wallpaper in the downstairs hall. In that way the walls of the bedrooms will not be hampered by pattern on the walls of the hall that leads to them.

Vestibules frequently can be papered in a very dramatic and unusual pattern because they open into a hall or living room which, as a rule, has plain walls.

Succeeding bedrooms which open off the same hall should not compete for attention with patterned walls if their doors are close together. Instead, it would be well to decorate one with a patterned paper, the next with a plain, a third with a stripe, and a fourth with a figured ceiling. In this way there is no competition and no feeling of monotony.

Patterned wallpaper should be selected cautiously.

In the selection of wallpaper, the pattern should be evaluated for the general effect of the design, rather than for the subject represented. It is in the way a design is handled that an artist gives a pattern usability, personality, and scale.

The usability of a pattern is perhaps the most important quality of all to consider in selecting a pattern for the walls of a room. Pattern is stronger and busier in large areas than it is in small. Unfortunately, sample wallpaper books show only a small area of the paper. As a result, the effect which is created by pattern multiplied many times over a large area is difficult to visualize. If it is at all possible, several rolls of the wallpaper should be hung side by side in the showroom or, better, in the room in which the paper is to be used, before a final decision is made. Only in this way is it possible to visualize how large areas of pattern intensify its effect.

The personality of a pattern should be considered when a wallpaper is being selected.

The master bedroom is one of the most mistreated rooms in the house, decoratively speaking. Too often the wife selects the wallpaper and furnishings according to her own likes and dislikes, quite forgetting that her husband has a 50 percent stake in the room.

For example, floral patterns that are simple and forceful are most appropriate for the master bedroom. Those that are dainty and feminine are out of place. A paper with a good geometric design or an interesting texture is a safe selection for this dual-personality room.

Your wallpaper might be selected as you select your clothes—according to your personality and tastes: tailored, formal, dainty, sporty, gay, quiet, or conservative.

For a masculine effect, a boy's room should be less fussy, more tailored, and in plain or striped wallpaper and fabrics.

The pattern of a wallpaper should reflect the decorative tone of the room. Rooms furnished in Early American furniture (*top*) look better when small-scaled patterned paper is used. Rooms that have a sophisticated or elegant tone (*left*) need large-scaled patterns for the walls.

A girl's room should be decorated according to her personality. Some girls like delicate floral patterns in pastel colors. Others prefer a more tailored effect, such as that produced by a paper with an interesting texture, a wide two-toned stripe, or a geometric design that is simple in style and strong and direct in color.

A boy's room done in a paper with a tweedy effect, a nubby texture, or stripes cannot possibly be called "sissy." Wallpaper with pictures of boats or airplanes may have an appeal, but a little thought will show that it is not practical as a background for the pictures, maps, and bulletin boards which most boys like to hang in their rooms. In addition, this pictorial type of paper becomes very tiresome after its novelty has worn off.

A guest room, like the master bedroom, should be papered so that either a man or a woman will feel at ease in it.

The scale of a pattern in relation to the room size is another aspect to be considered when wallpaper is selected.

Small rooms seem larger if the walls are plain. If a patterned paper is desired for a small room, the figure should be small in scale. If stripes are used, they should not be too bold. In fact, it is well to remember that any pattern at all reduces the room size and that the larger the pattern, the more it seems to draw the walls in by attracting attention to them.

Medium-sized rooms may have either plain or patterned walls. Small figures in wallpaper give a room a quaint effect. Medium-large figures make a room more dramatic. Plain walls generally make it seem larger. Like the medium-sized person, who can wear all types of clothes, a medium-sized room allows wide flexibility of treatment without endangering the artistic effect.

Large rooms will dwarf an average-sized figure in patterned wallpaper. Large rooms demand a strong, large-figured pattern, a texture, or no pattern at all. If a plain paper is used, it may be in a darker color than that used for a small room where light colors are needed to increase space.

Finally, in planning the use of pattern, keep in mind that the more personal things you display—such as pictures, collections, or books—the more important it is to keep walls and other large areas plain so as to have a background for the things displayed.

CHECKING YOUR KNOWLEDGE . . .

On a piece of paper write the numbers from 1 to 5. After each number write the word or words from those in parentheses that make a correct statement.

1. Using one color as either dominant or accent in all the rooms of a house (is dull) (lends unity).
2. Rooms connected by an arch (should be) (should not be) treated with blended color schemes.
3. It is (good) (wrong) to use a patterned paper in a hall that leads to rooms in which other patterned wallpaper is used.
4. Strong patterned walls in one room are (complimented) (ruined) by strong patterned walls in an adjoining room.
5. Plain walls in a living room (are enhanced) (look dull) if a patterned wallpaper is used in the dining room that opens from it.

USING YOUR KNOWLEDGE . . .

1. Select from an old wallpaper book six papers, each having green as a dominant. Choose one stripe, one conventionalized flower, one realistic design (scenic or floral), and one geometric design. Mount these on white paper and write under each the type of room you would use it in and the type of person who would enjoy it.
2. Select floral papers for four girls—one of whom is quaint; one, dramatic; one, very feminine; and one, dignified.
3. Select two variations of plain blue wallpaper—one to be used in a a very young girl's room and the other in a living room with a dull, soft blue rug.
4. Select colors or wallpaper patterns for the rooms of your own home, being careful that your choices reflect the tastes and characteristics of those members of your family who will use them.
5. When you have carried out the suggestion in Number 4, assemble the family and present your plans for each room, explaining the reasons for your choices. Give each a chance to comment on each selection and make careful notes of the different reactions. Report these to the class as the basis of a discussion on suiting decorating schemes to personality.

SECTION TWO: *Furniture in the Home*

The color filmstrips "Selecting Furniture for the Girl's Room" and "Arranging Furniture in the Girl's Room" have been prepared to correlate with this section.

CHAPTER 6: Furniture Selection

How many times have you heard people say, "Oh, if I had a lot of money to spend, I could have a beautiful home, too"?

Actually, money is not the most important requirement for creating a beautiful home. Many families have enough money to buy adequate furniture and furnishings, yet they do not have beautiful homes. The reason is that relatively few people are willing to put in the time and study required to find out how to produce a beautiful home. They do not realize that it takes as much ability to spend money effectively as it does to earn it.

Think for a moment how you would go about buying furniture if, by chance, you suddenly acquired enough money to refurnish your own room completely or to buy new furniture for your own home. Would you select a Hollywood bed or a studio couch? Would you choose a sofa, like the one in your own home, or a pair of love seats, like those used in the movie you just saw? Would you spend a large amount of money on a floor-model radio or buy a small one that would fit into a bookcase? Would you buy a rigid game table and four chairs or a lounge chair and a desk?

There are situations in which every one of these choices would be correct and others in which each would be wrong. To determine which is the correct choice for you, you must consider many factors. Buying furniture is not like buying a dress. If a dress is not appropriate or becoming, it will mean at most the loss of a relatively small amount of money and the dress can be hung in the back of a closet and forgotten. If, after a good piece of furniture has been purchased, it is discovered to be useless or for some reason unsatis-

The furniture here suggests an outdoor-type of family that lives in a casual, informal manner—quite different from the family who furnished the room shown on the opposite page.

factory, it not only means the loss of quite a large amount of money, but it prevents the purchase of the right piece because it cannot be put away and forgotten. It occupies too much physical space to be hidden.

Furniture should be selected according to the type of the family.

The first factor to be considered in selecting furniture for the living rooms of the house is the general type of the family. Most families tend toward a certain type, because of the personality and interests of the members, traditions in the family, or their social or economic status.

COURTESY ORIENTAL RUG INSTITUTE AND W. & J. SLOANE

The elegance and sophistication of the furniture in this room is suitable only for a formal type of family with different interests than the family suggested by the room on the opposite page.

The outdoor type of family that enjoys sports and likes to live close to nature may, by careful planning and selection, make their home or apartment seem like part of the outdoors. They might, for example, use split-bamboo or wrought-iron furniture with gay cretonne cushions. Both of these kinds of furniture have the outdoor feeling and are appropriate selections for the nature-loving family.

The formal type of family that likes to create dramatic effects might select alabaster lamps with gold shades, mahogany furniture upholstered with strikingly colorful fabrics, and long, heavy drawdraperies. They might use an occasional antique of excellent quality to add distinction to the setting.

The average type of family may also select mahogany furniture but have it upholstered in simple, informal fabrics. They will want simplicity of line and soft colors. They will select brass and pottery lamps with simple translucent shades.

The very informal type of family will probably select provincial furniture in light woods, short chintz draperies or Dutch curtains, and lamps of copper and pewter. Rugs might be handmade and table linens might be coarse-textured.

Furniture should be selected according to the family's pattern of living.

Another factor in selecting furniture is the pattern of life a family follows. For instance, the furniture selected by a family that likes to entertain a great deal should differ greatly from that selected by a family whose members prefer more studious and quiet activities.

A family that entertains needs more chairs to accommodate many guests. They need nests of tables that can be easily moved anywhere for serving refreshments, and teacarts for wheeling food around a room to serve a number of people. If their parties include much dancing, they should have rugs that can be rolled up, rather than wall-to-wall carpeting that is tacked down. If they play cards or have card parties, they will need rigid game tables, comfortable chairs, and proper lighting for the tables.

Families that spend more time working, reading, or conversing in small groups need large desks, bookcases, deep lounge chairs, and good lamps. If the members of a family generally scatter to their own rooms to entertain, read, or work individually, there will be a greater need for individual desks, reading lamps, bookcases, lounge chairs, and radios in the bedrooms than in the living room. Nowadays there is a definite trend toward more family-centered activities. Television is a rallying point for all members of the family. Movie projectors, viewers for colored slides, and long-playing phonograph records also bring the family together to enjoy an evening in a common interest. Furniture in the living room should be suitable for any of these interests.

What would you think are the main activities of the family who furnished this living room? Would you say they are people who stay at home much? Entertain friends at home frequently?

Furniture should be selected according to the needs of individual members.

The habits and needs of individuals in the family should also be analyzed when plans are being made for the selection of furniture.

Work needs play a large part in the selection of furniture and furnishings. If the husband, wife, or children do much desk work at home, their needs will have to be considered in deciding upon the specific pieces which are bought. Furniture that encourages their endeavors is a "must" and should have first consideration in the basic planning of the home.

Leisure-time activities of the family members should also be considered when furniture is selected. Hobbies and interests, which enrich life so much, need the encouragement of an adequate setting. People who collect recordings need shelves or cupboards 14 inches deep to hold carefully catalogued records. Those who collect first editions of books need plenty of bookshelves. Stamp collectors need a place for albums, a desk, and a good light for work. The model-train builder needs excellent light and a large work surface, as well as cupboards and storage space for equipment. He must also have space enough for a railway track where he can run his trains.

Personal habits should be thought about in the selection of furniture. Some people prefer a sofa in the living room so they can stretch out while reading or listening to the radio. Others would rather have a comfortable chair with a footstool. People who like to read in bed need a good bedside lamp and a good-sized bedside table to hold books and equipment. Others may prefer to have good lights on the desk or next to a chair. People who play "radio golf," tuning in on a new station every fifteen minutes, need a comfortable chair very close to the radio. The family that enjoys television needs a room planned with the maximum seating within the viewing area, movable rather than heavy chairs, and small tables for chair-side snacks.

Furniture should be selected according to physical needs.

The selection of furniture according to physical needs is sometimes ignored amid the multitude of other considerations.

Personal stature of the one who is to use the furniture must be considered in the selection. If you doubt this, consider the problem of the six-footer who tries to sleep in a normal-length bed. Think of the short person who tries to sit in a chair with a deep seat. Or, even worse, think of the long-legged person who tries to lounge in a chair that has a short seat. You will see very quickly just how important "fit" is in furniture. In fact, furniture should be selected to fit people just as clothes are. Tall people need extra-length side rails on their beds and extra-length mattresses. Short people need shallow-seated chairs. Each member of the family should try out the chair that is to be his own special possession before it is bought. It is the only way to be sure of comfort and fit. Any additional chairs can be selected for the comfort of the average guest who may use them.

Health demands must be analyzed in the selection of furniture. A person who is allergic to feathers should have furniture upholstered with foam rubber. People with weak backs need firm mattresses on their beds. People who are light sleepers should not try to share a double bed. All these points must be taken into account in the planning of furniture needs.

Furniture should be selected according to permanency of residence.

Some couples are fortunate enough to know, when they buy furniture, that they are going to be living in the same place for the next few years. Others know positively that they will be moving about for years. The buying of furniture by these two types of couples must be quite different, yet both can meet their particular needs by keeping their situations in mind when they plan furniture purchases.

Transients must be prepared for small as well as large rooms in their furniture buying. Double chests which demand large walls are not for them. They must buy small, compact single chests that can be placed separately on narrow wall spaces or side by side, if they so desire, when they find themselves even briefly in an apartment with large wall spaces. Beds without footboards make a small bedroom look larger. A narrow studio couch that can double as a guest bed would be a wise investment. A love seat that will make even a small living room appear to be of good size would be a much wiser purchase than a large sofa which, in spite of its beauty, might completely ruin the effectiveness of a small living room. A flat-top desk that can be used in front of a window should be their selection rather than a secretary that demands a wall. An extendable drop-leaf table with four upholstered chairs, which could be used in a living-dining room, should be their selection for dining-room furniture. In this way they would be prepared for the emergency of either a small or a large apartment.

They should select upholstered furniture "in muslin" that can be slipcovered to look cool for warm climates or warm for cool climates.

Wooden case furniture and tables must also be simple and impersonal enough to follow this same sort of transition.

Permanent residents, who feel fairly sure of living in the same house for ten or fifteen years, can be much more specific in their buying. If they want a large sofa and their living-room wall will accommodate it, they can buy it with a free mind. Their only duty is to check space carefully and buy to fit it. Some people hesitate to buy furniture that does not follow the architectural style of their home. This harmony is not as important as they think. True, it is very pleasant to come into a living room that seems to harmonize with the architecture, but sometimes people who want Colonial furniture find themselves forced to choose between a Modern- or a Mediterranean-type house. Naturally, they stifle their desire for a Colonial home, but there is no reason why they cannot still have Colonial furnishings. The interior of most houses can be adapted to the use of almost any type of furniture.

Furniture should be selected for quality.

After deciding on the kind of furniture that is needed to meet personal and family requirements, a couple will want to do a lot of looking and shopping around before making actual purchases. Then, when the time comes to buy, they will know about furniture construction, quality of wood and upholstery, and the reputation of the firm where the furniture is bought.

Looking for bargains may be wise in shopping for some things— but not for furniture. Cheap furniture goes to pieces quickly and, in the long run, is a waste of money. When good furniture is marked down, it is, of course, an excellent "buy." For this reason it is important to know the marks of good quality, so that sound evaluation of the furniture, rather than a quick judgment based entirely on the price, will be the determining factor in selection.

Construction of case furniture, such as chests and desks, and of light chairs can be easily checked for quality. A good way to begin is by examining the backs and the undersides of drawers and the bottoms of chair seats. A good piece of furniture is never rough anywhere. Backs, braces, and underparts are well smoothed off. A further check on the quality of cabinets or chests can be made by

Marks of Good Construction

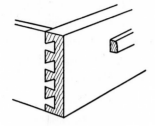

Dovetail joining

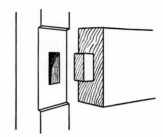

Mortise - and - tenon
joint

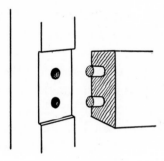

Doweled joint

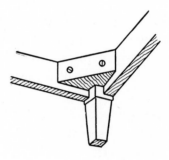

Screwed - in corner block

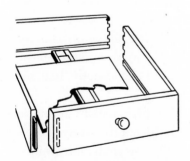

Center guide for
drawer

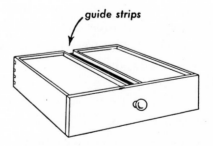

Bottom drawer with
center guide

For detailed descriptions of kinds of construction, see pages 108 and 110.

looking on the inside to be sure there are dustproof partitions between the drawers. Good pieces usually have them. There should also be a center guide or grooving on the underside of the bottom of each drawer so that it will pull out evenly and smoothly. The front of the drawer should be dovetailed into the sides. The corner blocks of case furniture, as well as chairs and tables, should be glued and screwed in, not nailed.

These fine points of construction can be seen easily. What cannot be seen must be accepted on faith, based on the reputation of the manufacturer or the firm being dealt with. The points of construction that cannot be seen are the doweling together of the frame, the use of mortise-and-tenon joining where great strain is anticipated, and the general quality of wood and workmanship. (See drawings on page 109.) Buying poorly constructed furniture, even at bargain prices, is an extravagance.

If a piece of furniture is highly decorated with a great deal of carving, it may be either beautiful hand carving or unattractive molded wood fibers. The first is a mark of excellent quality throughout. The second is a manufacturer's effort to cover basically poor workmanship. In average-priced furniture only a well-made piece, like a good dress, dares to be simple and plain. Good proportion, good line, and good quality need no decoration to attract attention or win approval.

Quality of wood in furniture used to be a problem, but now most manufacturers attach a tag which tells what wood has been used in the construction of the piece. Such markings can be trusted implicitly. Gumwood is sometimes used in underconstruction or for legs on inexpensive mahogany tables or chairs. This cuts the cost of manufacturing tremendously but does not weaken the furniture nor spoil its appearance, since gumwood stains exactly like mahogany.

The use of veneer is not, as some people think, a mark of inferior quality. Any furniture that depends for its decoration on matched graining must be veneered. It is the only way matched graining can be produced. Actually, a veneered table top is preferable to a solid piece of wood, because the cross-graining of the layers insures against warping.

If a piece of furniture is marked "mahogany throughout," it means that no other wood has been used. Often, however, top-grade mahogany desks and cabinets are made with oak drawers and shelves for greater strength and longer wear. In such a case, the variation from "mahogany throughout" actually means higher quality.

Quality of upholstery is another mark of value. A good piece of furniture can be bought in one of two ways: (1) "in muslin," which means that it is ready for upholstery or a slipcover, or (2) completely upholstered. In the first instance, every cent of the cost has gone into the frame and construction work in the piece. In the second, the quality of the piece as a whole is usually indicated by the quality of the covering, as well as by the finish of the wood. If the material seems "flashy" rather than "good," it is an indication that the frame construction is also of poor quality. The whole piece is probably cheap, and the covering has been selected to draw attention from the poor construction. A piece of furniture should never be bought with the idea of re-upholstering it with a better covering later on. In all probability the frame will not be worth re-upholstery, and the cost will be out of proportion to the total value.

The reputation of the firm that offers the furniture is one of the most important considerations, especially when buying upholstered furniture. It is obviously necessary to rely on the integrity of the firm in such invisible matters as construction of the frame, the number and quality of the springs, the number of times they are tied, the quality of the stuffing, and the quality of the webbing. If the salesman misrepresents any one of these items, there is no way to prove it until the furniture goes to pieces, and by that time the bill has been paid. For that reason it is necessary to deal with a reputable firm in buying upholstered pieces. A guarantee of any kind means nothing if the firm that gives it goes out of business.

Furniture should be selected for usability.

Nowadays, even people who are considered settled move two or three times during their lifetime. Most couples begin married life in a very small apartment and move when children are born and more space is needed. Then, as the children grow up and leave home, the parents move again—this time back into a smaller home or apartment. Or, sometimes the expansion of business districts in cities changes residential districts and forces people to move farther out from town. Social upheavals, such as wars and depressions, produce tremendous changes that are reflected in the increasing mobility of the population.

In consequence, the woman who now has a big living room, a small dining room, and no hall may find herself years hence with each of these conditions changed; yet if her furniture has been carefully bought, it will still be adjustable to the new surroundings. The kind of furniture that makes this type of adjustment possible is what is known as "multiple-use furniture."

Individualized storage pieces, such as chests, lowboys, highboys, and kneehole desks, are perfect examples of the multiple-use type of furniture. If these pieces are selected to harmonize with the furniture of the house as a whole rather than linked to any specific room by being part of a set of furniture, they can be used in many different ways and in several different rooms. Kneehole desks and lowboys can be used as desks in living rooms, as consoles in halls, as dressing tables in bedrooms, and as serving tables in dining rooms. The highboys and chests can be used in bedrooms to store clothes, in dining rooms for linen, in living rooms to store music or collections of some sort, and in halls to take care of the dozens of odd items that never seem to have a good legitimate home.

In contrast, single-use pieces of furniture, which are part of a set of furniture, can be used in just one room and for just one purpose. A dressing table, a dresser, and a buffet are excellent examples of single-use pieces. If it should turn out that the bedroom is too small to accommodate a dressing table, or if the dining room has a built-in buffet, or if the bedroom wall is too narrow for the dresser, there is no use for any of these pieces, since they cannot be adjusted to any other use or any other room. The similarity of design makes it impossible to divorce them from the set without immediate detection. A dresser which is part of a set, even though moved to another bedroom, shouts to the world: "I'm here, but I'm not supposed to be. I belong with the rest of the set in the other room."

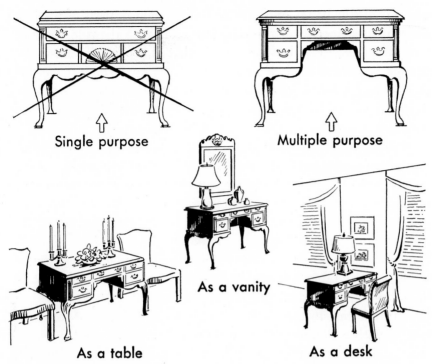

Single purpose   Multiple purpose

As a vanity

As a table   As a desk

The lowboy shown at the right can be used in many rooms and for many purposes, whereas the one on the left can only be used for storage.

But if individualized storage pieces are bought for the bedroom and dining room, they can be used equally well in other rooms in the house.

Interchangeable chairs also come into the class of multiple-use pieces. Upholstered host and hostess chairs can be used in the living room as effectively as in the dining room if they are covered in a color that is harmonious in both rooms. For example, a young couple might buy host and hostess chairs for the living room in their first apartment because they are less expensive than living-room upholstered chairs. Later, when they move to a larger home that has a dining room, these chairs can be used in the dining room when other chairs have been bought for the living room.

Dining-room chairs that are selected for their individuality can be used equally well as desk chairs, hall chairs, bedroom chairs, or game-table chairs in the living room. On the other hand, dining-room chairs or bedroom chairs that are obviously parts of a set can only be used successfully in the same room with the rest of the set.

An upholstered bedroom chair that is too small for comfort cannot be used in the living room, no matter how well its cover may harmonize with the living-room color scheme. If a little more money is spent for a slightly larger chair and the covering is carefully selected, it can be used in either place successfully.

Adaptable tables that have many uses are assured of a life of usefulness and are far better investments than tables that can be used in just one way. A dining-room table can only be used in a dining room, whereas an extendable table can start life in a small dinette, later be used in a dining room, and finally adjust to a living-dining room combination—all without any difficulty. A good-looking game table can start as a dinette table and later be used as a game table, a study table, a tea table, a serving table, or a breakfast table in a large dining room.

In contrast to these adaptable tables is the type of table that comes with a dinette set. This table can never be used anywhere but in a dinette, and even there it is not completely satisfactory. It harmonizes with neither the better living-room furniture nor the streamlined, modern furniture of the kitchenette or kitchen.

Furniture that has greatest use should be of highest quality.

In setting up a budget for furniture, the wise buyer economizes on the pieces that do not take a great deal of wear. For instance, the quality of wood in a bookcase is unimportant. The books it holds are the important thing. End tables and even coffee tables are scarcely seen. The lamps, magazines, ash trays, and objects of art which they hold are what people notice carefully. As a result, these pieces of furniture need not be top quality if the budget is small. The large bulk of the budget for the living-room furniture should be spent on such furnishings as desks, chests, sofas, and lounge chairs because they receive constant wear, and good quality is absolutely necessary. Economizing on such pieces is not advisable.

If the budget for the bedroom is a little slim, other items should be sacrificed, so that good springs and mattresses can be bought.

If a box spring is bought, legs can be screwed on or an inexpensive metal carriage used instead of a bedstead. If a bedstead is purchased, either a box spring or a coil spring may be bought for it. The only advantage of a box spring over a coil spring is that the box spring is encased in fabric, whereas the coil spring is not. Some women prefer the coil spring because they can get at the inside to clean it.

The type of mattress that is bought is a matter of personal taste. Some people prefer an innerspring mattress, whereas others feel they want foam rubber, hair, or cotton felt. All of these mattresses can be used with a coil spring or box spring. In any case, a mattress is not an item on which to economize. The greater part of the budget for furniture and equipment should be spent on articles such as these that will be subjected to constant wear and that must provide physical comfort. Savings can be made on pieces where comfort is not a primary consideration and where wear is negligible.

CHECKING YOUR KNOWLEDGE . . .

1. In what ways would your personal interests affect your selection of furniture for (a) a bedroom and (b) a living room?
2. What facts about your living patterns might determine the furniture you select for your own bedroom?
3. What physical needs of your own or a member of your family would influence the selection of furniture?
4. If you were buying a straight chair, what marks of quality would you look for?
5. If you were buying a chest, what marks of quality would you check?
6. Why is the reputation of the firm important in buying upholstered furniture?
7. Name two pieces of furniture in your own home that have (a) multiple use and (b) single use.
8. On what pieces of furniture is it possible to economize without sacrificing comfort or usefulness?

USING YOUR KNOWLEDGE . . .

1. List the activities which your family engages in as a whole and note the furniture that is now available for those activities. Also list the

furniture which would make these activities more enjoyable. What pieces of furniture or equipment would encourage more family-centered activities? Compare their cost with the estimated amount spent on out-of-the-home activities, such as movies, sports events, and parties.

2. Visit a furniture store and make a list of single-use and multiple-use pieces shown. Note relative prices, and list all possible uses for the multiple-purpose pieces. Then make a comparison between two like pieces of furniture—one that is single-use and one that is multiple-use—to determine cost versus usefulness.

3. Make an inventory of all the multiple-use furniture in your own or a relative's home. List all the possible uses and all present uses. Could any of this furniture be more valuable if it were moved to a place where it would be used in different ways?

4. Make a similar inventory of the homemaking center in your school. Compare the functions served by the furniture with the actual needs of the center. List the pieces which might be added which would help the center to meet those needs more effectively.

CHAPTER 7: Furniture in Your
Own Room

In this chapter we want to be much more specific and personal about the selection of furniture. We want to consider your particular furniture problem—the problem you face when you open the door of your bedroom after school today.

Has your room grown up with you, or is it just the same as it was when you were eight or ten? Does it recognize the fact that a large part of your time at home is spent in studying and that this requires space to work and a place to spread out books and papers? And, last of all, does it reflect your personal tastes and interests in a manner that is attractive and stimulating and that encourages you to enjoy your free time and use it to the best advantage?

It is possible for you to satisfy some of these needs and desires even though you sleep in one of the living rooms of the house or share your room with your sister or some other member of the family. Even lack of money is no excuse, because a great deal can be done without too much expense. And, since baby-sitting has become so popular, any high school girl can earn money. Knowledge is the real hurdle—knowledge of exactly how to go about making your room represent you.

If you do not have a room of your own, as is the case with many girls, you will want to respect the tone of the room you use. Even so, it is possible to build a personal area for yourself around a desk or study table which, properly placed, will serve as a night table as well. A good lamp, which serves both desk and studio couch, good-

Ingenuity has been used in this room to provide for sleeping, study, books, hobbies, and entertainment at very little cost. The day bed consists of mattress and springs on legs; the draperies are made of bedspreads; the coffee table is an old card table with legs cut down; and the desk is an old vanity with mirror removed and back covered.

looking book ends, a group of well-selected pictures over the couch, and a smartly tailored spread and bolsters for the couch itself will create a very attractive grouping that you will find enjoyable, personal, and useful.

If, on the other hand, you have a room of your own or one you share, there is even more you can do. Your first step is to determine exactly what furniture you need or would like to have in your room. Next, you will want to analyze what furnishings you have, and from that analysis you can plan how to remodel it to fit your desires.

Make a list of your needs and desires.

Pretend for the moment that you have no furniture at all and that you are going to furnish a room for yourself. Rule a large piece of paper into three columns. Head the first column "Needs and Desires," the second column "Major Pieces," and the third column "Minor Pieces." In the first column list everything you do or would like to be able to do in your own room if it could be managed. Your list will probably include most of the following items, plus a few that are strictly your own. (See Chart 12.)

Sleeping and dressing should be the first two items in the first column, since these are two basic daily needs for which every girl must provide in her bedroom arrangements.

In the other two columns list the major and minor furnishings that are necessary for each of these activities. For instance, under the heading "Major Pieces" and opposite the item "Sleeping," you would list "Comfortable bed," and in the "Minor Pieces" column you would probably list "Good bedding." In the second column opposite "Dressing" you would list "Chest of drawers" and "Ample space for hanging clothes." In the third column you might list "Boxes for hats, shoes, and accessories." A good mirror and a good light should also be added in the third column opposite "Dressing," because both are necessary to the achievement of a good personal appearance. If there were more full-length mirrors or small mirrors hung on closet doors at skirt-length level, there would be fewer slips showing, uneven skirt lines, and crooked stocking seams.

Studying and reading are other important activities of most teen-age girls. So, opposite this item in the second column of your

Chart 12: Furniture Needs for a Girl's Bedroom

Needs and desires	Major pieces	Minor pieces
Sleeping	Comfortable bed	Good bedding
Dressing	Chest of drawers Ample space for hanging clothes	Boxes for hats, shoes, and accessories Good mirror Good light
Studying	Desk and comfortable desk chair	Good lamp Wastebasket Bookshelves
Reading (in bed)		Back-rest pillow Good bed lamp Bedside table
Reading (daytime)	Lounge chair	Small table Good light Ottoman
Entertaining	Extra seating space	Games Radio, etc.

Plan for a Girl's Multiple-purpose Room

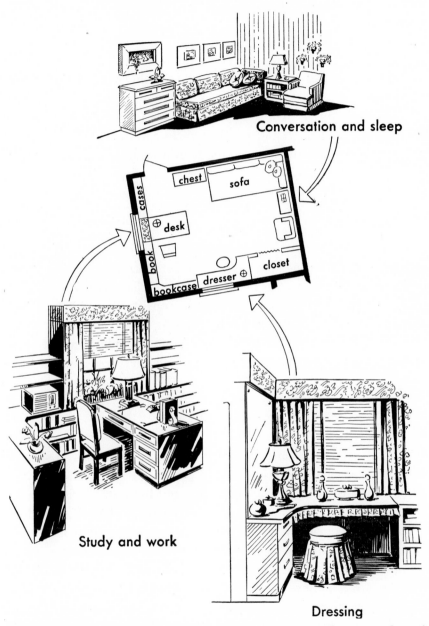

Conversation and sleep

Study and work

Dressing

Even a small room can be made to serve many uses without crowding if thoughtful planning is put into the selection and arrangement of furniture.

chart you would list "Desk and comfortable desk chair." In the third column you might list "Good lamp," "Wastebasket," and "Bookshelves."

If you happen to be a girl who likes to read in bed, it will be necessary to list some minor pieces opposite "Reading (in bed)," such as "Good bed lamp," and "Bedside table" to hold books and magazines.

Entertaining is a third activity that should be an item in the first column. Although big parties are important, it is the casual, day-by-day get-togethers that seem to add up to so much in lasting friendships. Girls seldom talk confidentially over creamed chicken served on Spode china, but cookies and milk in the privacy of a girl's room are likely to stimulate intimate, personal discussions and confidences. Because of that fact, some preparation for this sort of informal entertaining should be made. Opposite "Entertaining" the notation "Extra seating space" could be listed as a major piece. This might take the form of a bed turned into a studio couch with a tailored spread and bolsters, or it might consist of some flat pillows or mats that could be strewn on the floor. As minor pieces you might need cards for canasta or gin rummy, a radio, or a phonograph. (For further information on furniture grouping and arrangement, see Chapter 8.)

**Let your personal interests determine
the type of your room.**

Before you make any further plans for your room, you should do a little self-analysis. What kind of person are you? What do you like to do best? What are your main interests? Some girls have so many interests that it is impossible to say which is strongest. But in order to give your room individuality try to decide what your greatest interest is so that you can remodel your room according to some definite plan. These suggestions may help you.

The girl who likes frilly things will want her bedroom to be the boudoir type of room. She will want a dressing table with a billowy skirt. She will want a Hollywood bed with an upholstered headboard and a ruffled bedspread. Draperies for her room might be ruffled organdy or net, and the wallpaper could be a chintz floral design in soft pastel colors. Even the desk could be made to look a little less austere with a lamp made of a glass or delicate china base, topped with a lace-trimmed shade.

The girl who likes the outdoors will want a bedroom that is very simple and tailored. Plenty of storage space for ice skates, tennis rackets, or golf clubs will be more important to her than space for a dressing table. She will want either a simple pottery lamp or a metal planter lamp filled with greens. Lamp shades should be plain parchment. A bed for her room should be as tailored-looking as a couch. It should have no headboard or footboard, and the pillows should form a bolster along the wall. Her draperies should be of plain fabric that draw together smoothly and simply.

The lounge chair in her room should be deep and roomy and might be covered in a rough, homespun material. The desk should be simply designed and well proportioned. If it is possible, the outdoor type of girl might use split-bamboo furniture and boldly designed cretonne rather than mahogany furniture and chintz fabric.

The girl who likes to read will want to make her room into a combination study-bedroom. The first big need for her will be bookshelves in quantity, then a desk, a comfortable lounge chair, a good lamp, and a big ottoman. She probably also enjoys reading in bed. Therefore, she would need a large pin-up lamp directly over the bed head or a side lamp and table. Her choice in furniture might be as simple as that of the outdoor girl or as feminine as that of the girl who likes ruffles, but she might select as her fabric history-telling toiles. She might hang maps of historic spots or photographs of famous writers on her walls instead of pictures.

The girl who has a blend of many interests—as most girls do— will want some elements of each type that has been discussed, and perhaps many others. She would, doubtless, like her room to be a combination of a bedroom, a study, and a sitting room, with a perfectly recognizable bed and a big study desk. She might show a touch of sophistication by using a Hollywood bed, but she would be practical and choose a gingham spread for it so that her friends could lounge comfortably on it. The drama and utility of draw-curtains would be appropriate for her. Her provision for make-up would probably be confined to an in-a-door arrangement, consisting of a shelf under a mirror inside the closet door.

All four of these types of rooms have distinct individuality, yet each one can be produced from the stereotype bed-dresser-table type of bedroom which is the lot of most girls. The transformation can be achieved at an amazingly small cost, if ingenuity, knowledge, and work are applied. (See illustration on page 118.)

Suggestions for furnishing rooms shared by girls of different personalities are given on pages 133–137.

Remodel your furniture to fit your needs.

The first thing to do before remodeling is to think over the furniture you now have and the way it could be made to fit into your new room plan to suit your needs and your interests. Next you will want to talk your plans over with your mother to see whether or not she is willing to have you work out your remodeling scheme. It may be that the furniture in your room is too good to be changed but that you can take furniture from another room for your project.

Once the two of you have found furniture which can be cut apart, you may have to obtain recruits from the family or among friends to help you with the work. Making something lovely and useful out of something unlovely and inappropriate is an achievement that carries with it tremendous satisfaction for everyone who participates. Your plan may become a family project in which every member will be interested. The following are some ideas for remodeling furniture for your bedroom.

The bed is the most important piece of furniture in a bedroom, and it usually dominates the room. If the room is small, the bed should have a low headboard and no footboard at all because a footboard acts as a fence that breaks up the room. A high headboard can dwarf even a good-sized room.

Regardless of whether your bed is wood, brass, or iron, you can make it into a Hollywood type by using the foot of the bed for the head and sawing off the high headboard at the point where the crosspiece for the bottom of the headboard meets the side posts.

The crosspiece will in this way act as a support to keep the mattress in place, but it will be completely covered by the bedspread.

Now look at the new headboard of your bed—that is, the former footboard. Cut off any "gingerbread." If it has a molding that frames it completely, the center might be padded and upholstered.

If the bed is brass or iron, you will need a hack saw to cut off the headboard. The footboard, which becomes the headboard, should be padded heavily before it is upholstered or slipcovered. Use an old carpet as the base, so that the whole headboard will have an even rigidity. After old quilts have been added for softness, it is ready to be slipcovered.

An envelope slipcover can be made quite easily of muslin, chintz, cretonne, or sateen. All of these fabrics make excellent inexpensive slipcovers. The thinner materials are more effective if they are quilted. For more careful tailoring, you might box the slipcover, as shown in the drawing at the top of page 127. Edge it with a brush fringe for an especially smart effect.

Either the slipcovered or the upholstered headboard will be a complete change, and both will make the room look much larger.

A *desk* that is big enough to work on and to store ample equipment is a necessity in a teen-age girl's room in which homework is a daily occurrence.

A large table top that might be picked up in a secondhand shop is a splendid beginning for a big desk. The next step is to locate objects to support the table top and at the same time furnish storage space for work equipment.

Probably the least expensive way to obtain these would be by ransacking a secondhand store for an old triple-mirror dressing table made up of two commodes connected with a flat top. These commodes usually are about 30 inches high and, when separated, might be used for the end supports for your large table top to make it into a very useful kneehole desk.

Another way to make a desk out of a table top is to buy unfinished bookcases, which are available in most department stores and from mail-order houses. Select a pair that are about 20 to 25 inches long, because the length of the cases will determine the depth of your desk. Turn them end out from the wall, so that the backs

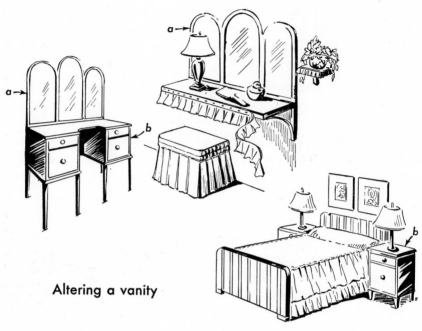

Altering a vanity

Altering a buffet

Remodel Furniture

Altering beds

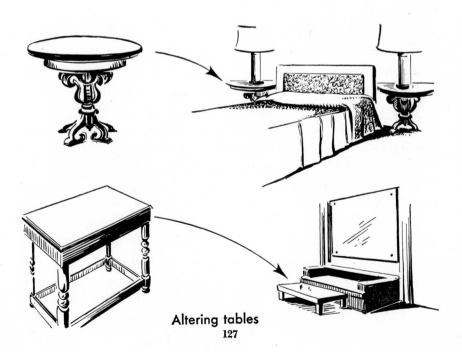

Altering tables

127

of the cases will form the inside walls of the kneehole space. The table top placed over the two will complete your desk. The bookshelves will be good to hold books, papers, and boxes, and they will be decorative as well.

A *chest or dresser* is another piece of furniture that is especially needed in a bedroom. Many a dresser is really a good-looking chest which has been completely ruined by the superstructure of a mirror attached by an ugly swing-arm arrangement. Fortunately, these dressers are so constructed that, by the removal of two blocks of wood held by four screws, the chest and mirror can be separated. If the mirror is then hung separately on the wall above the chest, the effect will be much improved.

If the mirror looks too small without the arms which held it to the dresser, you might enlarge the appearance of the mirror by hanging a pair of pictures or brackets on each side of it.

If the legs of the chest are unattractive, they can be either replaced with plain ones or sawed off so the bottom of the chest rests flat on the floor. It is frequently possible to add a great deal of charm and simplicity to a chest merely by replacing any overornate brass hardware with wooden knobs.

Chairs are another type of furniture that can take some remodeling, especially if they are ornate or fussy in style. If all the extra decorations and protrusions are removed from a chair, its beauty will be increased tremendously. If it is then padded well and slipcovered, it will be much more comfortable and more likely to harmonize with the room scheme.

A piano stool that has been padded and flounced makes a good dressing-table stool. If you need an ottoman, cut the back off a straight chair and cut down its legs. Pad it and give it a flounce. When it is placed next to a lounge chair, the combination will be as comfortable as a chaise longue.

Cabinets for storage of hobby or school equipment can be made out of old radio cabinets. The same process of simplification is necessary, however. Legs and extra decorations should be removed and shelves installed.

Tables that are quite hopeless-looking can be made into dressing tables, bedside tables, coffee tables, or occasional tables. A large table with ungainly legs can be completely masked with a dressing-table skirt. A smaller table can be cut in two and made into a pair of wall consoles for each side of a bed. The backs can be attached to the wall like a bracket or a telephone shelf, and the legs will support the front. Almost any old table can be cut down to make a low magazine table. If it is to be used next to a chair, it should be cut the same height as the chair arm. If it is to be used as a coffee table in front of a studio couch or window seat, it should be cut to the standard 18-inch height. (See drawing at the bottom of page 127.)

A *built-in buffet* in the dining room of an old house will need to be changed if the house is remodeled and the dining room is made into a living room or bedroom. To fit its new location and function, the built-in buffet would be changed as follows: First of all, the glass doors and mirror should be removed. If storage space is desired, some of the glass doors might be replaced by wooden doors. The open shelves remaining can be used for books, and the top drawer can also be used as a desk by hinging the front so that it can be let down to form a writing space. (See drawing on page 126.)

How you refinish furniture depends upon its condition and style.

Up to this point we have talked about form in furniture. This, however, is only half the problem. The finish is the other half, and there are several methods that an amateur can use to refinish furniture and achieve a good result. The method should be selected according to the condition and style of the furniture.

If the piece is structurally good and the design is pleasing, it might be given a natural-wood finish. First, get varnish remover, or paint remover if the piece is painted, and follow the directions on the can carefully. After the old finish has been completely removed, the wood should be smoothed with a fine grade of sandpaper. Then it is ready for waxing.

Waxing is the easiest way for an amateur to achieve a natural-wood finish. Simply apply a good clear furniture wax, and then polish. This waxing and polishing process should be repeated many times to build up a heavy surface that will protect the wood and give it a pleasing luster.

If the piece is nondescript in design and made of cheap wood, painting is a good way to refinish it. Start by sanding the whole piece with fine sandpaper in order to smooth the surface. For good results, the surface should be absolutely smooth before any paint is applied. Use several thin coats of paint in preference to one thick one, and let each coat dry thoroughly before applying another. Sand down any roughness that develops between coats.

If the room is small, painted furniture that matches the walls melts into the background and makes the room seem larger. One note of warning! Use just one color for each piece of furniture. Painting the spindles or other parts in a second color is the mark of an overenthusiastic amateur.

If the piece is simple and straight in its lines, it might be covered completely with wallpaper. Beautiful marbleized or interesting textured papers covering the entire surface of an ordinary piece of furniture will make it into something strikingly individual. The paper is put on with ordinary wallpaper paste. When it is thoroughly dry, it should be shellacked or waxed to give it a protective surfacing.

Painted furniture or furniture with a natural-wood finish may be decorated in three different ways.

There are three types of decorating which can be used effectively on painted furniture or furniture with a natural-wood finish. They are antiquing, découpage, and stenciling. All are interesting to do and are within the scope of an amateur.

Antiquing is the least conspicuous way to decorate furniture. In fact, it is merely a tone applied to a painted surface, rather than a pattern. Therefore, it can be used in a room with patterned fabrics or wallpaper.

All that is needed for antiquing is a tube of oil paint called "burnt umber," some thinner, and a cloth. The piece of furniture which is to be antiqued must first be smoothly painted and thoroughly dried. Next, squeeze out a small amount of the burnt umber on a plate, add turpentine or linseed oil for a thinner, and then mix

Stenciling is an easy way to decorate painted furniture.

the two. Dip a cloth into the mixture and rub it rather thickly over the surface. Do just one complete surface at a time. Let it stand for a moment and then rub it off gently, pressing harder in the center of the surface covered. A small amount of the dark color will remain around the edges. The center will look almost as it did before, but when you have finished, the whole piece will have an aged look that is distinctive and lovely. To test your skill, practice this decoration on a painted board before working on the piece of furniture.

Découpage demands real artistic ability, patience, and skill. Begin by selecting some decorative motifs from left-over or sample wallpaper that are interesting in color and not too intricate in design. Cut them out and plan their arrangement on a panel or the surface of the piece that is to be decorated. Then attach each motif to the furniture with shellac or glue. When it is thoroughly dry, cover the entire surface of the piece decorated with several coats of clear shellac to protect the decoration. The result will be a decorative effect that can, if well done, be the accent note of the room. Découpage is definitely patterned in effect and should be used only in a room that has plain walls and very little pattern in fabrics.

Stenciling provides a third method of decorating furniture. By using this method, you can apply decorations to any natural-wood finish or any painted piece of furniture. Cut-out stencils can be purchased at any art store. (See illustration on page 131.)

Select furniture finish according to setting.

The finish selected for furniture should be based not only on the style and condition of the piece itself, but on its relative place in the decorative scheme of the room in which it is to be used.

If the furniture is to be the accent of the room, it is possible to use a highly decorative treatment, such as découpage, stenciling, or papering. The furniture then becomes the dominant note in the room, and walls, floors, and draperies must be absolutely plain and unified in color.

If the furniture is to be part of the background of the room, it should be painted one of the background colors. It can then be antiqued or waxed. In this way it will demand no attention beyond that of utility or natural beauty of line. It allows fabrics or accessories to play the dominant role in the decorative scheme of the room.

If there are other wood finishes in the room, it is artistically correct and interesting to have one piece utterly different. It might be painted in the color of the wall or in the accent color of the room. Or, if most of the furniture in the room is painted, one piece in natural wood might add an interesting note.

Remember, however, that there must be a clear dominance of one kind of finish. There should never be an even division, such as two pieces of one treatment and two of another. It is possible to have a bed, a chest, and a table of natural wood and a desk of painted wood, but never have a bed and chest of natural wood and a table and desk of painted wood. On the other hand, the desk, bed, and table might be of painted wood, and the chest of a natural wood.

Shared rooms can have dual or single personality.

All this time we have been planning rooms for the use of one girl, while many girls share their rooms with a sister or someone else. Two girls who may thoroughly enjoy each other's company or who were brought up by the same parents in exactly the same way may be utterly different in type. One may be the tailored type; the other, the more feminine type.

Naturally, the question arises as to which type shall dominate in the decorating of the room. Of course, neither one should dominate, because each girl has an equal share in the room and has a right to have her personality expressed in some of the furnishings. Following are three methods of handling the furnishings of a shared room, each one of which recognizes equally the rights of both occupants.

Unified decoration is the easiest way to handle the decoration of a shared room when sisters or roommates happen to be similar in type. Upholstered headboards could be identical, except for names or monograms embroidered in the center. Identical desks and chests would further emphasize the similarity of types. The result is distinctive because of the repetition. Pictures, collections, or hobby displays should, however, be varied enough to suit each girl's individuality.

Divided-room decoration is a solution to the problem of a room shared by girls of different personalities. This plan is only possible in a room large enough to permit each girl to stake off her own claim and then decorate her section of the room according to her liking and personality.

The one point at which concessions are necessary in this scheme is the matter of backgrounds. The color and treatment of walls, floor, and draperies must, in general, be agreed upon by both girls, because they are to be the unifying factors in a scheme which is otherwise not unified. They will establish the dominant color.

Both sections of the room must be well done and each must be clearly distinctive or this plan will fail and become simply heterogeneous. There must be a clear-cut difference in tone and treatment. (See illustrations on pages 27 and 136.)

In unified decoration each girl has an identical bed, chest, dressing table, lamp, and desk. In this room, a pair of identical swivel chairs serve the girls for both desk (against wall) and dressing table (in center).

(COURTESY ARMSTRONG CORK COMPANY)

For instance, the bedspread of the girl who wants more feminine things must be a very ruffly-type spread. The other bedspread must be utterly different in style. It could be severely tailored with corded edges. The headboard and footboard of the bed could be cut down to an even height to make a day bed, or they could be cut off just below the mattress top to make a couch. In either case, pillows can be arranged along the walls in a bolster or stiff-pillow arrangement. The effect will be very tailored and entirely different from the bed of the other girl.

If both girls have chests of drawers, the feminine type could do hers in a dainty découpage, while the tailored type could use antiqued paint. Lamp shades and pillows also should be completely different. Those for the more feminine type ought to be frilly—in sheer material and edged with lace or embroidered ruffles. Those for the girl who likes tailored things should be simple and corded.

It might be possible, if the room is carefully planned, for the frilly type of girl to have a corner dressing table that would not take up too much room and would satisfy her feminine tastes. The balancing corner could be turned into a corner cabinet in which the other girl could display a collection of some kind.

Adjustment in decoration is the third method to use in shared rooms. Most master bedrooms are adjusted in decoration to suit the personality of the husband and wife, but this is the least satisfactory form of decoration for teen-age girls. In this method, the athletic, outdoor type of girl gives up having her hockey sticks crossed over her bed and allows her bedspread to be made with a dust ruffle, while the frilly girl gives up the feminine dressing table which she would like to have and accepts simple parchment lamp shades when she prefers silk ones.

The room, in consequence, would be a unified blend of the two types, but it would not represent the character of either girl strongly. This type of room is not as attractive to most girls because it is older in its whole approach and result.

The important point is to decide which arrangement best fits you and your sister or roommate. Analyze your types and your interests carefully. Check the size of your room and the possibility of divided-furniture arrangements, and then make your decision.

Plan for a Divided-room Arrangement

For details on divided-room decoration, see pages 133 and 135.

136

A shared room is an adventure in decorating, as well as in living, and it is fun to see how a room can be decorated to suit the personalities of two people without having either one dominate it.

Some day you will share a room with your husband. Here is a good opportunity to begin learning how you can harmonize two personalities, decoratively speaking, without offending either one.

CHECKING YOUR KNOWLEDGE . . .

1. How did you determine the pieces of furniture needed for your own bedroom?
2. Would the furniture needs for your best friend be the same as yours? Why, or why not?
3. What did you consider in determining the style of your room?
4. What are the different methods of finishing furniture?
5. What are the methods of decorating a shared room? Which would suit your situation best?
6. Under what conditions would each method of finishing furniture be appropriate?

USING YOUR KNOWLEDGE . . .

1. Divide the class into groups and plan a furniture-refinishing project. Get donations or buy a few pieces of case furniture—such as a chest, a cabinet, or a cupboard—that could be used afterward in the home-making center or the teachers' room. Each group might work on one piece. Hold two open houses—one while work is in progress, to demonstrate methods, and another to exhibit the finished job. Keep accurate account of cost of materials and hours spent.
2. Draw a diagram of your own bed at home, using squared paper to get the proportions accurate. Show how it could be remodeled, and estimate time and money required. Plan to do the work as a vacation project.
3. Make an envelope slipcover for the head of a bed at home, being sure that you use a fabric that harmonizes in color, style, and design with the other room furnishings.
4. Ask for the cooperation of the woodworking class in a desk-making project. Each girl might collect materials as suggested in the text and make detailed plans for the construction. With the help of the teachers, have the two classes meet to discuss and revise these plans. The construction might then be done by the woodworking class, the

girls paying for it on an hourly basis agreed on at the first meeting. The girls might do the refinishing. Pictures should be taken of the different stages of work to be exhibited with the finished product at an open house.

5. Invite a good upholsterer to help with a desk-chair project. Before his first visit, have each girl bring to class a chair, a bench, or a stool and a plan for remodeling it. The upholsterer would be able to advise the best methods of professional procedure in each case and might visit the class once or twice during the remodeling process to answer questions and evaluate the work.

6. If you sleep on a studio couch in the dining room or living room, plan a small desk with a big drop leaf that can be raised for work and dropped out of the way the rest of the time.

7. If you share a room, plan an arrangement and decoration that would satisfy both you and your sister or roommate. List both your needs and hers and plan to accommodate them as nearly as possible. Estimate what you would need and how much it would cost.

CHAPTER 8: Furniture Arrangement

The proper arrangement of furniture, like the proper use of color, follows definite principles which must be adhered to if beauty and comfort are to result. Attempts to arrange furniture without a knowledge of these principles have caused more strained backs and family discord than people care to admit. Men, as a rule, like to leave furniture as it is, and women usually like to change it. Both are right at times—the men, if the furniture is correctly arranged, and the women, if it is not.

When it is difficult to follow accepted principles of furniture arrangement because of too many large pieces of furniture in the room, the large pieces should be replaced by smaller ones. For example, the substitution of one or two small chairs for one or two large overstuffed chairs would not only make good arrangement of the furniture in a living room much simpler but it would make for more space and livability. Or, in a bedroom that is so crowded with furniture that effective arrangement is difficult, a large bed and dresser might be replaced by a day bed and a compact chest.

Furniture arrangement should be approached theoretically.

The best way to study furniture arrangement is to reduce the room and the furniture to workable proportions on paper. Beds, pianos, and sofas are not easily moved around. But if the whole room and all its furniture are reduced to a scale of one-half or one-quarter of an inch per foot on a diagram, it is possible to try the furniture in a number of different placements without any physical strain.

Outline of Room to Scale

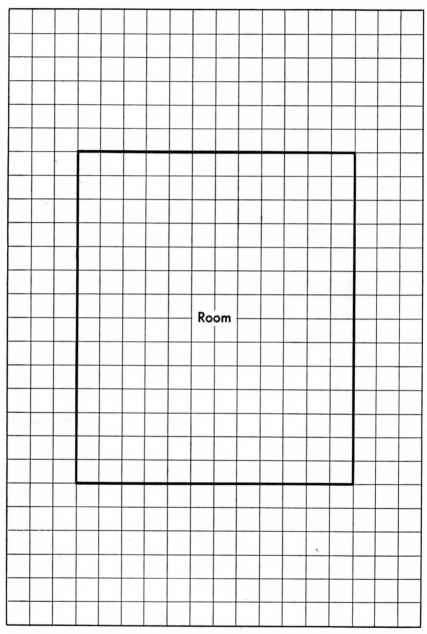

Room

To keep proportions right in diagramming a room and its furnishings, use ¼-inch squared paper, with each square representing 1 square foot.

Architectural Symbols

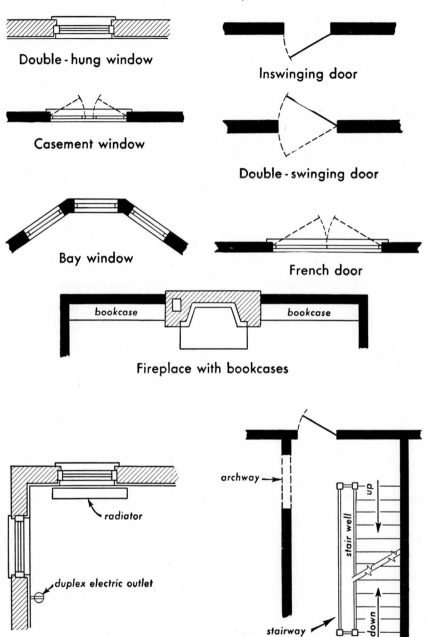

Double-hung window

Inswinging door

Casement window

Double-swinging door

Bay window

French door

bookcase   bookcase

Fireplace with bookcases

radiator

duplex electric outlet

archway

stair well

up

down

stairway

If you use the accepted symbols for architectural features when you diagram the floor plan of your room, you will have all the essential information when you are ready to plan the arrangement of your furniture.

Measuring the room according to scale and laying it out on squared paper is the first step. For example, if the room measures 12 × 16 feet, the diagram will be 3 × 4 inches, if a scale of one-quarter of an inch per foot is used. Turn to page 140 to see how this is done. Also take note of the diagrams on page 141 which show how to indicate windows, doors, archways, radiators, and electric outlets. All of these architectural details affect the arrangement of the furniture.

Measuring the furniture that is to be used in the room and scaling it for the diagram is the next step. The area covered by each piece on the floor is the only measurement needed for the diagram. Chart 13 gives the average sizes of most pieces of furniture, but the measurements of the actual furniture to be used should be taken. A variation of a few inches may make a big enough difference to prevent the actual placement of the furniture in the room as planned on the diagram. After the actual measurements of the furniture have been taken, they should be reduced to the same scale used for the room diagram and drawn on another sheet of paper. (See furniture diagrams on page 145.) These area diagrams of the furniture can then be cut out and sorted into major and minor pieces. When this is done, it is possible to start arranging the furniture on the diagram of the room.

Furniture placement is governed by principles.

Large pieces of furniture and cut-up wall spaces have been the cause of much trouble in the arrangement of furniture. Therefore, we shall start with the principle for the correct placement of large pieces of furniture.

The placement of furniture parallel to the walls is a principle that is both logical and artistic. It covers the placement of all case furniture, such as chests of drawers, cabinets, and desks, as well as all large pieces of upholstered furniture, such as sofas, benches, settees, and beds. Every inch of space is valuable in a house, and the placing of furniture parallel to the walls makes the best use of the floor space. The placement of furniture across a corner is unwise because it eliminates several square feet of floor space from all use. Artistically, diagonal lines create a sense of confusion, so from this point of view also, a cater-corner arrangement is not good. If there is no wall space large enough to accommodate a piece which should be placed against a wall, the piece should be moved into another room and replaced with a smaller piece.

Some large pieces of furniture are finished on all sides and so can be placed out in the room away from the walls entirely. Flat-top desks, sofas, grand pianos, and tables are examples. Even these pieces, because of their size, must be placed parallel to the walls of the room, in spite of the fact that they do not touch a wall at any point. Scatter rugs should also be placed to follow this rule of parallel lines.

Small movable pieces, such as single chairs, however, need not be set parallel if an informal effect is desired. If the chair has an accompanying table, the table should, of course, parallel the arm of the chair rather than the wall, because it serves that one piece of furniture and is considered a part of it. If, on the other hand, the table is a large one that serves two chairs, the table is the determining factor, rather than either chair, and—like all large pieces— it must be placed parallel to a wall. (See drawings on page 153.)

The alternating of wood and upholstery is another principle of furniture arrangement that is logical and artistic. Upholstery enhances the beauty and strength of wood, and wood is an excellent foil for the color, softness, and texture of upholstery. Therefore, alternating them in every grouping assures strength and beauty.

Think, for example, of the pleasing relief which upholstered host and hostess chairs lend in a dining room—a room usually filled with hard wooden dining-room table and chairs. The combination of a coffee table with a sofa is another example of effective alternating of upholstery and wood. A chair with an upholstered back combined with a high wooden secretary; upholstered chairs with a game table; and chairs with wooden arms combined with a sofa— all these are good examples of the effectiveness of combining fabric and wood. In fact, no grouping of furniture can be successful that does not follow the principle of alternating wood and fabric in its arrangement.

Chart 13: Approximate Measurements of Furniture *

Furniture	Inches
Living room:	
Baby grand piano . .	60 × 66
Barrel chair	27 × 30
Cabinet radio	16 × 28
Card table	30 × 30
Club chair	30 × 36
Coffee table	24 × 42
End table	15 × 24
Flat-top desk	20 × 40
Love seat	24 × 42
Piano bench	16 × 36
Secretary	18 × 32
Sofa	30 × 72
Straight chair	18 × 18
Upright piano	24 × 60
Wing chair	32 × 32
Dining room:	
Dining table	40 × 60
Sideboard	24 × 60
Straight chair	18 × 18
Bedroom:	
Chaise longue	28 × 60
Desk	20 × 40
Day bed	34 × 80
Double bed	54 × 78
Dresser or chest of drawers	18 × 40
Three-quarter bed . .	48 × 78
Twin bed	39 × 78

* *Note:* Most tables and desks are 30 inches high.

Furniture Symbols

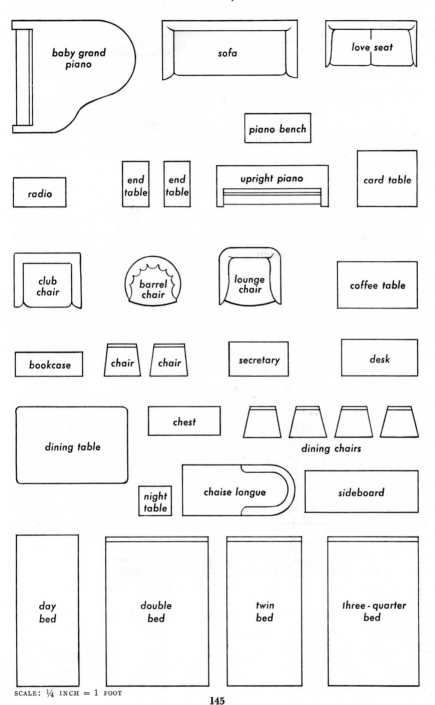

baby grand piano

sofa

love seat

piano bench

radio

end table

end table

upright piano

card table

club chair

barrel chair

lounge chair

coffee table

bookcase

chair

chair

secretary

desk

dining table

chest

dining chairs

night table

chaise longue

sideboard

day bed

double bed

twin bed

three-quarter bed

SCALE: ¼ INCH = 1 FOOT

145

By alternating upholstered furniture with wood furniture, each piece stands out and is shown to best advantage. In this room, the mirror over the sofa increases the apparent size of the room and helps to make the sofa grouping a focal point, or center of interest, in the room.

(COURTESY *The Stylist Magazine*)

Furniture should be grouped according to use.

The basic reason for having furniture is to serve a need, not to fill up a home. In consequence, every piece of furniture in a house should be arranged from the point of view of its use. Also, each piece should be placed in relation to the other furniture which helps it to serve its specific need.

Furniture groupings in Victorian days were isolated from one another by being placed in separate rooms. This was possible because the houses were made up of many small rooms, each planned for just one purpose. The parlor was used for formal calls. Chairs and settee were placed against the walls facing a table in the center. Everyone took part in the same conversation, and conversation was the only function which that room served. The dining room was for dining only, and it was used three times a day. The bedrooms were for sleeping only, and there was no provision made in their furnishing for reading, lounging, or working.

Furniture groupings in homes of today are not isolated in separate rooms. We have smaller homes because of the higher cost of building and heating, and we have fewer rooms but the rooms themselves are larger.

Some of the more functionally designed houses today have few if any interior walls. Draperies lend privacy when it is desired, but the house is really composed of a few immense rooms. By the grouping of the furniture, areas within these large rooms may be turned into eating, study, conversation, and sleeping units.

This type of plan, of course, is still unusual, but the need for grouping furniture to meet varied needs within rooms exists in most homes, because our living needs are just as varied as they were fifty years ago. The difference is that today each room must serve several purposes. The one large living room of today, for instance, must serve as a parlor, a music room, a library, and sometimes even a dining room. A bedroom serves as a sleeping room, a study, and sometimes as a living room.

This need for accommodating several types of activities in each room has brought about an entirely new system of furniture arrangement, which is known as "use groupings." Each grouping, complete

In large rooms the most effective arrangement of furniture is into use groupings. Here, the furniture has been grouped around the table for reading, around the desk for work, and around the fireplace for conversation. Note that the basic principle of placing all large pieces parallel with the walls has been adhered to.

COURTESY ARMSTRONG CORK COMPANY AND MODERNFOLD DOORS

One room can be made to serve many purposes by the way in which the furniture is grouped. In this room, the sleeping and cooking areas are separated from the living-dining room by folding doors. There is also a group for study, one for eating or games, and one for music, reading, or conversation—all in a relatively small room. (See illustration on page 67 of the same room with doors closed.)

as to furniture, lighting, and accessories, takes over the function of one of the small, single-purpose rooms of the old, larger homes, but all are housed in one big room.

The planning of use groupings begins with an analysis of functional needs. (Turn back to pages 119–122 in Chapter 7 to see how this was done for a bedroom.) First a list should be prepared of the things that people like to do in each room, accentuating any special hobbies or interests enjoyed by individual members of the family. The list for the living room of most families would include reading, writing, conversation, entertaining, music, and games. Each one of these functions requires certain major and minor pieces of furniture. In consequence, the space selected for the major pieces must be large enough to include the minor pieces also. For example, the place selected for the desk must be large enough to accommodate a chair, a lamp, a wastebasket, and a bookcase—as well as the desk—because this grouping has taken over all the functions of the library. The sofa should be placed out in the room or on a long wall that has plenty of space for one or two tables to hold lamps. Chairs to complete the conversational group can be set out from the sofa to form a semicircle, because this grouping has taken over the functions of the parlor. (See drawing on page 153.) The addition of tables and lamps to the conversational grouping will make it useful also for reading.

One of the reasons for this new emphasis on use groupings is that people do not "just sit" nowadays. They read, knit, listen to the radio, watch television, or talk with someone. The placement of every piece of furniture should recognize these activities and help to make it possible to carry them out. Fortunately, as in the case of the conversation-and-reading group, some furniture groupings can serve several purposes.

Furniture groupings should balance in the room.

The process of arranging furniture should begin with the balancing of the major pieces of furniture on the room diagram. This may be done by dividing the cut-out furniture pieces into two groups—major and minor pieces—and then by moving the pieces in the major group around on the floor plan until an ideal arrangement is worked out.

Formal balance, which is sometimes called "absolute balance," is the easiest kind of balance to use in arranging furniture. To create formal balance, a chair and a table on one side of a sofa or fireplace must be balanced by the same type of chair and table on the other side.

As a rule, formal balance is used within a grouping more often than between groups in the average room. A twin-bed grouping with matching tables and lamps and a sofa grouping with matching end tables, lamps, and chairs are quite common examples of formal balance within a grouping. Yet the bedroom or living room as a whole need not be arranged according to formal balance. The average room has to fulfill so many functions that it is seldom possible to build up two identical major groups. This is fortunate, however, because overuse of formal balance in a room produces a far too orderly appearance.

Informal balance, which is also called "occult balance," is the balancing of unlike pieces of furniture. It is more commonly used than formal balance in the arranging of furniture. For example, a sofa on one side of a fireplace may balance a wing chair, a table, and a lounge chair on the other side; a piano on one side of an archway can be balanced by a desk group on the other; or a conversational group of a pair of chairs and a table may balance a gametable grouping.

Balance between groups in which the size of the major pieces varies greatly can only be established by augmenting the major pieces of furniture with minor pieces to a point where the total effect of the group balances.

As an example, it is often necessary to balance a fireplace with a sofa directly opposite on the parallel wall. The sofa, no matter what its style, seems soft, heavy, and low when contrasted with a fireplace, which is narrow, high, and hard. Also, a sofa protrudes into the room, while the fireplace is back against the wall. A group of pictures may be hung over the sofa to make it seem higher and to balance it with the height of the fireplace. A pair of tables can be added to the sofa grouping to balance the wood or hardness of the fireplace. A pair of chairs and lamps can be used on each side of the fireplace to add the softness and bulk necessary to balance it with the sofa grouping. Thus an informal balance of mass, color, and height is achieved.

A flat-top desk that is placed at one end of a room to balance an upright piano at the other will have to be built up into a group with considerably more weight and height to produce an effect of balance. A high-backed desk chair will add height to the desk grouping. Bookshelves, pictures, or a map can be hung above the desk to raise the height of the grouping to that of the piano. And if the group still seems small, a lounge chair or wing chair may be added near the desk. The piano group, however, needs the softness

Grouping Furniture for Study

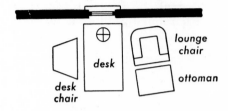

A flat-top desk with a lamp on it and a desk chair on one side makes an ideal study group—especially when the desk is placed end out from a window. The same desk can also be used as a table if a large chair and ottoman are placed on the other side of it.

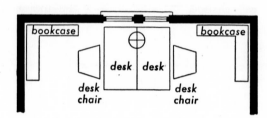

Two flat-top desks, placed back to back and end out from a group of windows, form a study group for two people. When bookcases for books and equipment are arranged so as to line the corners, the grouping is even more attractive and useful.

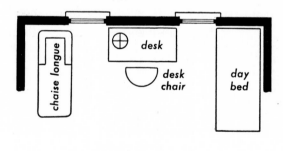

In a small room, where every inch of space is important, a desk with space for books is a convenience. If the desk can be set between two windows, it might serve as a table for a lounge chair, or chaise longue, as well as for a bedside table.

Grouping Furniture for Conversation

Furniture arranged in a semi-circle makes a convenient and attractive grouping for conversation. The usual pieces in such a grouping, as shown here, consist of a sofa, a pair of tables with lamps, two chairs, and a coffee table.

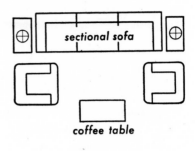

coffee table

A group of windows can be dramatized and the view enjoyed when furniture is arranged around the windows. A pair of love seats, tables with lamps, and a coffee table form an H-shaped group that is ideal for conversation.

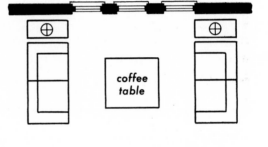

In a large room, an intimate semicircular grouping can be formed around a fireplace by placing a love seat or sofa in front of the fireplace and backing it up with a table and lamps. A pair of chairs with tables and lamps on each side of the fireplace and with a coffee table between completes the grouping.

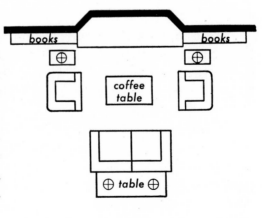

153

of a pad on the bench and a lamp to balance the variety of color present in the desk group.

In some rooms the fireplace is opposite a large entrance archway, so that it is impossible to balance it directly without blocking the entrance to the room. In such a case the fireplace might be balanced by two smaller groupings placed on each side of the archway, each of which would have approximately the same height and each the same blend of wood and upholstery. The fireplace grouping would also have to be softened and built out in mass, as has been suggested.

In some rooms the long wall, ideal for the sofa, is opposite a large, low picture window that should be framed rather than blocked by furniture. The solution here is to balance the one big grouping of the sofa by two smaller ones placed on each side of the large window. This type of informal balance, in which two small groups balance one large one, is like the balance on a seesaw when a big boy sitting on one end is balanced by two little girls on the other.

Often in a bedroom the bed must balance a desk group. This balance can be managed if the desk chair is upholstered and a lounge chair is added to the desk group. The bed group, which is soft in effect, should have a bookshelf and a bedside table added to it in order to balance somewhat the wood of the desk group.

Furniture arrangement should accentuate architectural beauties.

Some rooms have an architectural feature of great beauty. It may be a fireplace, a group of windows, or a picture window. Whatever it is, this architectural feature should be accentuated by the furniture arrangement. It should be made the focal point, or center of interest, in the room.

A *fireplace* should always be treated as the focal point in the room, with chairs, tables, and lamps arranged around it to give it importance. If the fireplace is not a real one, the furniture arrangement must not admit it. As long as it is in the room, it must be accepted as the center of interest of the room. To put a table or chairs in front of a fireplace is like announcing, "This fireplace is a fake."

The fireplace may be used as the focal point in a room around which to arrange furniture (*above*) or a group of windows might be used with a furniture arrangement to provide the center of interest in a room.

Instead, the inside of an artificial fireplace may be painted black, so that no one will realize that it is not real. Any artificial equipment should be removed and real birch logs that look as though they could be burned at a moment's notice should be substituted. The reality of the logs and the black chimney will give a feeling of cheer that an empty fireplace or artificial logs never can achieve.

A good picture or a beautiful mirror should be hung over the fireplace. If the chimney slants so that nothing can be hung on the wall above it, decoration should be placed on the mantel. A lovely shelf clock or green plants in a container, flanked by candelabras, would be interesting and attractive.

A *group of windows* is another architectural feature which could well be the focal point of the room. The group is particularly effective if it overlooks a beautiful view. One of the best ways to make a group of windows the focal point is to build a window seat under it and group chairs on each side of it. A sponge-rubber pad will make the window seat really comfortable, and if a coffee table—to hold magazines, books, and flowers—is placed in front of it, the charm and comfort of the entire grouping will make it the center of interest in the room. If the windows are high enough, a low bookcase placed under the window will be an interesting treatment and will not block the view. (See illustration on page 155.)

If a high radiator under the windows makes a window seat impossible, a grouping of furniture can be used to emphasize the window. Matching groups, each composed of a chair, a table, and a lamp, placed on each side of the windows and at right angles to them, will call attention to the beauty of the windows as well as to the view.

If the windows are high, a sofa can be centered under them. Flanked with matching tables and lamps, the grouping will, in effect, frame the window, yet by its own beauty it will minimize the unpleasant height of the window sill.

A *doorway vista* can be thrown into relief or made important by using a pair of matching mirrors, sconces, or wall brackets with plants on each side.

When there is no architectural feature which can be used as a focal point in a room, the furniture may be grouped so as to make a center of interest. Here, the break front serves as a focal point for the formal-balance grouping, which becomes the center of interest in the room.

Furniture alone can be used to create a focal point in the room.

No room is effectively arranged if there is no spot to which attention automatically turns. If there is no architectural focal point in the room, a center of interest can be effectively created with furniture. For instance, a sofa with lounge chairs, tables, and lamps grouped around it can be a very beautiful focal point. (See illustration on page 146.) A low bookcase with a beautiful picture over it and flanked by a pair of love seats is another type of important furniture arrangement that can be used as a focal point. A tall secretary or a dramatic break front is also large enough to be an adequate substitute for an architectural accent. (See illustration on page 157.)

Furniture arrangement should minimize architectural faults.

There are very few houses that do not have some architectural faults. It may be the proportion of a room. It may be an archway that is too large. Whatever it is, the careful management of furniture arrangement can help to disguise or hide these faults to an amazing degree.

A *long room* that seems too narrow can be made to appear shorter—and therefore wider—by placing large pieces of furniture at the extreme ends of the room. For example, a long bedroom can be shortened by placing the bed at one end of the room and a dressing table on the opposite wall. A long living room can be made to look shorter by placing a piano or secretary at one end of the room and a sofa at the other.

In each case the bulk of the pieces will seem to move the walls in considerably. Also, the long horizontal lines of the bed or sofa at the end of the room will seem to broaden the room, making the length less noticeable. Imagine the difference if these long pieces were placed along the long walls. Immediately the narrow room would look narrower and longer.

A second way to make a long room seem shorter is to arrange the furniture on the long wall so that it extends out into the room, cutting into the length. For instance, a flat-top desk can be placed end out from the long wall. A game-table grouping can be set out from a wall, breaking into the length of the room most effectively. A pair of love seats can be used end out from a window with the same result.

A *large archway* that is out of proportion to the rest of the room can be minimized by the building of narrow shelves on each side within the opening. These can be used to display accessories and books. Or, a four-leaf screen can be divided in half and used as two screens, one on each side of the archway. The decoration and color of the screens will make beautiful backgrounds for groups consisting of a chair, a table, and a lamp. In addition, the screens will give privacy and cut down drafts.

A *wide room* can be made to look longer by using furniture with long, low lines on the long walls. A long, low bookcase, a long window seat, or a long sofa will all help to make the room look longer and, therefore, appear to have better proportions.

Furniture should be arranged for best use of space.

In addition to the need for balance and accent in the arrangement of furniture, there is also the need for adjusting furniture to fit the space of the room. The clearing of paths from room to room in a house, the assignment of space for furniture groupings according to use, and the planning of large open spaces are some of the ways in which space is recognized in good furniture arrangement.

Natural paths, or traffic lanes, can be analyzed quite easily if the steps taken in a normal day's routine are reviewed. Paths from one room to another, to the front door, to the telephone, to closets and cupboards are the natural traffic lanes which should be planned for in arranging furniture. (See drawings on pages 410 and 411.)

If a hall is only moderately wide, any furniture in it should be placed along one wall, so that there will be a straight, easy path through the hall. If the living room acts as the hall to the dining room or to a stairway, the furnishings should be so arranged that a direct path, unblocked by coffee tables or chairs, is open.

In a bedroom the natural paths to closets and entrances should not be blocked by furniture.

Space assignment to furniture groupings must be made according to use. If one part of a living room is cut off from the rest of the room by a traffic lane, it is well to recognize that fact by assigning to it furniture that can function in isolation. It might be a desk group, a lounge-chair reading group, or a piano music group—any one of which is not dependent on the other groups of the room to function well. Conversational groupings should be placed away from traffic lanes, of course.

The position of windows may also affect the placement of groups of furniture. A dressing table should be placed so that the light will fall on the person rather than on the mirror. For that reason, a wall space between two windows is a perfect place for a dressing table with a hanging mirror. If the mirror is of the easel type, the dressing table could be placed directly in front of the window. A flat-top desk should be placed end out from a window so the light falls on the desk top instead of in the writer's eyes.

Open living spaces are as important to the beauty and usefulness of a room as the furniture. A small bedroom will look much larger if the bed is placed against the wall so that it does not divide the floor space into small areas. Twin beds in the center of a small room will almost fill it. If they are pushed against opposite walls or arranged at right angles in a corner, the center of the room will be clear and the room will look considerably larger. The center of a small living room should be kept as clear as possible in order to give a feeling of space. There should be no large coffee table blocking it. Low lounge chairs are better than high wing chairs in such a room, and chairs with no arms will add to the feeling of space. Beds without footboards are especially good for small rooms, because a footboard on a bed fences off part of the room area, making the room seem smaller.

Broken areas are important, however, in large rooms which might otherwise have a tendency to look like ballrooms. A big living room should be treated like a series of small rooms. There are many space-breaking schemes: A desk may be set end out from the wall; love seats may be used end out from the fireplace; a full-sized sofa might be placed in the middle of the room, facing a fireplace, with a desk backed up to it; and lounge chairs might be placed to form a semicircular, square, or oblong conversational grouping with a sofa. Any of these group arrangements will break up large open spaces into pleasant, useful groups and eliminate any effect of being as scantily furnished as a skating rink. The illustration on page 148 is an example of a large room in which furniture has been arranged to break up floor areas.

Any extremes of space are bad artistically. Rooms with very large open spaces and rooms with too little open space are both unpleasant. Good furniture arrangement seeks to reduce both extremes to the gracious medium which is invitingly intimate yet spacious in effect.

CHECKING YOUR KNOWLEDGE . . .

1. Why are use groupings essential in a large room?
2. Name the use groupings necessary in your own living room.
3. What two types of balance are used in furniture arrangement?
4. What furniture must always parallel a wall?
5. What piece of furniture can be placed at an angle?
6. How do traffic lanes affect furniture placement?

USING YOUR KNOWLEDGE . . .

1. After you have familiarized yourself with the approximate furniture measurement listed in Chart 13, measure accurately pieces in your own home and in stores to train your eye to estimate variations from the standard sizes. A test of your ability would be to estimate sizes of furniture pointed out at random in the homemaking center or other rooms of your school.

2. Make a shoe-box model of several different rooms that you actually know. Use the same measurements, the same window and door placements. Make, or buy at the dime store, scale furniture and try out different arrangements based on different use groupings and the needs of different types of families.

3. Make an arrangement with a local furniture dealer to allow the class to visit the store after closing time and have the opportunity to try out arrangements of furniture. Divide the class into groups and let each arrange one of the model rooms or display sections. The class could then criticize and evaluate each other's work.

4. Divide the class into several groups and let each submit a scale diagram for a new arrangement of furniture in the homemaking center. Each group, through a spokesman, should present its plan, giving reasons for each decision. The entire class could then select the best parts of each arrangement and help rearrange the furniture accordingly.

5. Analyze the habits and tastes of the members of your own family and then plan a rearrangement of your living room accordingly. Present the plan to the family and report the family reaction to the class, as well as any changes that resulted from the suggestions.

CHAPTER 9:   Furniture Styles

An understanding of furniture styles is as important as a knowledge of furniture quality. Yet only in recent years have we realized this fact. In consequence, many people still think that the amount of money they can spend should determine the style they select in furniture. They will say unhesitatingly, "We are going to buy Early American maple furniture. It is inexpensive and good." They may also add, "Mahogany furniture is good, but it is too expensive." They seem to be unaware of the fact that nowadays both mahogany and maple furniture can be bought in all qualities, at many different prices, and that *good* maple furniture is as expensive as *good* mahogany furniture.

Some people say, "I'm not going to use period furniture. I like Modern." These people do not realize that every "period" design in the world was "modern" at the time it was created. They forget, when they buy their furniture on the basis of what is new instead of what is appropriate for them personally, that the furniture will become "period furniture" before it wears out and thus will not at all fulfill their desire for the "latest style" in furniture.

The style of furniture should be selected to reflect in a very real though subtle way the type and personality of its possessors, as well as their way of living.

Furniture should harmonize with the way of living.

Fortunately there are furniture styles that have been beautifully designed to fit every personality and every type of life. Some furniture is as smoothly sophisticated as a slim black evening dress; some

Provincial furniture is informal, casual in feeling, and fairly small in scale. Consequently, it is especially appropriate for small rooms and for homes in the country.

is as informal and casual as a sweater and skirt; and some, like a good suit, is so functionally designed that it can be either formal or informal, according to the kind of furnishings and accessories used with it.

The reason furniture has this wonderful variety nowadays is that manufacturers are not only designing contemporary furniture but they are reproducing furniture styles which were designed and planned to fit the needs of many different kinds of people in many different times and many different places.

For instance, the early settlers in New England needed furniture that was suited to a very simple, informal life. As a result, designs for furniture developed which, with only slight variations, still suit people in the twentieth century who wish to live in a setting that is similar to that of early New Englanders.

In all furniture styles similar parallels exist between the furniture needs of the people of the time in which they were created and the needs of certain types of people today. So, in order to select a style that is appropriate for our needs, we should know about the type of people for which the various styles were designed.

Of course, much of the furniture designed during any period is not being reproduced today because the people for whom it was designed found it unsuitable after use. Therefore, the designs were discarded. The same is happening today with Twentieth Century, or Modern, furniture. Many of the earlier designs were found to be impractical and are not being manufactured or are being redesigned to suit our needs. Therefore, the only furniture pieces from past periods that are being reproduced today are those that have proved their worth over years of use. These authentic designs, accumulated through centuries of time, are today being reproduced by the manufacturers, and we may select any style from them to suit our personality, temperament, or way of living.

Provincial furniture harmonizes with informal living.

Provincial, or country, furniture, used with artistically correct accessories, makes a home that is simple, comfortable, casual, and informal. This is the furniture for people to select who live casually and informally.

There are just two types of provincial furniture generally available—the Early American and the French Provincial.

The spirit of provincial furniture is exactly suited to an unpretentious family. It has a forthright, direct simplicity and sincerity that is charming and informal. The Early American variation is expressive of the very frugal type of life that existed in America at the time it was designed. The French Provincial furniture has a little more elegance and comfort, because in Central and Southern France, where this style was most popular, the sun shone all day long, crops grew luxuriantly, and the people in that country were quite well-to-do.

The woods which were used originally for this style, and which continued to be used, were those found close at hand in the countryside. Walnut, maple, pine, and fruit woods were and are the most popular woods for provincial furniture. Sometimes several kinds are used in one piece of furniture.

The designs of provincial furniture are primarily simple and informal in type. They were created to fill the needs of the people at that time. Three-legged stools that would stand level on an uneven floor, drop-leaf tables that would conserve space, and chests for storage were typical necessity pieces in both France and America. Chairs in America were apt to have higher backs to cut off the breezes of a cold New England winter and smaller seats to suit thin, spare people. French chairs, designed for a milder climate, had lower backs and were wider to suit plumper people who had more money for food and to accommodate the fuller-skirted dresses of the women.

People in France had more fabrics than the Americans, so many of their chairs had cushions covered with quilted fabrics, while in America the chairs were made with rush-bottomed or splint-bottomed seats.

Present-day furniture factories have deepened and lowered chair seats in provincial furniture so as to suit the casual slouching of people in our times, who do not sit in the bolt upright position of these earlier people. They have added springs and cushions for increased comfort. Some manufacturers of provincial furniture still make candlestands and cobbler's benches, which were used with this style originally; but because these pieces do not fit into twentieth-century living, wise buyers will not be tempted to purchase them. Nowadays people need big lamps that cast strong light for long periods of reading, instead of a flickering candle. They need a large flat-top coffee table that will hold quantities of magazines and newspapers or accessories rather than a cobbler's bench,

Salt-box house

Lamp

Chairs

Corner cupboard

Windsor

Wing

Ladder-back

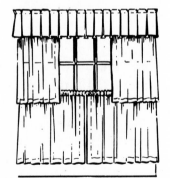

Dutch curtains

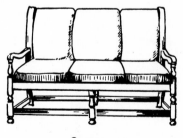

Settee

Furniture and Furnishings

Silver

Pewter

Fireplace

Chest - on - chest

Mirror

Highboy

Four - poster bed

Butterfly table

French Provincial house

Chairs

Armchair

Side chair

Grandfather
clock

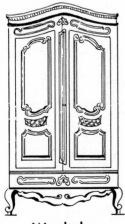

Wardrobe

Curtains

168

Furniture and Furnishings

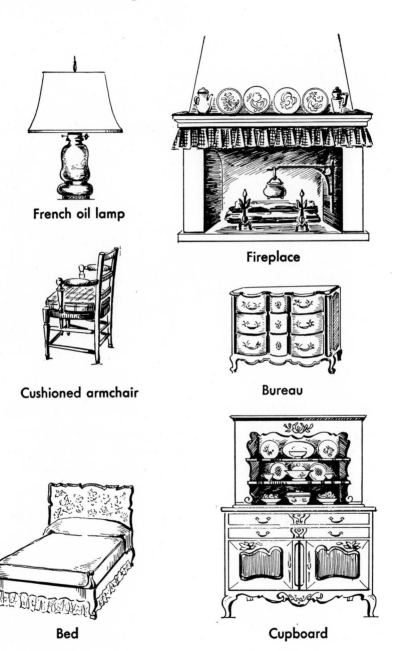

French oil lamp

Fireplace

Cushioned armchair

Bureau

Bed

Cupboard

which is divided into small sections that will not accommodate any of our present-day equipment.

The fabrics and accessories which were used with provincial furniture originally, and which are proper artistically now, were simple in design. Materials were coarse, hand-woven cottons and linens. These are still appropriate and effective for draperies and table linen with provincial furniture. Ruffled net curtains are as artistically wrong for this type of furniture as a ruffled chiffon blouse would be with a denim skirt.

Floors, in those early days, were covered with small rugs made of scraps of fabric, either hooked, braided, or woven together. Unfortunately, the smooth floors and streets of today have made us unaccustomed to lifting our feet as we walk, so these small rugs are a hazard and an irritation as we stumble over them. In consequence, even though plain, simple carpeting is less authentic with this informal style of furniture, it is a wiser choice. The more authentic small rugs may be reserved for the bedrooms, where there is less traffic.

Accessories of pottery, pewter, wrought iron, and brass were used, and still are most appropriate artistically, with this type of furniture.

Eighteenth Century furniture is adjustable.

The current vogue for Eighteenth Century English and American furniture and early Napoleonic furniture is not at all surprising when we consider the very obvious parallels between the period that produced the original designs and the period in which we are now living. Its selection by many people today is therefore quite natural and easily explainable.

The spirit of this furniture—used in the Eighteenth Century in England, America, and France—is mainly one of adaptability. The reason for this quality is that during this time—when William and Mary, Queen Anne, the Georges, and Napoleon were ruling and men like Thomas Chippendale, Sheraton, Hepplewhite, and Duncan Phyfe were designing furniture—the buyers were mainly middle-class people who were constantly moving ahead financially. Fortunes were being made in trade and commerce, and a great deal of

Eighteenth Century furniture has an adaptable quality, so it can be used for either formal or informal living.

Georgian house

Lamp

Chairs

Tilt-top table

Anglo-Chippendale

Chippendale

Draperies

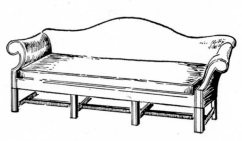

Chippendale sofa

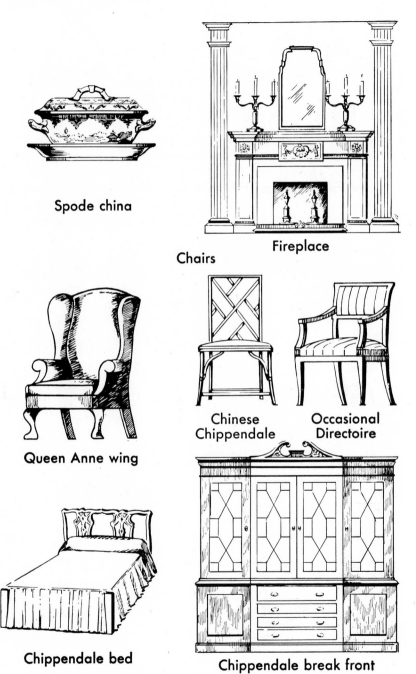

Spode china

Fireplace

Chairs

Queen Anne wing

Chinese
Chippendale

Occasional
Directoire

Chippendale bed

Chippendale break front

173

Colonial house

Lamp

Chairs

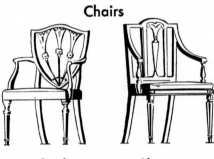

Hepplewhite

Sheraton

Sheraton secretary

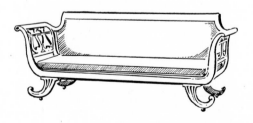

Duncan Phyfe sofa

174

Duncan Phyfe table

Chairs

Fireplace

Adam   Duncan Phyfe

Sheraton bed   Draperies

the furniture that was bought for modest homes had to be usable for very large and elegant homes later on. As a result, the furniture had to be designed to adjust harmoniously to such changes.

The medium scale of the pieces made them appropriate in the rooms of a small home. The dignity and beauty of line made each piece important later on in a large and impressive home. The dark, rich finish added importance and dignity to any fabric, from chintz to damask, with which the pieces were upholstered or combined. They were designed for many uses.

How natural it is that this same furniture is so popular and so appropriate here in America now, where many young couples start married life in a modest apartment and within five or ten years are able to build or buy a home.

The woods which were used originally in Eighteenth Century furniture, and which are now used in the present reproductions of it, reflected the far-flung interests of their buyers.

During the eighteenth century, ships belonging to middle-class merchants left England and France laden with merchandise for the New World of the West Indies and Central America. They returned loaded with mahogany, which was first piled into the empty ships for ballast but which very soon was found to have great value as a cabinet wood. Then, as now, its fine grain, its color, and its workability made fine carving and beautiful finish possible. As a result, furniture of this wood became tremendously popular. The word "imported" had just as much glamour in the 1700's as it has now, and businessmen capitalized on this fact.

The designs of Eighteenth Century furniture were created for adjustability in function. Thus the furniture was always useful to the people who were moving from house to house as they progressed economically and socially. Break fronts, which were most popular, were and still are equally beautiful when used in dining rooms to hold china, in living rooms to hold books, and in halls to hold art objects. Upholstered host and hostess chairs were equally at home in living rooms and dining rooms. Dining-room chairs were so beautifully designed that they were used also as living-room chairs and desk chairs. Chests and highboys were designed with beautiful pediments so they could be used effectively in bedrooms, living rooms, halls, and dining rooms.

How very understandable it is that this adjustable furniture should find widespread popularity in America nowadays, when many people move frequently. How understandable it is that there has been no need for changes or modifications of this style by manufacturers. It fits perfectly into our present-day way of life and our ideas of comfort and beauty.

The fabrics and accessories originally used with this furniture varied from the simplest to the most elegant. Curtains ranged from chintz to damask, and we still find the range artistically right and economically convenient. All types of china, silver, glass, and linen were and still are appropriate on the polished table tops of mahogany furniture. Polished brass, decorated china, Oriental porcelain, or painted tôle—all these were, and are now, artistically right with this furniture. In fact, now, as then, it is possible to give tone to this furniture with these accessories. For this reason Eighteenth Century English and American and early Napoleonic furniture are considered the most flexible and useful styles of furniture that exist.

French furniture is sophisticated and feminine.

Girls who have their own apartments and women who have a separate bedroom or an upstairs sitting room that is completely their own are justified in selecting completely feminine furniture. They are the ones who can turn unhesitatingly to the French furniture of the 1700's—the world's most feminine and elegant style of furniture. At that time women controlled the whole social and much of the political life of France, and the furniture was designed to please them. Louis XV was swayed by Madame de Pompadour and Madame Du Barry. Louis XVI was dominated by Queen Marie Antoinette. Consequently, both these styles—Louis XV and Louis XVI—are especially comfortable for women and are charmingly feminine.

The spirit of this furniture is one of femininity and elegance. It is, of course, quite unsuitable for a man's domain, especially if he is the husky, outdoor type.

House with Mansard roof

Figurine lamp

Louis XV chairs

Armchair

Side chair

Draperies

Chaise longue

178

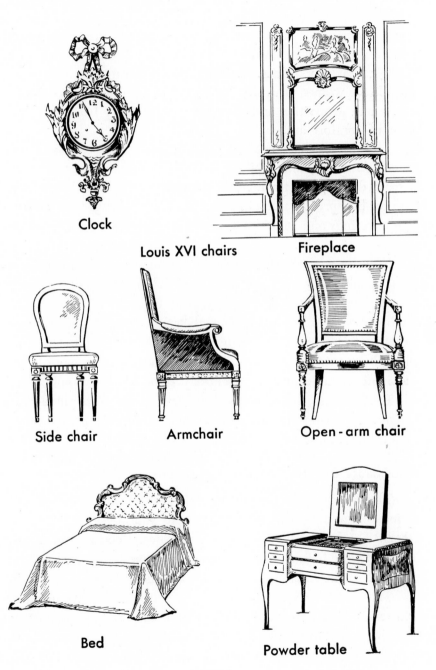

Clock

Louis XVI chairs

Fireplace

Side chair

Armchair

Open - arm chair

Bed

Powder table

The woods used most frequently in this type of furniture were, and still are, satinwood and mahogany. Painted woods decorated with gold were also used.

The designs of these periods in their best forms are especially delightful for girls and women. Even its proportions are planned to fit their own proportions. In fact, French furniture is more comfortable for women than any other kind of furniture. It is beautiful in line and proportion and completely satisfactory from the standpoint of comfort and artistic appeal.

The fabrics and accessories which were used originally with French furniture, and which are still appropriate artistically, are elegant, dainty, and feminine in the extreme. Silks and laces were used for bedspreads; rich tapestries and Oriental rugs were used for floor coverings and hangings. Chandeliers were of crystal, gold, and silver.

Nowadays, the trend in home furnishings is toward simplicity. It is possible, however, to achieve that simplicity even though French furniture is used. Plain, delicately colored fabrics can be combined with toiles and chintzes; the rugs can be plain broadloom; the lamp bases and shades can be simplified in design. The result will still be extremely feminine, but the room will be more livable and more suitable to the present-day trend toward simplicity.

It is unwise, however, to buy French furniture on a small budget. Cheap reproductions of French furniture are shoddy and have little real beauty.

Renaissance furniture is massively elegant.

The Renaissance periods in Italy, Spain, and England were periods of great wealth for some people and abysmal poverty for others. The homes of nobility were castles. Rooms were 20 feet high and were ballroom size. Floors were stone or tile, and the general tone of the interiors was impersonal and formal.

The present-day version of this elaborate Renaissance furniture, as a result, harmonizes only with institutional interiors. It does not fit or harmonize with any but the largest and most palatial homes. It dwarfs the average home and chokes its rooms.

Renaissance furniture is ornate in decoration and massive in scale. It is appropriate in very large rooms, such as this one, but overpowering in most homes of today.

The spirit of Renaissance furniture is one of impersonal, massive elegance which is all right for a spacious hotel lobby or club but not for the average home. In fact, it is almost impossible to create an informal, homelike personal atmosphere around this style of furniture.

The woods used for the furniture of the Renaissance period were oak and walnut. The weight and toughness of these woods lend themselves to the heavy carving and the straight lines characteristic of its style.

The designs are overpowering, straight-lined, formal, and ornate. Beds were tremendous in size and were hung with curtains for privacy and warmth. Tables were long and narrow because people usually sat on one side only. Chairs were thronelike. Present-

Manor house

Lamp

Spanish chair

Spanish side chair

Italian side chair

Draperies

Italian credenza

182

Candelabra

Italian fireplace

Italian X-chair

English refectory table

Spanish desk

English canopy bed

day manufacturers, as a rule, reproduce this furniture in these same proportions, and for that reason the furniture is out of scale for the homes of today.

The fabrics and accessories demanded by the Renaissance periods were originally, and still are, heavy, ornate, and elegant. Marble, bronze, damask, velour, velvet, tooled leather, oil paintings, large tapestries, and Oriental rugs—all were and are appropriate with this furniture.

Modern furniture has charm and severe simplicity.

Modern, or Twentieth Century, furniture makes an immediate appeal to those who like utilitarian furniture that is severe and simple. It suits people who want their home to have sophistication and yet simplicity. It suits the people who are pioneers at heart.

The style first appeared at the Paris Exposition in 1925. Since then it has gone through drastic changes of line and form. In fact, it has followed rather closely the changes that have taken place in the modern automobile. Both the car and the furniture began with the high, angular build of the model T Ford, and both have gradually evolved into the smooth, low simplicity of present-day designs.

A similar process of evolution has, to a greater or lesser degree, taken place in the development of every other style of furniture which we know about. No style has ever sprung full-blown into complete acceptance.

The spirit of Modern furniture is basically one of simplicity, impersonality, and adjustability. Modern furniture that meets these requirements is truly good furniture.

The woods used in Modern furniture are numberless—mahogany, oak, walnut, pine, and many others. As a rule, though, these woods are bleached to a light blond or a grayed blond. The blond finishes are very practical because they do not show dust and therefore do not present a constant dusting problem in a metropolitan area.

The designs of Modern furniture have not as yet settled down completely, but certain very definite characteristics are beginning to show up.

Modern furniture is simple of line and yet sophisticated. It is adjustable to the needs of twentieth-century living.

Twentieth Century house

Castleton
chinaware

Chairs

Side chair

Side chair

Lounge chair

Individually assembled units

Sectional chaise longue

Furniture and Furnishings

Planter lamp

Fireplace

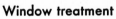

Window treatment

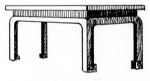

Coffee table

Hollywood bed

Planter bookshelves

1) Versatility of function, or adjustability, seems to be the first and most basic of the design characteristics that distinguish Modern furniture. Sectional sofas are so designed that they can be used as single chairs or as two-, three-, or four-seated settees. Tables are made so they can be used as card tables and dining tables and also be lowered to coffee-table height. Small tables are designed so they can be used individually beside chairs or put together to form one large coffee table in front of a large sofa. Wooden storage furniture is made in units of drawers, shelves, and cupboards that can be arranged in endless combinations. Such designs as these express versatility of function, which is a distinctive characteristic of Modern furniture that seems likely to persist.

2) Smooth, simple line is a second characteristic which seems to be basic and probably will last. We like this line in clothes, in cars, and in architecture. Certainly this type of line will last, even though certain interpretations of it may change.

3) Storage space in cabinets, dressers, and chests, specifically designed to hold wearing apparel or household equipment, is a third characteristic of Modern furniture designs. Divided, shallow drawers for wearing apparel are easy to keep in order. Specially designed storage drawers for household equipment make chests and cabinets of great importance as housekeeping aids.

4) Softness of appearance is an attractive characteristic of some of the Modern furniture. The deep springs and fabric-enveloped frame, with little or no wood showing, give Modern upholstered pieces a luxurious, comfortable appearance.

5) Lightness in appearance of occasional chairs is achieved by using interlaced straps, thin foam-rubber cushions, or molded plywood for seats and backs.

Some of the weaknesses of Modern furniture designs are also beginning to show up, and in consequence some of the designs are already being discarded.

1) A great many of the chairs and sofas are much too large in scale for the average-sized room. A few of these oversized pieces choke a room, limit its usefulness, and make good furniture arrangement difficult, if not impossible.

2) The solid-box bases of some of the upholstered pieces make them very unwieldy. Homemakers find them difficult to move when cleaning, and hosts find them almost impossible to move around when an adjustment in grouping is desired.

3) The stark, impersonal simplicity of line of some of the more angular pieces is likely to become tiresome. This is particularly true of the wooden pieces, such as tables and chairs.

4) Some of the upholstery on the inexpensive Modern is garish in color and overscaled in pattern. These two features increase the apparent size of the pieces and thus decrease their usability in average-sized or small rooms.

The fabrics and accessories for Modern furniture have made greater changes in home interiors than has the furniture itself. The modern trend in fabrics has proved that plain fabrics can be beautiful if they have lovely color and interesting texture, produced by variations in weave and yarn. It has outmoded the whole group of dull, ineffectually patterned fabrics whose main reason for being was that they "blended with everything."

The modern trend has introduced a whole new field of drapery fabrics that have a spongy, soft texture produced by nubby yarns and new weaves. These fabrics in heavier form make strong, durable upholstery fabrics.

The modern trend in accessories is toward a strikingly functional type of design. Ash trays are large enough to be useful. Vases and plant containers are designed to hold a luxurious quantity of flowers or greens advantageously. Picture frames are strong and simple. Book ends are heavy and structural in design.

The tendency toward a sparing use of accessories with Modern furniture accentuates the importance of each accessory. Each is, therefore, usually selected carefully so that it will play an important part in the color and decorative scheme of the room. In a well-decorated Modern room, there is no such thing as a clutter of accessories.

Metal furniture has been found increasingly useful.

Metal furniture has had a great increase in popularity in the last few years. The reason is probably that metal is the most work-

Lacy metal furniture is practical and popular for indoor and outdoor living.

able material ever known. It has tremendous strength, even when it is reduced to finely drawn wire. It also lends itself to an endlessly wide range of designs and styles.

The spirit of metal furniture is almost as varied in kind as the many forms that metal can take. The only generalization that can be made is that almost every type of metal furniture has a clean, outdoor look that is satisfying and very appropriate in some settings.

The designs roughly divide into three types: (1) the clinical, chromium-pipe style that is good in kitchens, lavatories, and bathrooms; (2) several outdoor styles that range from the strictly functional style to the ornate lacy-leaf designs similar to those used in the French Quarter in New Orleans; and (3) a weathered-looking green metal style in beautifully graceful designs that combines modern sophistication with traditional grace and charm of line. Glass tops give the tables of this green metal type a light feeling, and cretonne-covered cushions lend a softness to the chairs and settees that make them equally attractive indoors and outdoors.

The fabrics and accessories that are used with the clinical style must be very simple, modern, and impersonal. Anything made of fabric to be used with this metal furniture—such as curtains, pillows, or lamp shades—should be water-repellent and strong in color or design. Ash trays, lamp bases, and plant containers should be utterly plain or very simply decorated pottery or chromium to harmonize with the furniture. Nothing should be used that is quaint or cute.

The accessories for the New Orleans type can be more decorative, but the fabrics should be the smooth-surfaced type.

Accessories for the green metal type can be selected from a wide variety of styles because the furniture itself is so adjustable and sympathetic in style. Nearly any kind of smoothly sophisticated lamp base of pottery, plaster, or glass with a parchment shade is appropriate. Sailcloth or cretonne makes perfect draperies and pillows. Pictures should be glass-covered and unframed, or they should be framed in simple natural wood frames. Plants or simple Oriental figures for decorative accents harmonize and contribute to the delightful, graciously modern out-of-doors atmosphere which this furniture produces.

The cost of upkeep of metal furniture is very little, which is a great advantage. The only disadvantage of metal furniture is its coldness. In a warm climate this is, of course, an advantage, but in a northern climate it is bound to seem inappropriate in the winter.

Some furniture pieces blend with all styles.

There are certain pieces of upholstered furniture which are so simple in line that they blend with any style of wooden furniture. They take their style from the fabric in which they are upholstered or slipcovered and from the pieces of period furniture with which they are used. (See drawings on page 192.)

The Lawson sofa is one of these pieces of furniture. It is a simple, straight-line type of sofa that harmonizes with Modern furniture, with Eighteenth Century furniture, with provincial styles, or with the Renaissance period. In fact, it is like a well-tailored suit—

Furniture that Blends with All Styles

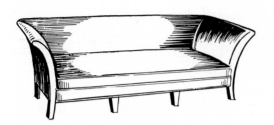

Tuxedo sofa

Barrel chair

Lawson sofa

Club chair

Charles of London sofa

Lounge chair

it looks well anywhere and depends entirely on such factors as color, quality, and type of fabric for its character.

The Charles of London sofa is another piece of furniture which has no period and no special affiliation. Because of its weight and its straight lines it is sometimes considered to be Jacobean, but actually it is as adjustable as the Lawson, except that it harmonizes better with slightly more masculine or heavier types of furniture from any period.

The Tuxedo sofa is a third piece which is simple, straight-lined, and periodless. Because of its high arm, it has a little more formality than the Lawson sofa, but it, like the Lawson, takes its character from its fabric covering.

The wing chair, the barrel chair, and the channel-back chair are all standard chair forms that were used all through the late seventeenth and eighteenth centuries in England and on the Continent. They also are as adaptable as the three sofas listed above and can be blended according to their upholstery.

CHECKING YOUR KNOWLEDGE . . .

1. Considering harmony of design, what furniture would you select for a kitchen with white streamlined refrigerator, stove, and sink?

2. Why are modern adaptations of provincial furniture more comfortable than the originals for present-day use?

3. Is it wise to buy authentic copies or originals of such things as cobbler's benches and candlestands? Give reasons.

4. Which would you select for a small living room—Italian Renaissance furniture or Eighteenth Century mahogany?

5. Why is Louis XV and Louis XVI furniture seldom used for living rooms?

USING YOUR KNOWLEDGE . . .

1. Write a letter to any museum, art institute, important club, or college in your area inquiring what authentic period furniture they have in their possession and whether your class may see it. Then arrange a trip, using a chartered bus or cars driven by parents. Take notes on both furniture and settings to form the basis of class discussion. Check particularly on the harmony between fabrics, accessories, function, and furniture.

2. Discuss with the head of your leading furniture store the possibility of a group or individual survey of the authentic period furniture in his shop. Find out what period furniture is on the market and how many pieces illustrated in this chapter can be found in the store. Note their cost.

3. List people you know who would enjoy the following styles of furniture: (*a*) informal, provincial; (*b*) adjustable, middle class; (*c*) sophisticated, feminine; (*d*) and massively elegant. Tell why you think so.

4. Select the type of furniture you would like in your own home and bring to class information about five pieces of that style which you have seen in stores or catalogues.

5. Tell about one book or story you have recently read in which there are descriptions of room furniture in a style discussed in this chapter. Tell what the period was, analyze the type of people and the life they lived, and decide whether the furniture was well selected for their uses.

6. Make a survey of the furniture in one of the rooms of your school, your home, or some public building. Analyze the period, the setting, and the function of the room, and decide whether the furniture was well selected.

7. Do the same with the rooms shown in three movies you have seen lately.

SECTION THREE: *Fabrics in the Home*

The color filmstrip "Fabrics in the Girl's Room" has been prepared to correlate with this section.

CHAPTER 10: Beauty out of Whole Cloth

Most girls and women enjoy selecting and working with fabrics for their clothes. Selecting fabrics for a room or a home should be equally enjoyable because bedspreads, draperies, and slipcovers are the clothes of a room. Fabrics can accentuate the personality of a room in the same way that clothes can accentuate the personality of a girl or woman. Therefore, the fabrics for a room should be selected to meet the same tests as those used in selecting dress fabrics.

Tests used when buying clothes may be applied when buying fabrics for homes.

Because fabrics for furnishings can be considered the clothes of a room, we apply the three tests in their selection which most women apply automatically when buying clothes: (1) Will it be appropriate for the functions for which I plan to use it? (2) Will it be suitable for the climate as well as the locale? (3) Will it harmonize with my personality and enhance my appearance?

If these three tests were applied when fabrics are being selected for the home, many mistakes would be avoided and the fabrics in each room would be functional, appropriate, and individually beautiful.

Test 1: Is the fabric appropriate for the functions of the room? The changes in the functions of bedrooms within the last few years have necessitated a change in the types of fabrics used in them. For

A boy's room—for study and entertaining—should be done in fabrics that will not crush easily and will not show soil.

instance, when bedrooms were sleeping rooms only, it was possible to use white or crushable taffeta bedspreads. Nowadays, a girl's or boy's bedroom is also a study and a place to entertain friends; consequently, the bedspread must be made of material that does not show soil and will not crush when the bed is used for sitting or lounging. Master bedrooms have also gone through some changes in use. Previously, when bedrooms were sleeping rooms only, even master bedrooms were likely to be decorated in a feminine style. Nowadays, when both parents may spend an evening in their room while the young people of the family are entertaining in the living room, fabrics not only must be in harmony with the new functions of the room but they must be appropriate for the man as well as the woman.

Test 2: Is the fabric suitable for the climate and locale? Extremes of heat and cold in climate will quickly show the need for this test in selecting the fabrics for a home. A bearskin rug or a deep-pile plush upholstery fabric would be as ridiculous in the tropics as a fur coat; while slick-surfaced grass matting, chintz, sheer organdy, smooth sateen, and cool muslin are examples of fabrics that are more pleasing during hot weather than when the temperature is below zero.

In a cold climate, heavy curtains that help to shut out the breezes will add comfort to living. Deep-pile fabrics, such as velveteen and frieze, and wool fabrics of all kinds are particularly appropriate. Even slipcovers made of spongy or nubby fabrics, such as corduroy and antique satin, will give an effect of depth and warmth. If smooth fabrics are used, they can be quilted to give them the additional weight and depth so appropriate for a cold climate.

Test 3: Does the fabric harmonize with the personality of the room? The personality of the room should, of course, express the personality of the occupant. So, a girl who likes tailored clothes should use such fabrics as gingham, linen, and sailcloth in her room. A girl who likes dainty things should use dotted swiss, organdy, or sateen. A boy who enjoys outdoor sports should go to the other extreme. He should have coarse, heavy materials, such as homespun, burlap, or heavy drill, in his room.

Color often helps greatly to determine the personality of a

For warm climates, slick-surfaced, smooth, cool fabrics are appropriate. If used on a porch, they should also be waterproof.

fabric in a room. For instance, a corded poplin would be an excellent choice for a girl's room if it were in light pink, and it might also be right for a boy's room if it were in cocoa brown.

Pattern also helps greatly to determine the personality and therefore the use of a fabric. A cretonne with a conservative tree-of-life design in soft, rich colors blends perfectly with traditional furnishings in a living room, dining room, den, or man's bedroom. The same fabric with a dramatic modern design in bold colors is an excellent complement to metal porch furniture or modern living-room furniture.

**Fabrics should be selected for their
practical qualities.**

Fortunately, it is no longer necessary to sacrifice the beauty of fabrics for the sake of practicality. It is possible to obtain fabrics

For cold climates, deep-pile, heavy fabrics are more appropriate because they look and feel warm for brisk days.

that have all the practical qualities desired and that are, at the same time, so beautiful that they add charm and individuality to the room. The important thing is to check the fabric you are considering so as to be sure that it does possess the necessary practical qualities.

Unfortunately, most of the practical qualities of a fabric are hidden and cannot be discovered by inspection. Even an expert cannot always tell at a glance whether a fabric is colorfast, whether it has been preshrunk, or whether its surface finish is permanent, semipermanent, or temporary. Yet all these qualities influence the utility of the fabric and help to dictate its use. Other qualities, such as strength, weight, and durability, are more obvious, but must also be considered in making a selection.

The hidden qualities of a fabric will be more important throughout the lifetime of a fabric than they would seem at first. Only by carefully reading the tags and labels attached to the fabric, by look-

Personality of Fabric Designs

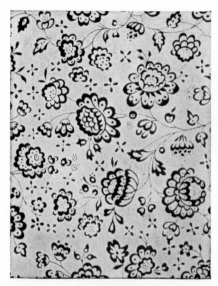

PEASANT

TRADITIONAL

MODERN

These three designs vividly express the varieties of personality possible in pattern. The one at the top (*left*) is quaintly simple and direct in its delicately strong black-and-white all-over design. The one directly above has sophistication and elegance in its muted grays and sweeping lines. The one at the bottom has strength and force in its austerely plain lines and strong, heavy pattern.

(ALL PHOTOS BY COURTESY *Interiors*)

ing at the printing on the selvage of the material, or by questioning the salesperson about a fabric can a buyer get information about the hidden qualities which are so important. These three hidden qualities are colorfastness, shrinkage, and type of finish.

1) Whether or not a fabric is colorfast is very important. Some fabrics are advertised as being satisfactorily colorfast to washing and some to be colorfast to sunlight. Some firms specialize in using dyes that are as near sunfast as possible, and a well-trained salesperson will know that fact. Actually, no fabrics are guaranteed to be absolutely colorfast, but some are far more sun-resistant than others. Selvage markings and tags usually indicate whether the color of a fabric is tubfast and sun-resistant—qualities which will make it possible to use colored fabrics even though they must be washed frequently and are to be used on or near sunny windows.

2) Whether or not a fabric has been preshrunk or how much it will shrink when washed is just as important as its colorfast quality. Some cotton and some wool fabrics are now treated to reduce shrinkage or stretch to a minimum, but this treatment is more frequently used for dress goods than for materials for furnishing. If no label is attached, it might be wise to buy a small amount of material, cut it in half, and wash one of the pieces. It will then be possible to determine exactly the amount of shrinkage to expect. It is also possible to check the colorfast quality in the same experiment. If, in the experiment, there is a considerable amount of shrinkage, the material should be preshrunk at home before it is made up. This preshrinking will make it possible to fit slipcovers, bedspreads, or curtains accurately when they are being made without having to allow for shrinkage.

3) Whether a finish is temporary, semipermanent, or permanent is another matter which should be checked at the time of purchase. The desirability of one finish over another depends entirely upon the purpose for which the fabric is to be used.

Wax and starch finishes on chintz add a temporary luster and smoothness that are beautiful to look at and that shed dirt effectively. Wax and starch finishes, however, must be replaced each time the material is washed. Some finishes that look like wax or starch are semipermanent and last for several washings. Merceriza-

FEMININE FABRICS

(ALL PHOTOS BY COURTESY *Interiors*)

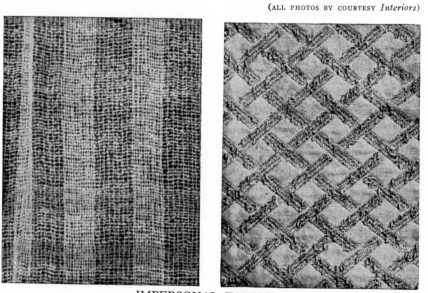

IMPERSONAL FABRICS

Fabric Weaves

COURTESY *Interiors*   COURTESY *The New York Times*

MASCULINE FABRICS

Feminine fabrics are so called because of their delicacy of fiber, design, color, or weave. A fabric that is feminine from all four points of view should only be used in a girl's or woman's room. A fabric that has only one or two feminine qualities may be used in a master bedroom or guest room.

Impersonal fabrics are equally useful for both men's and women's rooms so far as fiber, weave, pattern, and color are concerned. They are especially usable in traditional living and dining rooms because they have more strength than feminine fabrics yet are not so strong as to overpower the fine carving and delicate inlay of traditional furniture.

Masculine fabrics have a roughness or coarseness of weave, a strength of fiber, and a simplicity and boldness of pattern and color. Woven patterns, such as stripes and tweeds, often fall into this category, and all masculine fabrics have a casual, functional feeling which makes them especially suitable in contemporary rooms as well as in men's and boys' rooms.

tion is a manufacturing process that adds luster to yarns. Fabrics woven of these yarns have a smooth satinlike sheen that gives them a rich and elegant appearance. Permanent stiffness is a third quality which is now being added to sheer fabrics, such as organdy and voile. This quality increases their usefulness and is supposed to last for the lifetime of the fabric.

Check selvage printing and labels for information about all of these less obvious qualities. They completely change the possible uses of fabrics. For example, organdy to which a permanent stiffness has been added can be used in a steamy kitchen or bathroom—an impossibility for ordinary organdy. Cretonne that has been water-proofed may be used on porch furniture because it will withstand morning and evening dews.

The obvious qualities of a fabric are strength, weight, and durability. A good shopper can, as a rule, identify these qualities by a casual examination of the material. Bedspreads often must take heavy wear and should be made of a strong, heavy, serviceable fabric, such as corduroy, velveteen, quilted cotton, homespun, or chenille. Slipcovers, stretched tightly over chairs or couches, should also be made of strong, durable fabrics. Closely woven strong wools and cottons that will not pull out at the seams are good examples of fabrics that wear well and that are easily recognized even by an inexperienced shopper.

Fabrics for furnishings that are not subjected to heavy wear can be as delicate and fragile as is desirable or obtainable. Curtains, for instance, may be made of fabrics that are loosely woven and sheer without impairing their usefulness. A dressing-table skirt in a girl's room or a canopy on a girl's bed can be made of delicate fabrics because they receive no hard wear. But there are very few instances where the durability of fabrics can be ignored. When up-holstered or slipcovered chairs need a plastic covering to protect them from the daily wear and tear of the family they were bought to serve, it is a sign that the fabrics in which they were upholstered or slipcovered were not well selected. A bedspread that cannot take daily use and must be saved for special occasions is not only made of a fabric that is too fragile, but of a fabric that would be inap-propriate for the room at any time. Every fabric that is used in a room should be able to meet the demands of everyday living in that room. It should not have to be protected, except at points of special wear.

Fabrics for windows should be selected with three requirements in mind.

The three things to be kept in mind when deciding on fabrics for windows are: (1) the placement of the windows, their number, and their proportions; (2) the type of the room and its decorative scheme; and (3) the exposure of the windows and the setting of the house. These conditions should be analyzed so the window treatment can be planned and the fabrics selected accordingly.

The placement of windows, their number, and their proportions should be noted first in order to determine whether or not the windows are worthy of being given decorative importance in the room. If the windows are well placed, not too numerous, and well proportioned, it is possible to add a great deal of beauty to the room by accenting them. This can be done by curtaining them with fabrics that contrast with the walls in color, in value, or in both. If the walls are plain, a figured curtain can be used for additional contrast. The use of any one of these methods of contrast is like saying, "Look at these windows. They are important."

If windows are badly proportioned but are well placed in the room, curtains can be hung in a way that will apparently improve the proportions and make the windows worthy of decorative emphasis. In fact, when curtains are properly selected and appropriately used, they can do all the things for a window that the right clothes can do for a woman. (See drawings on page 208.) When windows are too short, the curtains should be floor-length, and a cornice or valance may be set up on the wall above the window. This will increase the apparent height of the window, just as a long dress or a high-crowned hat will seemingly add to the height of a short girl.

When windows are too narrow, the curtains should cover the casing only and hang out over the wall, leaving all the glass of the window exposed. This treatment will make the window seem wider.

When windows are well proportioned, the curtains should be

Treatment for Difficult Windows

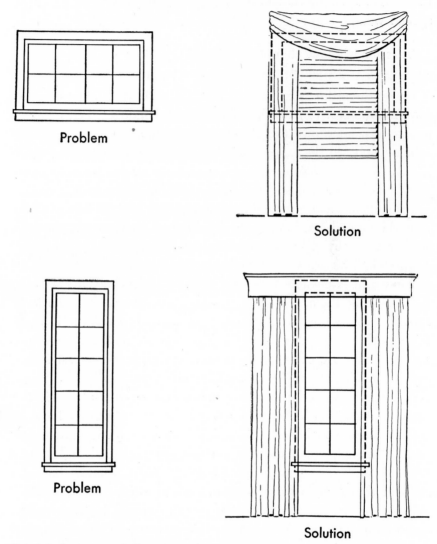

Careful placement of draperies and cornices can completely transform windows that are poorly proportioned.

hung so as to cover the window casing at the top and sides, thus preserving the good proportions established by the architect.

If the windows are too numerous or badly placed, they should be made inconspicuous by being curtained with a plain fabric that matches the wall in color and value. Many people prefer curtains in fabrics that match the color of the walls even when the windows are well placed and well proportioned, because this treatment of windows enlarges the appearance of the room and allows attention to center on beautiful pictures, a rug, or some other object that has more personal or decorative importance than the windows.

The type of the room and its decorative scheme should be accentuated by the fabrics selected for the windows, just as clothes are selected to accentuate the personality of the wearer.

For instance, curtains of muslin or plaid could be used by the girl who loves the out-of-doors, sports, and simplicity; whereas organdy, cotton taffeta, and Glosheen would be right for the room of a girl who is dainty, feminine, and petite.

The exposure of the windows and the setting of the house often dictate the type of curtain and therefore the fabric to be used for the windows.

1) Glass curtains are so called because they hang next to the glass in one long panel or in short panels attached to the window sash itself. They are usually made of transparent net or gauze and are kept drawn for privacy. Windows that are directly opposite those of a neighbor or close to a street should be curtained with glass curtains. The personality of the room would, of course, dictate whether the curtains should be made of fine, coarse, filmy, plain, or decorative net or gauze. Glass curtains of fine net, organdy, or voile are particularly good in a room for a girl. A coarse net, such as theatrical gauze or fishnet, would be right for glass curtains in a boy's or man's room. Plain marquisette or net, hung very straight and gathered in deep folds, would be appropriate for rooms that are used by both men and women, such as a guest room, a master bedroom, or a living room.

In any of these situations, the glass curtains can be given weight and decorative importance by edging them with colored tape or brush fringe or crisscrossing the entire curtain with trimming to form large diamonds or squares.

Another way to assure privacy or shut out a bad view is to use Venetian or bamboo blinds, which can be kept down without cutting out too much light. (See illustrations on page 225.) This type

COURTESY *Popular Home*

The draperies in both of these rooms were well selected to suit the personality and uses of the rooms—durable, functional, short draperies for a playroom; decorative, long, and graceful draperies for a dignified living room.

COURTESY *Better Homes and Gardens*

of window treatment is appropriate in any but a very feminine room.

Contrary to popular belief, Venetian blinds are as appropriate with Eighteenth Century furniture as with Twentieth Century furniture, because they were made and used in colonial times. There are two disadvantages to the use of Venetian blinds, however, with any kind of furniture: (1) They can never be moved to a window of different size. (2) They are difficult to keep clean.

The use of growing plants, set close together in an inside or outside window box, is a more unusual method of achieving partial privacy. If complete privacy is desired, plants can be set on shelves that divide the window evenly, or they can be trained to grow on a trellis made of bamboo fishing rods which can be bought at a hardware store. Such a trellis can be made by nailing the fishing poles together at each crossing and tying them with raffia. The use of plants for privacy should not be adopted when a room has more than two windows, because too many plants would have to be used and the room would resemble a greenhouse.

2) Draw-curtains are the kind of curtains that hang on each side of a window during the day but are wide enough to be drawn across the window at night to prevent outsiders from seeing in or to avoid the glare produced by the glass on the interior of the room at night. Draw-curtains can be used for windows that do not require daytime privacy but need it at night when the lights are on. They not only provide nighttime privacy but give the room charm both day and night. The fabrics for draw-curtains may be plain or figured, heavy or light, but they should be of a soft material that can be drawn easily and that will hang gracefully.

3) Draperies [1] are heavy, decorative curtains that hang on each side of the window. Draperies are usually not wide enough to be drawn and are sometimes used with glass curtains or blinds. Sometimes draperies are used alone at windows that need neither daytime nor nighttime privacy. The main purpose of draperies is to decorate and soften the outline of a window. Draw-draperies, like draw-curtains, may be used for large picture windows to shut out too much sunlight during the day or to assure privacy at night. They

[1] Draperies should never be referred to as "drapes." The word "drapes" is a verb.

may be made of most of the same fabrics used for side draperies, and they may be lined or unlined.

In order to control the light from windows for daytime naps, for movies or television, or for the protection of furnishings, window shades, which can be purchased in translucent, semitranslucent, and absolutely opaque fabric, are the most useful. They can be kept rolled up inconspicuously under a cornice or valance when not in use. They can be obtained in any colors so they will blend with the color of the curtains or the wall when they are pulled down.

Fabrics for room furnishings should enhance the furniture.

Fabrics for bedspreads, slipcovers, and upholstery must enhance the wood of the furniture or harmonize with it in color, texture, and weight, and should blend with the design of the furniture as well.

The color, texture, and weight of furniture woods vary considerably. Satinwood, lacquered woods, bleached mahogany, walnut, and fruit woods are all fine-grained, light in color, and capable of taking a high polish. Fabrics for slipcovers and upholstery for furniture made of any of these woods may vary from slick-surfaced chintz to elegant velvet. The only fabrics that do not harmonize with these woods are the heavy, nubby, coarse fabrics. These fabrics are appropriate for furniture of bleached or natural oak, because oak is a coarse-grained, tough wood.

The design of the furniture also must be considered in selecting fabrics for upholstery, slipcovers, and bedspreads. If the furniture is plain, patterned fabrics may be used with it. If, however, the furniture is carved or decorated to any extent, the fabrics for its upholstery, slipcover, or bedspread should be plain so that the decorated wood may be the center of interest.

If the furniture is small in scale, any design that might be present in the upholstery or slipcover fabrics should be small in scale also, so as not to be overpowering. If the furniture is large and massive, the fabric designs can be correspondingly large in scale.

It is well to remember that a fabric or a color which would not be practical for upholstery might be perfectly practical for a slip-

The way in which fabrics are used enhances their beauty and helps to determine the tone of the room. Here, the formal swags emphasize the dignity of the room. The upholstery fabric—in its strong, yet conservative, stripe—repeats the stripe effect of the louvred shutters and harmonizes with the simplicity of the Directoire chairs.

cover, because slipcovers, unlike upholstery, can be removed and cleaned periodically. Furniture that is to be covered with slipcovers may be bought "in muslin" at a considerably lower cost than an upholstered piece of the same quality. Slipcovers nowadays—thanks to zippers and snap tapes—have all the trim smoothness of a good upholstery job. They are no longer in the class of protectors for better upholstery. They have definitely graduated to a place of importance and effectiveness equal to that of the upholstery itself.

CHECKING YOUR KNOWLEDGE . . .

1. What are the tests used in buying fabrics for clothes that can be applied in buying fabrics for home furnishings?
2. What practical qualities influence the use of fabrics and yet are not obvious at first glance?
3. What practical qualities that are apparent to any good shopper influence the wearability of fabrics?
4. What three things should be known about windows before the fabrics are selected to curtain them?
5. What are (a) glass curtains, (b) draw-curtains, (c) draperies, (d) draw-draperies?
6. What type of fabric can be used with furniture that is made of light, fine-grained, highly polished wood?
7. What type of fabric is appropriate with oak?
8. Is it artistically correct to use a patterned fabric on a chair that has a great deal of carving?

USING YOUR KNOWLEDGE . . .

1. List the fabrics which could be used correctly in three rooms of your home. Check each with the tests listed in the chapter.
2. Visit a drapery department and make a list of all the practical qualities given on fabric tags or printed on selvages that would be important in determining the use of a fabric.
3. Pretend that you are selecting fabrics for three special purposes. Which of the fabrics examined in Number 2 would you select, according to its practical qualities, for each of the uses?
4. Analyze the windows in the kitchen or dining room in your own home or in the homemaking center at school. Consider light control, view, and style of the room. With these facts in mind, plan one

window treatment that uses fabric and one that uses plants, shutters, or some other fabric substitute.

5. Find a poorly proportioned window in your own home, a friend's home, or your school. Plan how you would curtain it to minimize the effect of the bad proportions.

6. Analyze three windows, each of which could be treated with a different type of curtain—(*a*) glass curtains, (*b*) draw-curtains, and (*c*) draperies with glass curtains or blinds.

7. Visit a furniture store in your community. Ask the cost of a piece of furniture "in muslin" and the cost of the same piece covered in an upholstery fabric of your own choice. Then ask the exact cost of slipcovering that same piece of furniture. Estimate the difference in cost and list the advantages of each type of covering.

CHAPTER 11: Fabrics that Fit Your Room

After learning about the selection of fabrics, as you did in Chapter 10, you can begin to make that information important to you personally by taking the next step—deciding how fabrics should be selected and made up for your own room. In order to make that decision, analyze yourself to be sure that the style you select for your fabric furnishings will harmonize with your personality.

Use a style for your fabric furnishings that will harmonize with your personality.

In deciding on a style to use for the curtains, bedspread, and slipcovers in your own room, pretend you are selecting a pattern for a new dress or skirt. Fabric furnishings are the clothes of your room, and they can help to establish its tone and personality just as the style of your clothes enhances your personality.

If someone asked you, "Which do you prefer—a plain, a ruffled, a circular, or a pleated skirt?" you could probably answer immediately. In that answer lies an excellent style guide to use for your curtains, bedspread, dressing-table skirt, or slipcovers. They, too, can be plain, ruffled, circular, or pleated.

Even the length of skirt you prefer for your clothes might be used as a guide in determining the length you make your curtains. Street-length skirts in dresses have their counterpart in short, apron-length curtains or Dutch curtains. If you love to swish around in a

COURTESY ARMSTRONG CORK COMPANY

The fabrics in a bedroom should express the personality of the occupant, harmonize with the style and type of furniture, and give individuality to the room.

housecoat or in a formal, you will enjoy floor-length curtains—particularly the kind that draw.

You will enjoy ruffles on curtains, around the top of a dressing-table skirt, and around your lamp shades if you like them on dresses. If you prefer smooth, softly tailored lines in your clothes, you will prefer straight-edged curtains that hang from a smoothly upholstered or painted cornice. You will want corded seams on bedspreads and, for decoration, a well-designed initial in the center of the spread.

The fabric furnishings in your room can and should have all the individuality of your own clothes. For instance, you can even repeat dressmaker details in your curtains, bedspreads, and dressing-table skirts to personalize and individualize your fabric furnishings. Study the latest fashion magazines and adapt the details of dress design to the fabric furnishings of your room. (See drawings on opposite page.)

Buy room fabrics that are within your budget.

In planning an expenditure for fabrics, girls are likely either to allow too much money or to underestimate the cost. The same standards of cost should be maintained for home furnishings that are maintained for clothes. The type of shopping ingenuity that secures beauty in clothing without great expenditure should be used to secure beauty in fabric furnishings.

The actual cost of fabrics for a room varies as much as the cost of fabrics for clothes. Perhaps the most helpful thing to remember is that suitable materials may be obtained from many sources other than the drapery department in a department store. One of the most useful materials for curtains is Indian Head, which is very inexpensive. Gingham, from the dress-goods department, makes smart curtains, bedspreads, and dressing-table skirts. Bath toweling, from the household linen department, denim, and ticking all make unusual curtains and bedspreads. Curtains and bedspreads can also be made from bleached or unbleached sheeting. Awning material is splendid for cornices in boys' and men's rooms.

The hidden cost of room fabrics, which is quite different from the cost per yard of material, should be carefully considered in buying. For instance, in estimating the cost of window curtains, you may find that single-width panels of 36-inch material are ample, in which case it would be wasteful to buy 50-inch material. On the other hand, it may be that a 50-inch fabric can take the place of a panel made of one-and-a-half widths of 36-inch fabric. Thus, if the 50-inch fabric is $2.00 a yard, and the 36-inch fabric is $1.50 a yard, the selection of the 50-inch fabric would be a clear saving, not only of 25 cents a yard, but also of labor in cutting and sewing the widths together.

It may be that 50-inch material will cut to much better advantage for slipcovers. Bedspreads, for even a twin bed, must be 39 inches wide, so anything narrower than 40-inch material adds immeasurably to the labor as well as the cost of bedspreads. For that

Your room fabrics can be styled according to your tastes in dress—tailored, flouncy, ruffly, plain, or fancy.

By the clever use of fabrics, a room can be made attractive and interesting at very little cost. This grouping consists of crates for the dressing table; an old mirror with a fabric-covered frame; an old ice-cream-parlor chair; and an old piano stool—but how new and fresh the pieces look when covered with a few yards of cotton fabric!

reason, buying a 36-inch fabric for a bedspread, even at a lower price, would be an extravagance.

Another hidden cost is that of the extra yardage which must be bought when patterned fabric is used to allow for matching designs at seams or centering designs in panels of curtains, on sofa cushions, or on the tops of bedspreads. The amount wasted depends upon the size of the design. The larger it is, the greater the probable waste of material. Of course a plain fabric is the most economical of all because there need not be an inch of material wasted in the use of the fabric.

Fabrics that must be dry-cleaned are much more expensive over a period of years than fabrics that are washable, even though the original price of the nonwashable fabric is less. A slipcover or curtain made of an inexpensive, nonwashable fabric must be dry-cleaned—an expensive process compared to washing. On the other hand, a slipcover or curtain made of an expensive cotton or linen that is washable is a good investment because it will save you more than its cost in the elimination of dry-cleaning bills during its lifetime. If, however, the slipcover or curtain is made of an expensive fabric that has very delicate fibers or is so loosely woven that it will not stand washing, you will have the cost of its upkeep in addition to the original cost. Therefore, a wise buyer will not only check the cost of a fabric per yard but will also check these hidden costs. Remember the price on the price tag is only the initial expenditure.

The total cost of fabric furnishings is greatly reduced if you can make things yourself. For example, the cost of material and equipment for curtains and slipcovers which you make yourself may be less than half of the total cost of a finished product which is made to order. Even when you buy ready-made curtains or slipcovers, what you are paying for labor is high in comparison with the cost of the material. By making your own fabric furnishings, you can really save a great deal of money and, at the same time, you will have more individuality in the style and design.

There are simple basic rules for the making of all fabric furnishings which, if followed, will produce an article that is professional-looking and will give you great satisfaction. Making curtains or slipcovers is less complicated than making a dress, so why not try your hand at it now in your own room?

Before you curtain your windows, learn about window construction.

In order to do a good job of curtaining your windows, you should know that windows are not all constructed alike. There are several different kinds of windows, each of which has its advantages and its disadvantages. Curtains or draperies must be adapted to any limitations imposed by architectural variations and, in addition, they must accentuate the beauty of the windows. Most windows will fall into one of the following classifications or types of construction. (See drawings on opposite page.)

Double-hung sash windows are the most common and the easiest to curtain because there is nothing about them to interfere with cornices, curtains, or blinds. If the windows are well proportioned, curtain rods can be hung at the edge of the wooden casing to save the plaster. If they are poorly proportioned or too small, they can be improved as suggested in Chapter 10 on page 207.

Outswinging casement windows are fairly easy to curtain because there is nothing about them to interfere with a cornice or curtains. However, it is obviously impossible to use glass curtains, shelves, or other unusual treatment on windows that open out. Another disadvantage of these windows is that they are difficult to screen.

Inswinging casement windows present no problem in screening, and they are easy to clean. However, these windows do present problems in curtaining. Curtains must be hung on swing arms or on rods that extend far enough over the plaster so that the curtain can be pushed back when the window is opened. Cornices must be set up on the casing or placed sufficiently high above the window to allow the free opening and closing of the window.

Dissimilar-sized windows in the same room should be made to look as uniform in size as possible. Sometimes this can be done by placing the cornices so that the window heights appear even and by extending the curtains out over the wall to make narrow windows appear wider.

Differences in the heights of window sills from the floor can be disguised by placing furniture in front of the high windows and by using floor-length curtains on all the windows. Actually, however, people are far less conscious of the differences in height of the sills than they are of other dissimilarities among windows.

When there is too great a discrepancy in the size of the windows, it is difficult to curtain them. They are best treated by covering up some of the windows entirely. For example, in a bedroom

Types of Window Construction

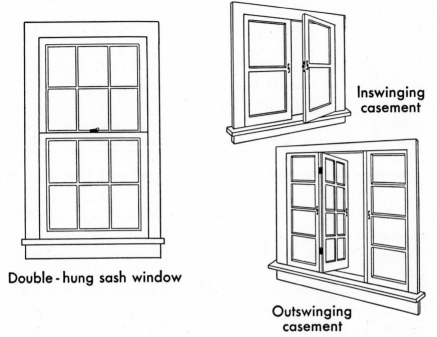

Inswinging
casement

Outswinging
casement

Double - hung sash window

Consider the type of window before planning for curtains or draperies. The double-hung sash window allows greatest freedom in curtaining. Inswinging casements interfere with cornices, unless they are placed high enough to clear the window when it is opened. Outswinging casements are difficult to curtain with glass curtains but will take unusual cornice treatments. (See page 222.)

a mirror can be placed so as to cover completely a very small window and its casing, and a dressing table can be used beneath it. Very small living-room windows can be covered by bookcases—an especially good arrangement for hiding the little windows on each side of a mantel. (See drawings on page 224.)

Groups of windows, no matter how large, must be treated as one unit, never as separate windows. This treatment may also be used for two windows that are separated by a wall space, if it is desired. If the wall space between the windows is not as wide as the windows, this treatment is especially effective. In any case, the entire grouping may be unified by the use of only one pair of cur-

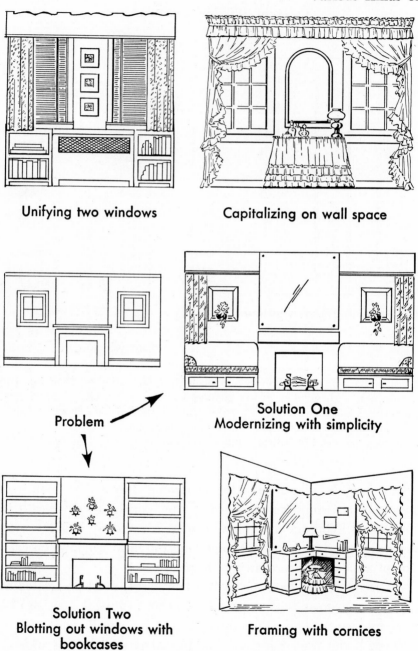

Unifying two windows

Capitalizing on wall space

Problem

Solution One
Modernizing with simplicity

Solution Two
Blotting out windows with
bookcases

Framing with cornices

All of these windows have been treated as a group rather than as individual units, and in each case they also become a part of a furniture grouping.

Window Treatments

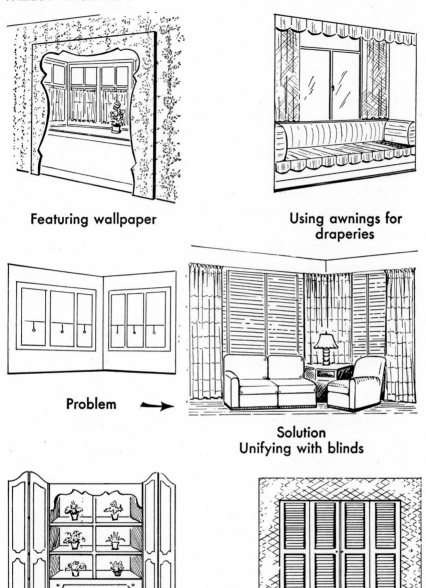

Featuring wallpaper

Using awnings for draperies

Problem ➞

Solution
Unifying with blinds

Curtaining with screens

Curtaining with shutters

Some windows may be best treated with drapery substitutes—such as wall-paper cornices, shutters, or screens. Others can be unified with blinds.

tains and one cornice placed over the two windows and the wall space. The wall space between the windows may be decorated with pictures, a mirror, or brackets.

However, if there are three windows or more on one wall—all separated by wall spaces which are equal to or wider than the windows themselves—they should be treated as separate units. In such a case, the curtains should match the color of the wall exactly so as to be as inconspicuous as possible. Six or more panels of contrasting material on one wall would demand too much attention.

A group of windows around the corner of a room should be treated to reflect the tone of the room. If the room is traditional in style, three panels of curtains are necessary—one for each of the two outside edges of the group and one for the corner. If the tone of the room is Modern, even though there is wall space at the corner, curtains should be used only at the outside limits of the group of windows. The corner wall space may be decorated with pictures, plants, a lamp, or mirrors.

With these points in mind, look your windows over carefully, at the same time keeping in mind the matters of privacy and view which were discussed in Chapter 10.

Your curtains and draperies should be well tailored.

Just as an irregular hem or a badly fitted sleeve will ruin the total impression of a woman's ensemble, so poorly tailored curtains, slipcovers, bedspreads, and dressing-table skirts will ruin the effect of an otherwise well-furnished room.

The tailoring of curtains should be done according to professional rules. Compared to making a dress, making curtains is simple if you follow the methods of those who do it professionally. Sometimes it is a temptation to skip the fine points, as we do when we give ourselves a home manicure, but if you do, the curtains will not have the professionally tailored appearance which they should have.

Taking measurements for curtains is the first step in curtain planning and making. Measure from the top of the casing to either the bottom of the window apron or the floor, depending on your decision as to length. (Check window terms in diagram on opposite page.) To that figure add 9 inches. This will allow for a single 3-inch

How to Measure for Draperies and Curtains

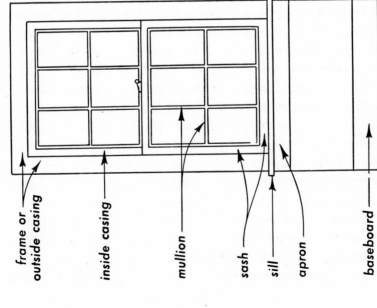

Legend for letters in drawing at right: Basic measurements for (*a*) floor-length draperies, (*b*) apron-length draperies, (*c*) sill-length curtains, and (*d*) draw-curtain width.

Terms Used for Parts of a Window

frame or outside casing

inside casing

mullion

sash

sill

apron

baseboard

hem at the bottom and a double 3-inch hem at the top for stiffness. Next, figure an allowance for shrinkage if the fabric is washable. (Review the discussion of shrinkage on page 203.) And last, if the material has a pattern, measure the size of the unit of the pattern and allow that much for matching the pattern at the top of each curtain. Each panel must have the units placed in the same position at the top of the curtain.

In planning draw-curtains, remember that pinch pleating requires double fullness. For example, if the rod length from wall out, across the window, and back to the wall is 33 inches, plan to have a total of 72 inches of material in the total width of the two panels in order to allow for twice the length of the rod plus two side hems 1 inch wide and a lap of 2 inches for each panel in the middle where the curtains come together.

In planning the amount of material needed for proper fullness in ruffles for curtains, double the length plus the width of the curtains. For example, if a curtain is 2 yards long and 1 yard wide, a ruffle on the inside and bottom of the curtain will require 6 yards of material the width of the ruffle. If a very full ruffle is desired, use three times the length plus the width of the curtain, or 9 yards of material the width of the ruffle.

Cutting the curtains by first drawing out a thread will ensure an accurate job. The only exception to this rule is in the cutting of a printed fabric, which should be cut according to the printed design rather than according to the weave. Do all the cutting of the material at one time, so that you reduce the fabric yardage to workable lengths as quickly as possible and know immediately if you haven't estimated your yardage correctly.

Tailoring the curtains begins with the removal of all selvages. This will keep the curtain from pulling up at seams and hems. If two or more widths are to be used in each curtain, the next step is to sew them together. Then measure, press, and sew the 1-inch side hems. Top and bottom hems come next, handled with the same routine of measuring, pressing, and then sewing. After that the French pleats should be put in, by following the steps shown in the drawings on page 230. Then the rings should be sewed on or the pins inserted. The pins should be placed about halfway between the top

COURTESY ALEXANDER SMITH & SONS CARPET COMPANY

If you want a patterned fabric for your bedspread, you should use plain fabrics for draperies, slipcovers, and floor coverings.

of the curtain and the base of the French pleat so that the top of the curtain will come to the top of the window casing and cover the rod. People who are experts in making curtains fold them in deep pleats to make them hang evenly. When the curtains are finished, they are folded as dictated by the pinch pleats and tied with tapes. The curtains are left folded thus for twenty-four hours to train them into proper folds without producing a rigid line, such as would result from pressing.

Be sure you get the right equipment for your window hangings.

The installing of curtains is as important as the making. In order to do it properly, you must know the types of drapery hardware which are on the market. (See drawings on page 231.)

How to Make French Pleats

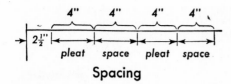

Spacing

The distance between pleats and spacing from edge of curtains depends upon the width of the fabric and the desired width of the curtain or drapery when finished. (*Note:* Measurements suggested are average.)

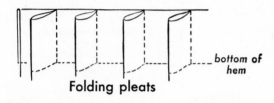

Folding pleats

Fold pleats desired size, and stitch each pleat from top edge of curtain to bottom of hem. Reinforce ends of stitching to prevent ripping.

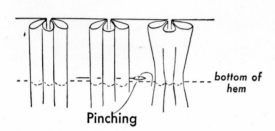

Pinching

Fold each pleat into three small pleats of equal size. Pinch together and sew securely at hemline.

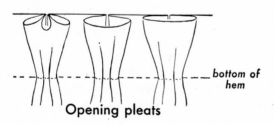

Opening pleats

Open out the top of the pleat.

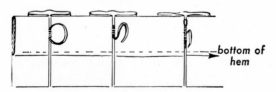

Attaching hooks, pins, or rings

Attach sew-on rings or pin-in hooks to back of each pleat, halfway between top of pleat and hemline.

Hardware Accessories for Draperies and Curtains

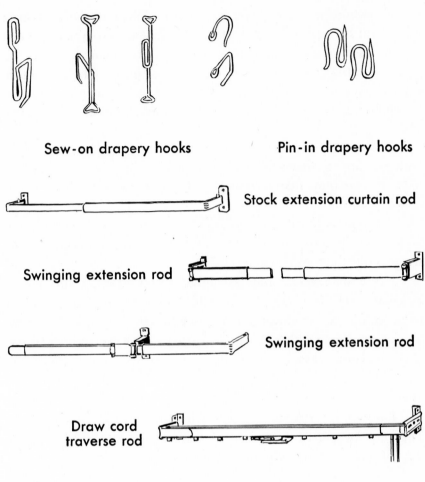

Sew-on drapery hooks   Pin-in drapery hooks

Stock extension curtain rod

Swinging extension rod

Swinging extension rod

Draw cord
traverse rod

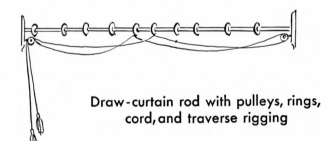

Draw-curtain rod with pulleys, rings,
cord, and traverse rigging

Hardware for window hangings should be selected according to specific needs. Each of these accessories has a value for a particular kind of window or a certain kind of window treatment.

Custom-made solid brass rods are excellent if the curtain is heavy and strength is needed. However, they are expensive and can only be used on the window for which they are planned.

The extension curtain rod comes in two forms. One kind holds the curtain close to the window glass; the other has a curved end which brings the curtain out beyond the extension of the window sill.

The swing arm, which is used for side curtains, is usually used with inswinging casement windows. Some of these are rigid. Others have an extension feature which makes it possible to use a wider panel of curtain.

Custom-made traverse rods, made to fit one window or a group of windows exactly, are very satisfactory for draw-curtains of any weight, but they are very expensive.

Extension traverse rods are quite a new product and a very welcome one. They may be used for draw-curtains on all except large groups of windows and are relatively inexpensive. Heretofore, equipment for draw-curtains was custom-made and expensive. Now, however, traverse extension rods are available at hardware and drapery stores, so it is possible to equip all but the largest groups of windows inexpensively.

Pin-in drapery hooks are especially good for washable curtains. They are inexpensive and a great laborsaving device, both at the time of making and at the time of each laundering.

Your bedspread will be one of three types.

Bedspreads should harmonize with room styles. If the room is done in a tailored style, a plain, simply corded spread with an unruffled flounce would be the best selection. If the bedroom is furnished in an extremely feminine style, you would want a deeply ruffled flounce on the bedspread. If the room is in between the two styles, a pleated or circular flounce would probably harmonize most effectively. But quite aside from the individualized styles of bedspreads, which vary as widely as the styles of dresses, the basic patterns can be divided into three types.

COURTESY *The Stylist Magazine*

The use of a two-piece spread allows for a combination of both patterned and plain fabrics. When much pattern is used elsewhere in the room, this combination must be reversed—a plain spread for the top and a patterned fabric for the dust ruffle.

The one-piece spread that includes enough material to cover the pillows is the simplest type. The top of the spread should be the width of the top of the mattress, plus bedding, and the length of the mattress, plus an allowance (20 inches) for tucking under the pillows. The depth of the flounce is determined by the distance from the top of the bed, when it is made up, to the floor, plus seam and hem. To make a plain flounce, use twice the length of the spread, plus the width, plus two 6-inch crossovers (12 inches) at both of the foot corners where the flounce separates for the bedposts or the footboard. To make a gathered flounce, you will need one-and-a-half to two times the amount of material needed for a plain flounce. For a pleated flounce, you will need three times the amount.

The two-piece bedspread is composed of a top spread and a separate dust ruffle. The dust ruffle is attached to a piece of fabric which is the exact size of the top of the springs and lies between mattress and springs. The top spread is made long enough to tuck under and then cover the pillows. It also drops down the side far enough to cover the bedding and the top of the dust ruffle.

The bedspread with separate pillow-cover spread consists of a spread for the bed, plus a pillow-cover spread, or pillow sham, of the same material.

In making any of these spreads, apply the same rules that were given for curtains—cutting by the drawn thread or by the design and pressing before sewing.

Make your dressing-table skirt in the same style as your bedspread.

The skirt for a dressing table should be in the same style used for the bedspread. There should be no break in tone, even in a master bedroom. Women sometimes erroneously think that because a dressing table is such a personal and exclusively feminine article, it can be extremely feminine in treatment even though the rest of the room is tailored.

If you use snap tape to attach the skirt to your dressing table, or the dust ruffle to the fabric between mattress and springs, it can easily be removed for laundering. The use of snap tape on furnishings made of washable fabrics is a boon in city homes where the battle against dirt is constant. The tape is inexpensive, absolutely inconspicuous, and easy to apply.

Take accurate measurements before making slipcovers.

Slipcovers should be made as carefully as a tailored suit. Baggy slipcovers are as outdated today in home furnishings as the Mother Hubbard apron is in clothes. Great pains must be taken to fit the material to the chair or sofa at each step. It cannot be done by guesswork.

Estimate yardage for a slipcover by measuring the piece of furniture carefully. (See drawings on page 236.) If the material has a pattern, allowance must be made for centering the motifs on back, arms, and pillows of chairs or sofas, and on the pillow-covering and top of the bedspread.

Preshrink the material before cutting, unless it has been pre-shrunk in manufacturing. To preshrink wool, press with a damp cloth. Although some allowance can be made for shrinkage by pressing in darts and allowing extra material in the length, it is easier to make well-tailored slipcovers if all material has been preshrunk.

Pin the material to the chair or sofa, following the diagram on page 236. If the material is figured, be careful to center the pattern on back, arms, and cushion. After the material has been fitted to the chair and pinned securely, cut it. Pin the pieces together before removing them from the chair. Insert cording or other trim in seams, and stitch. Add the skirt. (See drawings on page 237.)

Use zippers or snap tape to produce a smooth, professional fit and a neat closing. Either one is as important to a well-tailored and tightly fitted slipcover as it is to a smoothly tailored dress. In fact, it is almost impossible to make a well-tailored slipcover without using one or the other.

The trend in slipcovers for living-room furniture is toward a plain skirt, with a kick pleat at the corners, rather than a pleated or ruffled skirt. But it is still considered good taste to use slipcovers with pleated or ruffled flounces in bedrooms that are feminine or informal in character.

CHECKING YOUR KNOWLEDGE . . .

On a piece of paper write the numbers from 1 to 6. After each number write the word or words from those in parentheses that makes a correct statement.

1. Ruffled net curtains (are) (are not) extremely feminine and therefore (are) (are not) appropriate in all types of rooms.

2. If windows are badly placed architecturally, curtains should be selected that (match) (contrast with) the wall.

3. If the windows are grouped together, they should be treated (individually) (as one unit).

4. A washable cotton fabric (is) (is not) more economical than a more elegant fabric at a lower price that must be dry-cleaned.

5. If a window is 40 inches wide and is to be hung with draw-curtains, 50-inch fabric at $3.00 per yard is (better than) (not as good as) 36-inch fabric at $1.75 per yard.

How to Make

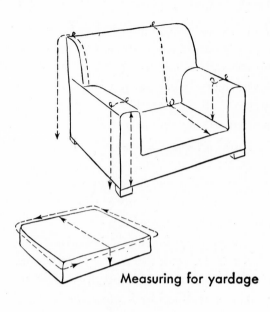

Measuring for yardage

Remove the cushion. Measure chair from the floor at the back and down the front to the edge of the seat. Add 4 inches for tuck-in allowance where back and seat meet. Now measure from front edge of arm to floor. Add twice the measurement from floor across arm to point where arm and seat meet. Again, add 4 inches for tuck-in allowance and 1 inch for each seam allowance. Measure cushion separately.

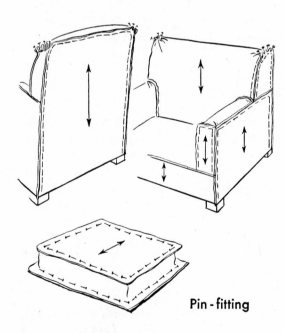

Pin - fitting

The arrows mark the placement of the length-wise grain of the fabric. Pin the preshrunk fabric, with wrong side up, smoothly over each measured section of the chair. Slash the fabric carefully when necessary to continue fitting. Work the fabric into small darts over the curved section of the chair. Allow 4-inch tuck-in fold at seat edge of back and arms. Remove cover; insert cording in seam before stitching.

a Slipcover

For width of flounce, add ½ inch to desired width for top-seam allowance and 1½ inches for hem. For a gathered skirt, add one or two times the measurement around the chair for fullness.

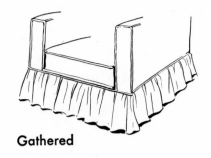

Gathered

For a box-pleated skirt, allow three times the measurement around the chair.

Box pleated

For a tailored skirt, add 10 inches to each side to be covered. Fold in 5 inches to the left and 5 inches to the right of each corner. Stitch top of pleat to prevent slipping.

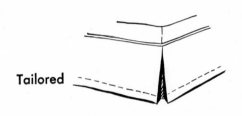

Tailored

For good tailoring, a closure may be made in the back seam of chair by attaching a zipper or snap tape to underside of back flap.

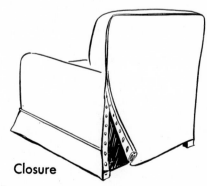

Closure

6. A painted or fabric-covered cornice would be (less) (more) appropriate than ruffled net curtains for a tailored room in a warm climate.

USING YOUR KNOWLEDGE . . .

1. Make arrangements for the class to visit a workroom of a curtain department in one of the local stores to see exactly how work is done. Take note of equipment used and discuss the possibility of having similar equipment installed in the homemaking center.

2. Invite the head of a drapery workroom to come to school and advise you on the best way to install a minimum of equipment for making curtains and slipcovers. The students might check costs of such equipment and discuss possible ways of raising the money. Approach the proper school authorities to see what part of the expenditure they might allow from the department budget for this purpose.

3. Hold an open house at which the subject of making professional-looking curtains and slipcovers could be discussed.

4. What kind of bedspread would you use in your own room? In your brother's room? Plan them carefully. Figure yardage, and use your ingenuity to find inexpensive, practical fabrics to make them both. Consider the upkeep and wearing qualities. Make a bedspread for your own room as a class project.

5. Find pictures or sketches of curtains or cornice treatments that would be appropriate for your own room. Find other pictures of another style that would be right for a boy's room. Measure the windows and figure the yardage necessary for each. Plan to make the curtains for one of the rooms as a summer project, using suggestions learned at the open house suggested in Number 3 to produce professional results.

CHAPTER 12: Floor Coverings

Floor coverings affect the appearance of our homes as well as our enjoyment of living. What we put on the floor often establishes the tone of the room, and what we walk on has a definite effect on our mood. Deep-pile rugs or carpeting make a room seem warm and luxurious and make us feel majestic. Polished wood, smooth matting, linoleum, tile, and stone make a room seem cool and make us feel energetic and brisk.

Floor coverings have even left an impression on our everyday language. Almost everyone uses the expression "called on the carpet." This expression originated back in feudal days when the lord of the manor was the only one who owned a carpet, and it was placed in front of his large thronelike chair. When he wished to speak to people, they were summoned onto the carpet.

Nowadays, carpets and rugs are no longer the exclusive prerogative of people of power and wealth. True, some floor coverings are still completely out of the financial reach of the average family, but there is a variety of attractive floor coverings in all price ranges, so that every family can, if they try, find something that is appropriate and that suits their budget. Aside from price, floor coverings should be selected with artistic and practical considerations in mind.

**Floor coverings should be selected to harmonize
with the decorative scheme of the room.**

The first requirement in the selection of a floor covering is that it harmonize with the decorative scheme of the room. The decision as to its color and its decoration should be made according to the

COURTESY *The Stylist Magazine*

A soft floor covering gives warmth and elegance to a room. Note how the softness of the rug in this room, by contrast, accentuates the severity of line of the furniture.

other furnishings and the general decorative scheme. The following factors should therefore be taken into consideration in selecting a floor covering.

The color of the floor covering. The relative importance that the floor covering is to have in the decorative scheme of the room should be the deciding factor in determining its color. If the floor covering is to be in the accent color of the room, it must be a fairly strong, intense color and different from the color of the walls and ceiling. If the floor covering is to be a part of the background, or dominant, color of the room, it must be in a tint or a shade of the color selected for the dominant. That is, it must be a part of the 60 percent of the room surface which is used to establish the dominant color of the room.

If a bright color is selected from the design or pattern of the floor covering for the accent of the room, one of the softer colors in the floor covering should be used for the walls of the room.

Whether the floor covering is to be patterned or plain. Patterned floor coverings should be used only when the upholstery and walls are to be in plain colors. If the floor covering is an Oriental rug, a copy of an Oriental, or an outstanding patterned domestic rug, the beauty of the color and design justifies the sacrifice of all other patterns. But an ordinary patterned domestic rug or an inexpensive, nondescript linoleum rug is not worth the sacrifice of pattern in the room on walls, draperies, or upholstery.

Two-toned marbleized or striped floor coverings do not demand as much attention as a multicolored patterned floor covering and so can be used with patterned draperies or upholstery. A floor covering of this kind may even be used with patterned wallpaper if the floor covering is separated from the wallpaper by a plain dado.

Plain floor coverings can be used with plain or patterned walls, draperies, and upholstery. A plain floor covering allows for flexibility in decorating because the room can be changed in tone and style at will—a fact which is important if the floor covering may be used in different rooms during its lifetime.

An absolutely plain floor covering that is very light or very dark in value is hard to keep clean. A floor covering in a middle-value color will present much less of a cleaning problem.

When a realistic patterned rug is used, nearly all other fabrics and areas in the room should be plain. (See Chart 3 on page 45.) Note the way this patterned rug draws the eye to the floor to the exclusion of all other objects in the room.

(COURTESY *Better Homes and Gardens*)

**Textural effects increase the practicality
of plain floor coverings.**

Many times people are tempted to settle the question of patterned or plain floor coverings on the basis of practicality. Obviously, a patterned floor covering demands less care than a plain one. But floor coverings in the new textural effects have the advantage of being as practical as patterned floor coverings from the standpoint of cleaning, while at the same time giving the effect of being plain.

Textural effects in soft floor coverings are produced by twisted yarns and unusual weaves, of which there are several types.

1) Twisted-pile rugs and carpets, which are called "frieze," look as if they were woven of dark and light yarn, because the twisted ends catch the light in different ways. These rugs do not show footprints and soil as easily as a straight-pile rug does. In this respect they are easier to keep clean than a plain rug with a straight pile, but at the same time they give the same effect as a plain rug.

2) Looped-pile rugs and carpets, like twisted-pile rugs, do not show footprints, despite the fact that they may be woven in one plain color. The shorter looped-pile rugs have the effect of a finely hooked rug. They wear well and are easy to keep clean. The longer looped-pile rugs are rather rough in effect.

3) Carved-pile rugs and carpets give the effect of a sculptured pattern. This effect is created by the clipping of the pile at different heights. In some rugs this effect of pattern does not last long because the pile mats down and the carved effect is lost. In other, more closely woven rugs, the carved effect lasts indefinitely. In either case, the effect of design has a tendency to mask footprints and to make the rug a little more practical than a plain, straight-pile rug.

Textural effects in hard floor coverings are produced in several different ways.

1) Marbleizing is the most common method of producing a textured effect in hard-surfaced floor coverings. When the marbleized design consists of closely blended colors, the floor covering does not seem to be patterned, but—like a patterned rug—it does not

show footprints or dust. If, however, the design consists of strongly contrasting colors or values, the floor covering has a patterned effect rather than a plain but textural effect.

2) The use of a jaspé, or a blended, stripe is another way that textural interest is produced in hard-surfaced floor coverings. An example of such a textural effect is a softly blended block pattern with stripes running in different directions.

3) Spattered mottling is a third method of producing textural effect in hard floor coverings. When blended colors are used, the floor covering appears soft and unobtrusive like that of a plain floor covering. When contrasting colors are used, however, the effect is the same as that of a patterned floor covering, and the rug must be treated as a patterned floor covering when the decorative scheme for the room is planned.

Floor coverings affect the apparent size of rooms.

In the past when all floor coverings, both soft and hard, were made only in stock sizes, people bought the largest one they could afford so as to cover as much of the floor as possible. They did not worry about the margin of floor which showed in varying widths all around the edge. These floor coverings were, as a rule, patterned, with a border around the edge.

Nowadays, when floor coverings are both plain and patterned, and when they are available not only in stock sizes but by the yard, in widths varying from 27 inches to room width, their purchase demands more thought. It is now possible either to cover the floor completely or to fit the room closely, allowing only small, even borders of wood to show. The choice between the two is a matter for careful consideration.

Stock-sized floor coverings that leave a border of floor uncovered reduce the apparent size of the room, regardless of whether they are patterned or plain. If the floor covering has a border, it will reduce the size of the room even more. However, if the floor is beautifully finished, the floor surface itself becomes a decorative asset which may more than offset the apparent loss in size. If the room is a large one, the reduction in apparent size may even be an advantage.

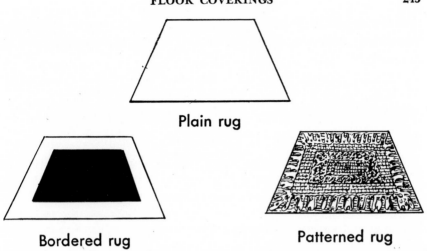

Plain rug

Bordered rug   **Patterned rug**

All of these rugs are exactly the same dimensions. Which looks largest? Which smallest? What does this prove?

Patterned floor coverings, regardless of their size, make a room seem smaller because the pattern demands attention. To check this fact, look at two different kinds of lawns. The lawn that is broken up with garden plots, bushes, and walks seems much smaller than the one that is an unbroken expanse of well-kept grass. The same optical illusion applies to a room according to the kind of floor covering used in it.

Plain floor coverings, regardless of their size, make rooms seem larger than they are. The lack of design or border creates the optical illusion of greater space.

Wall-to-wall floor coverings eliminate all borders and stretch the apparent room size to its greatest limits. In proof of this fact, check your own reactions to the drawings of three kinds of rugs shown at the top of this page. Which looks the largest to you? After you have made your decision, measure them to see whether you are right. If you are like most people, you will think that the largest rug is the plain one that extends from wall to wall and leaves no borders showing. The rug that looks smallest to you will probably be the figured rug that has a woven border, in addition to a margin of floor, showing all the way around the rug. Your eye just naturally deducts the width of any border—even the wood floor margin—from the total floor size. Even the narrow line of contrasting color that is often inset in hard floor coverings and is called a "feature strip" makes a room seem to shrink to the size of the area inside the border it marks off.

Broadloom and strip carpeting each have advantages.

Many people erroneously believe that the term "broadloom" refers to the quality of carpeting. Actually, all qualities of carpeting are made in the 27-inch width, as well as in broadloom, which is so called because it is woven on a loom that is at least 36 inches wide. Carpeting 27 inches wide—the standard for strip carpeting for many years—is woven similarly but on a 27-inch loom.

It is now possible to carpet a room from wall to wall with broadloom carpeting as well as with 27-inch carpeting sewed together. Rugs of any size can also be made of both broadloom and 27-inch carpeting. A selection should depend on whichever seems to suit the existing situation best, and to make that decision it is necessary to know the advantages and disadvantages of each kind.

Carpeting 27 inches wide is the most economical selection for wall-to-wall carpeting for any room whose width is a multiple of 27 inches and which thus can be covered with 27-inch carpeting without waste. The possibility of being able to remake the carpeting into rugs of different shapes is most important to young brides. Their furnishings will probably have to be moved to several different homes with rooms of different sizes before they settle in a permanent home, and floor coverings that can be adjusted to such changes are a definite advantage and saving.

Even if a border of floor is to show, 27-inch carpeting is a good selection because worn spots can be eliminated by the simple process of removing one strip and replacing it with another from the hall or from another room. Such adjustments are a great saving of money. By resewing 27-inch carpeting, it is often possible to avoid the expense of replacing a rug that has been badly worn in spots.

Broadloom carpeting is the most economical selection for wall-to-wall carpeting if a room is regular in shape and is a size that fits one of the stock broadloom widths. All cost of sewing and all seams are eliminated. If the room is slightly wider than one of the stock broadloom widths, the carpeting can be bound at the edges and laid as a rug.

Broadloom carpeting can be cut into smaller sizes and bound, but it is more difficult to increase the size or eliminate worn spots in broadloom than it is in strip carpeting. The seams in an otherwise unseamed rug or carpet will make it look patched.

Wise buying of rugs and carpets involves five considerations.

Wisdom in buying rugs and carpets does not come to anyone automatically with the need to buy. Instead, it is the result of real study and research. There are five main points to consider before making a decision, and the amount of money involved in the purchase of this large item of home furnishing indicates the importance of knowing them.

1) Get the most for your money. The best way to get the most for the money spent is to get a plain rug or plain carpeting. In the case of a plain rug or plain carpeting, every dime spent goes into the rug or carpet itself. Therefore, better quality of material is assured in a plain rug or carpet than in a patterned one at the same price. In the manufacture of a plain rug or carpet nothing goes for artist's fees, new-loom adjustments, special small-quantity dyeing of yarns, or special handling of material, which are all included in the price of a patterned rug or carpet. The making of a one-color rug is the simplest type of rugmaking, and its price represents its quality far more accurately than does the price of any other kind of rug. In the case of plain 27-inch carpeting, every inch of the carpet is used. This is not true in the case of patterned 27-inch carpeting because the design has to be matched in sewing the strips together.

2) Select the best price range. Many people feel that the best grade of rug or carpeting is the wisest purchase. Actually, a medium quality rug or carpet will look as well on the floor and will wear for at least seven years.

When buying rugs or carpets for the first apartment, a couple should realize that the floor coverings they buy when they are first married will probably have to be adjusted to other rooms in a few

In addition to selecting a floor covering for color, pattern, and style that is appropriate for the room in which it is to be used, there are five important factors to consider in buying a rug or carpet for any room. (See pages 247–250.)

years when they move to a larger apartment or a home. For that reason the wisest purchase for them is a medium-quality floor covering that can be used later for a bedroom, den, or hall in a home. When the financial condition of a couple allows it, more expensive rugs or carpets can be bought for the living rooms of the home.

3) *Check the quality against the price.* Domestic rugs and carpets can be judged on these points of quality: (1) the height of the pile; (2) the closeness of the pile, or weave; and (3) the quality of the yarn and backing used.

The comparative height of the pile can be seen by holding rugs of different qualities side by side and noticing the differences. High pile alone is not an indication of quality. It must be combined with a close pile, or a close weave, and even an amateur can easily see the closeness of the weave on the back of a rug.

Only people who work with rugs and carpets constantly can judge the quality of the yarn. Therefore, the buyer has to take the salesman's word on this point. For this reason it is well to deal with a reputable firm that will stand back of its products. A verbal statement from a reputable merchant is worth far more than a written guarantee from an unreliable firm that may go out of business before any flaws that might be present in the rug or carpet become apparent.

The price of 27-inch carpeting per running yard is less than the price of the same quality of broadloom carpeting per square yard. This difference is explained by the fact that the yard of 27-inch carpeting is only three-quarters as wide as the yard in broadloom carpeting, which is 36 inches wide. Thus the total price of two equal-sized rugs would be the same for equal quality, even though the price per yard is different.

When selecting carpeting, a buyer must know exactly what the price per yard covers so that when shopping comparisons are made they can be made on the same basis. Some firms quote a price per yard that covers the cost of sewing, binding, padding, and laying. Some, however, do not include any of these.

4) *Consider upkeep and care.* The pile rugs and carpets that demand least care are those which are patterned, two-toned, frieze (or twisted-pile), and looped-pile. These types of rugs show footprints and soil less than a plain-colored or straight-pile rug. But any rugs or carpets in a middle-value color, regardless of weave, are easier to care for than those that are very light or very dark in value.

The rug or carpet that is easiest to clean thoroughly is the one with a straight pile—that is, a velvet weave. It can be washed on the floor and will look almost new. The pile stands up straight after washing, and the rug or carpet feels deeper and looks richer.

Some companies claim to manufacture frieze rugs that have a permanent twisted pile, but the pile on most frieze rugs gradually untwists after several washings by the effect of the water and the friction of the scrub brush. Therefore, the lack of permanence of the twist should be kept in mind when a frieze rug is being considered—especially if the rug is so light in color as to require frequent cleaning.

5) *Ensure the life of a rug with padding.* The life of any rug or carpet is lengthened tremendously if it is laid over a good pad which

COURTESY MARSHALL FIELD & CO.

Cut-pile cotton rugs are ideal for a bedroom because they are casual but somewhat luxurious. They are easily washed and come in a variety of colors.

will soften the grinding action of heels and thereby reduce the wear. A medium-priced rug laid over a good pad will have the feel of a much more expensive grade of rug. Stair carpets are usually laid with double pads on the stair treads. Pads made of sponge rubber are especially good under small rugs used in halls or at the foot of a stairway because they lessen the possibility of slipping. Nothing can remove entirely the possibility of stumbling over small rugs.

Mothproofing also is important to the life of rugs and carpets, but it is not a permanent process. It must be renewed every few years or after each thorough washing. The cost of this process is estimated by the square yard.

**Substitutes for wool floor coverings are
varied and inexpensive.**

There are several varieties of inexpensive floor coverings now available that not only give good wear but are very attractive. Each

COURTESY *The Stylist Magazine*

Wallpaper and chintz, heavily coated with wax or shellac, are possibilities for floor coverings in powder rooms or bedrooms.

year new styles are brought out because there is such a large demand for low-priced floor coverings.

Long-looped and long-cut pile cotton rugs, which were at first used only in bathrooms, are now available by the yard and can be used in many rooms in the house. The long loop or cut pile of these rugs gives them a casual but luxurious appearance that is good with Modern or with masculine furnishings. (See illustration on page 250.)

Many people baste small rugs of this type together to make bench covers, bedspreads, or room-sized rugs. When they become soiled, the basting can be ripped and the small rugs can be washed in a home-sized washing machine.

Wallpaper or chintz, heavily surfaced with many coats of wax or shellac, is another type of floor covering that is gaining favor because of its decorative possibilities and its low cost. Some wallpaper houses have covered their showroom floors with wallpaper so

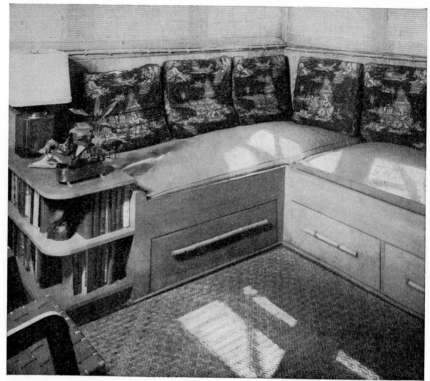

For a closed-in porch that is tailored in style and cool in feeling a grass matting is ideal for the floor covering.

as to prove its effectiveness and practicability to doubting patrons. (See illustration on page 251.)

Grass matting is a decorative as well as a utilitarian floor covering with many possible uses. It has graduated from its original position as an inexpensive covering for porch floors and can be bought in stock-sized rugs or in lovely woven squares that can be sewed together for either wall-to-wall carpeting or room-sized rugs. It is exactly right in sunrooms, breakfast rooms, recreation rooms, or any room that has an outdoor atmosphere.

Cotton rugs, in flat, cut-pile, or nubby weaves, come in a far wider range of colors than wool rugs and carpets. They can be used in any room of the house, and they wash well.

Felt carpeting is still in the experimental stage, and the small color range in which this carpeting is manufactured limits its usefulness. However, if the color scheme of the room is carefully planned around the colors in the carpeting, it is an effective floor covering that is much less expensive than a wool rug or carpet. Some couples use a felt carpet for a year or two and then lay wool carpeting over it, using the felt carpet as a pad.

Handmade rugs can be artistic and inexpensive.

A handmade rug can be a makeshift for temporary use, or, if it has been made with great care and artistry, it can be far more valuable than any domestic, machine-made rug. Its value depends on the workmanship and talent which have been put into it. There are three common types of handmade rugs.

Braided rugs, like those made by the pioneers in the early days of our country, can be a collection of everything in a scrap bag, or they can be works of art. They can be sophisticated or provincial, according to their color and design. They can be the multicolored type which our great-grandmothers made, or a one-color type that is appropriate in many styles of rooms. Rugs of one color look well in sophisticated living rooms, in all kinds of bedrooms, in recreation rooms, and in nurseries. Rugs of many colors are best for rooms with a pleasant, informal tone.

The type of braided rug selected should be decided by the tone of the room. If the room is to be somewhat dignified, the rug should be made of just one color and as near the room size as possible. Small oval rugs give a casual, informal tone that is not in keeping with the dignity of a formal room. One girl made a lovely blended beige rug for her bedroom out of discarded stockings. By using the lighter stockings in the center of the rug and gradually working in the darker stockings toward the outside of the rug, she produced a rug that was softly blended and in perfect harmony with her bedroom, which was smartly tailored in style.

In making a braided rug, be sure to braid firmly and to use the same weight of material throughout so the rug will wear evenly.

COURTESY *Better Homes and Gardens*

Hooked rugs may be made or bought in a variety of sizes. They are generally patterned and are most appropriate with Early American furniture.

Hooked rugs, made of mill-end fabrics or scraps cut narrow and hooked through burlap, are usually patterned. Sometimes the pattern, or design, is a very soft, two-toned geometric figure that has dignity and distinction. If the design or pattern in a hooked rug is strong in color and in contrast of light and dark values, the rug can only be used in a room that has plain walls and plain upholstery. The design for such a rug can be copied out of a book on historic design, or it can be an original one, created to suit the room.

The main thing to remember in planning the design for a hooked rug is that it will be seen, and must look right side up, from every side of the room. Therefore a realistic picture of a bold schooner in full sail on a bounding sea, which was so popular in early American days, is not appropriate for a good rug design. Such a design must be seen right side up to be attractive. It should be used as a picture hung on a wall and always seen right side up. Rug designs must have no up and down. They must appear right side up from any point in the room.

Scraps of material that are to be used for hooked or braided rugs should be selected according to weight as well as color. An even weight ensures even wear—a factor that is very important in getting the most wear out of a rug.

Needle-point rugs are usually made on burlap, although sometimes needle-point is embroidered on a one-color crocheted rug. In either case, the tone of the rug is entirely determined by the color and pattern of the design. If the colors are closely blended and the design is a formal one, the result will be a sophisticated effect, whereas if the design is an informal one and the colors are numerous and bold, the rug will be more appropriate in an informal atmosphere.

Most needle-point rugs are made of many small squares sewed together like a patchwork quilt. A large one-piece needle-point rug is very difficult to make.

Utility determines the selection of hard-surfaced floor coverings.

Hard-surfaced floor coverings originally were used only because of their utility value for kitchens, bathrooms, halls, and vestibules. Now, however, since manufacturers have developed so many new designs and types of floor coverings and have put color and charm into all of them, the situation is quite different. People have begun to appreciate the decorative and utilitarian values of these floor coverings for many other types of rooms.

These smooth, colorful, hard-surfaced floor coverings are appropriate because they are cool, easy to clean, and decoratively beautiful in any room in the house. In any climate they are suitable for a nursery, where cleanliness is of utmost importance; in a sunroom, where an outdoor effect is desired; or in a boy's or man's room, where simplicity and severity are appropriate.

There are so many different kinds of hard-surfaced floor coverings that it may seem difficult to decide which one to select for a particular room. Some of the following information about each may be helpful in making a proper selection.

Wood has many advantages, the first of which is its beauty. A handsomely grained, medium-dark wood floor has the same rich-

Linoleum that repeats the colors of the woodwork is both practical and decorative for a hall where traffic is heavy.

ness and quality as a beautiful piece of furniture. The darker the floor is, the more perfect it is as a background for beautiful small rugs and dark wood furniture. Its disadvantages are the need for constant polishing and the refinishing which it sometimes requires, especially in spots which are subject to heavy wear. Light wood floors are beautiful with blond furniture.

Linoleum has the advantage of a tremendous range of beautiful colors. Its borders or feature strips and its insets of decorative motifs can add immeasurably to the decorative effect of a room. In the past it was made to imitate ceramic tile. As a result, it was considered "second best" or merely a substitute for tile, just as synthetic fabrics were looked down upon when they first appeared as "artificial silk." Now, however, both these products are standing on their own merits. Linoleum is made in colors and styles that have no relationship to tile. Therefore, it is now used in many places where tile would not have been considered.

Colorful linoleum and other types of hard-surfaced floor coverings are ideal for nurseries. Linoleum is warmer than ceramic tile and not nearly so hard, yet it can be cleaned readily. Halls carpeted in soft-colored, marbleized linoleum are smart in tone and a wonderful saving in housekeeping as well as in upkeep cost.

Linoleum comes in several grades or thicknesses. The quality chosen should be decided by the amount of wear anticipated, the permanence of the room arrangement, and the comparative quality of the rest of the furnishings. Linoleum will, of course, take far more hard wear than wood without looking shabby, and if the quality is good, the only repair necessary for many years is rewaxing and polishing.

Its disadvantage is that, like all hard surfaces, it does not absorb the sounds in a room as do the soft-surfaced floor coverings.

Rubber tile is made in very beautiful soft colors. Because of its block formation, it can be easily repaired by the replacement of a few blocks in worn places. Another advantage is its comparative softness. It is pleasant to walk on and, like linoleum, it can be put over wood because it is pliable and will not crack.

Its disadvantages are that it shows wear unless it receives a great deal of care, it absorbs grease unless specially surfaced, and it is expensive. Many people feel that these disadvantages are more than made up for by its great beauty. It is most attractive in halls and sunrooms, where it has much of the elegance and charm of marble.

Asphalt tile will probably take harder wear than almost any other floor covering except ceramic tile. It is amazingly easy to care for and is especially good for use in basements or garages where there is some dampness or moisture. Its asphalt content resists the moisture which might rot other floor coverings. Like rubber tile, asphalt tile comes in block form and is easy and inexpensive to repair.

Unlike rubber tile, asphalt tile is brittle and cracks if its base is uneven. It should be laid over cement for the best results.

Cork flooring is coming into considerable favor because of its harmony with wood colors, its relative softness, and its feeling of warmth and charm. It is laid in squares, is relatively easy to keep clean, and wears well.

Ceramic tile and terrazzo have the advantage of being almost absolutely durable. They are available in a tremendously wide range of colors and designs. Both have a clean, cool look that makes them excellent for use in warm climates, and both are easy to clean.

Their disadvantages are high original cost, hardness of surface, and the necessity for having a heavy underconstruction to withstand their weight.

CHECKING YOUR KNOWLEDGE . . .

1. What two qualities in a floor covering will add space to a room?
2. What form of carpeting is easiest to adjust to changed room sizes?
3. What rugs or carpets give the most quality for the money spent? Why?
4. Is top quality the best selection in a rug or carpet under all conditions? Why, or why not?
5. Name four floor coverings with hard surfaces and tell where they should be used for best results.

USING YOUR KNOWLEDGE . . .

1. Invite two women to demonstrate the making of hooked and braided rugs.
2. Arrange a trip to an Oriental rug shop to see how rugs are mended.
3. Survey the homemaking center and plan an economical, yet effective, renovation of its floor coverings. Take careful measurements and get comparative estimates on costs to be submitted to the principal.
4. Make an ideal floor-covering plan for your own home, using the floor coverings discussed in this chapter.
5. Measure your own room and get an estimate on two types of floor coverings which would be appropriate to use in it.
6. Make a good floor-covering plan for a five-room house for a family that lives in Florida and one for a family in Canada.
7. Design a hooked or needle-point rug that would be appropriate in your own room, taking the pattern from either an architectural motif or a beautiful piece of pottery you have seen. Collect the materials, keeping accurate account of all costs, and plan to make a rug as a summer project.

SECTION FOUR: *Accessories in the Home*

The color filmstrip "Accessories in the Girl's Room" has been prepared to correlate with this section.

CHAPTER 13: Accessories for Use and Beauty

The accessories in your room were probably the first things about which you felt any sense of possession when you were a little girl. A china dog with big eyes, a cat with prickly whiskers, a lamp with a rabbit on the base—these things were yours in a room of large pieces of furniture about which you had little personal feeling.

Not until you grew older did the possibility of doing anything about big things, such as furniture, ever occur to you. Perhaps it is a carry-over of that first interest in accessories that makes all of us especially enjoy buying accessories, even after we grow up. But whether this is the reason or not, most people are much more susceptible to a bargain in accessories than they are to a sale on larger items, and our rooms and homes show it. Most of us have been sold small novel articles much too easily and much too often.

If you doubt this, take an inventory of the accessories in your home. The chances are you will find quite a few that are unnecessary in your own room and in some of the other rooms of your home. You will also probably discover a number of little vases, figurines, and knickknacks gathering dust on shelves or stored away in closets. Many of these, of course, have been gifts, but some of them were bought with your own or your father's hard-earned money. You probably wish now that you had never seen them, because they are difficult to dust and have given you little satisfaction either from the standpoint of beauty or usefulness. You realize that they were a fad or a bargain that you picked up in an impulsive moment.

"But," you may say, "how can I avoid such mistakes in the future? How can I be sure I am buying the right things?"

The first way to avoid buying knickknacks is to close your purse when you are tempted and apply the three tests which all accessories should meet.

There are three tests of good accessories.

If an article meets the three tests of good accessories, it is a safe buy. If it does not meet them, no matter how impressive the "bargain" or the sales talk, it should not be purchased.

Test 1: Is the object functionally sound? In order to test whether an accessory will function well, consider first the use which the object was designed to serve. In the case of a vase, for example, its chief use is to hold flowers. Thus the test for a vase would be whether or not it would hold flowers well. Some vases have such a small neck that the flowers are crowded together; others hold so little water that the flowers wilt almost immediately.

In buying a clock, note first whether it can keep time. In the case of a lamp, the consideration should be whether it gives good light.

Regardless of how attractive anything is, it must serve the purpose for which it has been created. Otherwise it is not good functionally and should not be purchased.

Test 2: Is the object individually beautiful? In order to test an object for its beauty, evaluate its form, color, and decoration. First, look at its form without regard to decoration. Is it simple and well-balanced, or is it a weird shape to attract the unwary buyer? Good artists and craftsmen do not have to distort objects to attract attention. The beauty of good proportion, simplicity of line, and the material itself should be sufficient.

Next, look at the color of the object. Is it a lovely one that you immediately like, or is it garish or drab? And, last, look at the decoration, if there is any. Is it a structural type of decoration that seems to fit the object and be a part of it? If the decoration has been stuck on, like the Victorian wool roses on a fly swatter, not harmonizing with either the shape or the function of the object, turn

How well does each of the accessories in this room meet the three following tests for accessories: (1) Is it functional? (2) Is it beautiful? (3) Does it harmonize with the other room furnishings?

your back on it firmly. Accessories that are worth buying are right in shape, color, and decoration.

Test 3: Does the object harmonize with the room furnishings in color, size, and style? First, the object must harmonize with the color scheme of the room. If the color scheme is made up largely of grayed, or muted, colors, even accessories that are used for accent should be in softer colors than those used for accent in a room in which the color scheme is made up of strong colors. Color is relative, and an accessory that looks fairly dull in one room can be the intense accent in another.

Second, the object must harmonize in size with the room. No matter how perfectly designed an object may be in itself, its size should be in proportion to the size of the room in which it is used. A picture that is worth a fortune can be a handicap, from a decorating point of view, if it dwarfs a room by its massive size. The same holds true with a lamp that is so tall that it looks down loftily on all the other furnishings of the room. Pictures that are too small and lamps that are too small are equally impossible, because they become so insignificant that they simply clutter the room.

Third, the object must harmonize in style with the room. An alabaster lamp or a brass clock may be beautiful in a sophisticated room but completely out of place in a more casual, provincial style of room. A wrought-iron, wood, or heavy pottery lamp, at one-third the cost, and a simple wooden clock would be worth far more, from a decorative viewpoint, in this simple type of room.

Only after you have mastered these three tests are you in a position to evaluate accessories. But once you know them, you can select the well-designed vase from the dime store with the same confidence you would feel if it came from the best shop in town. (See illustrations on page 265.) Knowledge frees you from the tyranny of prestige and price. It frees you to shop in musty secondhand stores, and it also admits you to the fraternity of those who enjoy the beauties of the past as well as the present. Museums, art institutes, antique shops, and private collections will all become a part of your world, and their beauties will enrich your life. Start now consciously to train your eye to see and your mind to evaluate the accessories you see around you.

Each of these objects cost less than 50 cents, yet all of them are simple in line and in good proportion.

**An accessory should not be used
unless it serves a purpose.**

Any accessory for a room must meet one more requirement: Is it really needed? An accessory can meet all the tests given above, but if it is not really needed or does not serve some purpose in a room, it should not be purchased. New accessories can, of course, from time to time be substituted for old ones. By the process of substituting new and better things for old ones, it is possible to keep the accessories of a room useful, according to changing interests and changing needs.

**The three tests of good accessories should
be applied when buying lamps.**

Lamps have gone through very important transitions in function and importance since the early days when they were the only source of light. The advent of gas, and later electricity, gave us powerful enough light to illuminate a whole room—inadequately, it is true—by means of a center fixture. At first this center light was accepted as a wonderful improvement, but very quickly people began to realize that it gave a very cold, impersonal light that was either glaring in its intensity or inadequate for close work. Lamps placed the light where it was needed and lent a friendly, intimate atmosphere that was far more attractive. Consequently, lamps began to come back into our homes, first as notes of color and decoration, now as the main source of light. For this reason it is especially important to re-evaluate lamps and be very sure that they meet the three tests of good accessories.

Test 1: Is the lamp functional? A lamp is functional only if it meets the requirements for good lighting. A proper evaluation of lamps on this functional basis should include four points: (1) the height of the lamp, or its placement in relation to the area needing light; (2) the spread of light to the area needing light; (3) the strength of the light; and (4) the color of the shade as it affects the light.

The proper height of a lamp is the most obvious point to be checked. Many table lamps are so low that they throw the light on

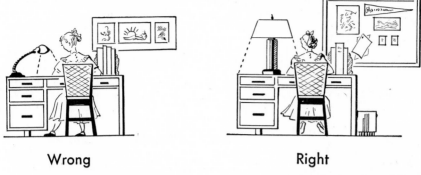

| Wrong | Right |

A low desk lamp throws light on a small section of the desk only, while a higher lamp with a larger shade throws a light over the entire top of the desk.

| Wrong | Right |

Reading by a low lamp encourages stooping, poor posture, and eyestrain. High lamps make reading easier and encourage good posture.

the table rather than on the book or work of the person sitting next to it. Lamps should be 28 to 30 inches high if they are used on medium-height or low tables.

A light on the headboard of the bed or on the wall behind it should extend forward at least 10 or 12 inches so it can throw light in front of the head and onto the reading matter of the person in bed.

The spread of the shade, a second point of evaluation, is especially important if the shade is opaque. A small barrel-shaped shade will throw the light up on the ceiling and down on the table but will not allow it to spread out at all.

The strength of the light cast by the lamp is determined by the size of the bulb used. Ideas of what constitutes adequate lighting have changed considerably in the last several years, and as a result there are many lamps still in use that are now known to give inadequate light. In 1925 people were satisfied with 5 foot-candles of power for reading. Five foot-candles is the amount of light cast by five candles held 1 foot from a work or reading surface that is perpendicular to the candles. Nowadays, we consider that entirely inadequate. Study Chart 14, which gives the amount of light now considered a minimum for different activities. (See also pages 334–336 in Chapter 16.)

Unfortunately, many homes are still lighted by lamps designed for bulbs with the power of 5 foot-candles. Stronger bulbs have been inserted in some of these old bases, but, because the lamps were not designed to give the stronger light, a glare is produced which is as fatiguing to the eyes as too little light. The reflector bowls used in modern lamps are almost essential for eliminating the glare of very large bulbs.

The fourth point in evaluating the functional efficiency of lamps is the matter of the color of the shade as it affects the light. Actually, there are only a few colors which are good for translucent shades. The only colors through which light can be sifted without distorting other colors in the room are cool neutrals, such as gray and white; warm neutralized colors, such as cream and beige; and tints of yellow. Consider, for example, a rose-colored shade, so often used on dressing-table lamps. Rose-colored light absorbs most of the red from a complexion, and a girl will probably use far too much rouge and lipstick if she applies her make-up under a rose-colored light. Test this color reaction by looking at the girls near you as you stand under a red stop light or near a red exit light. You will find that a perfectly healthy person will look wan and ghastly under rose or red lights.

The color and type of light of the bulb are also somewhat important both in the matter of eyestrain and in the effect on complexion and furnishings. The pure white incandescent lamp or bulb in common use makes a minimum change in color and complexion, but it does not give the clarity of light of the white fluorescent tube nor produce the flattering effect that is given by the pink fluorescent tube. Unfortunately, fluorescent lights come in long tubes which are

Chart 14: Foot-candles Required for Adequate Lighting

Type of place or activity	Foot-candles required
Halls Stairways Conversational groups	5 to 10
Reading large print Playing cards Working in kitchen Working in laundry	10 to 20
Reading newspapers Reading textbooks Sewing on light-colored materials Knitting Doing exacting shopwork	20 to 50
Reading difficult material for a long time Sewing on dark fabrics Doing fine needlework Doing detailed drawing	50 to 100

Foot-candles produced by bulbs

    25-watt bulb: 5 foot-candles of light at a distance of 2 feet
    50-watt bulb: 13 foot-candles of light at a distance of 2 feet
    60-watt bulb: 17 foot-candles of light at a distance of 2 feet
    100-watt bulb: 32 foot-candles of light at a distance of 2 feet

not adaptable to the generally accepted ideas of lamps and lighting fixtures for homes. So we continue to use incandescent lamps more than the fluorescent tubes in our homes.

The new circline fluorescent tube, which is becoming more generally available, is an attempt to meet this situation. Without a doubt this new kind of tubing—especially in the new pink color—will increase the acceptance of this type of lighting in homes. In addition to giving greater clarity of light, fluorescent tubing gives much more light per watt and is, therefore, much less expensive to operate than incandescent bulbs.

Test 2: Is the lamp beautiful? The test of beauty should be applied to the base of a table lamp just as if it were a separate vase. The shade also must meet this test, but in addition it must be in good proportion to the height of the lamp and it must harmonize in shape and style with the lamp. (See drawings on page 271 for examples of good proportion.) If the lamp base is square and simple in line, the shade should have some straight lines and be made of parchment, parchment paper, or undecorated stretched silk or rayon. A round lamp base that is decorated with dainty, Dresden-like flowers should have a round shade decorated with a narrow ruching or a stretched-lace binding.

Passing fads in lamp shades—such as ones trimmed with over-sized ruching, frills, or ruffles—should not be purchased because they will date the lamp and make it look out of style in a short time. A good lamp shade should last for years and therefore should be basically and conservatively designed.

Test 3: Is the lamp harmonious in color, size, and proportion with the other furnishings? The color of a lamp base is especially important because it is always spotlighted. Because it is relatively small, it can be fairly strong in color, and it can be patterned if it is used with a plain shade against a plain wall. Of course it must blend with the established color scheme of the room.

Many a well-designed lamp fails to be effective simply because it is too slim or too massive for the table, dresser, or desk it serves. It is difficult to give measurements for heights of lamps because the combined effect of the bulk of the lamp itself and the furniture around it is something that cannot be reduced to a slide-rule meas-

The lamp shades in the top row are all poorly proportioned and badly designed. The shade on the left is too shallow to cover the bulb; the other two
shades are too fussy and are unrelated to the smooth, simple lines of the bases.
The shades in the bottom row are well-proportioned, well-designed, and appropriate for the bases on which they have been placed.

urement. Instead, the eye must be trained to recognize good balance
between the mass of the lamp and the size of the furniture. This
ability can only be cultivated by repeated evaluation of good and
bad combinations.

One way to avoid a bad combination is to try out different
lamps with units of furniture at the store before the furniture is
bought. Most stores have a variety of lamps in different heights and
with different types of bases and shades. When the right one is found
for each unit of furniture, it should be measured carefully as a
guide to be used later when the lamp is purchased.

Not only must lamps harmonize with the other furniture in the

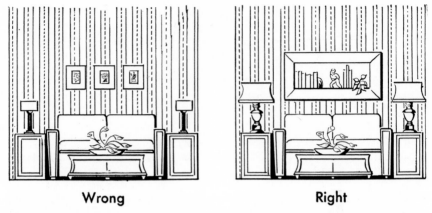

Wrong   **Right**

The size of lamps selected should be in proportion to the size of the table or chest on which they stand or the size of the furniture grouping in which they serve. Pictures should be large enough individually or in a massed group to decorate adequately the wall space on which they hang.

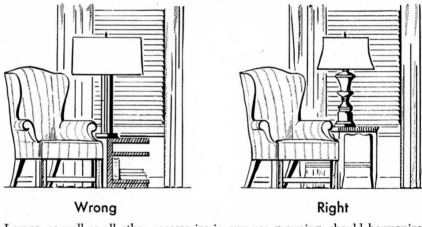

Wrong   **Right**

Lamps, as well as all other accessories in any use grouping, should harmonize in style and line, as well as in size, with the major pieces of furniture in the group. Why are the lamp and table at the left not appropriate for this chair?

room, but they must also harmonize with the other lamps in the room. All shades in any one room should be harmonious in color and texture. A rose shade here, a sand one there, and a gold one on the other side of the room will look like Christmas-tree lights rather than good general lighting. Shades of parchment skin or parchment paper can be used in the same room with shades that are made of heavy stretched silk or rayon because they are all tailored in effect. It is better, however, to use shades of the same color and the same type of material. Never should a chiffon shade, for instance, be used in the same room with a shade made of parchment or of a coarse cotton fabric because the tone of these materials is so different.

It is quite proper to use different types of lamps—table, floor, and bridge lamps, for instance—in the same room. In fact, it is desirable to do so for the sake of variety. But the material of the bases on all of the lamps must be in harmony. A lamp with a glass base and prism drops should not be used in the same room with a floor lamp that has a wrought-iron base. Polished brass, however, is such an adaptable type of metal that lamps made with polished-brass bases may be used harmoniously with lamps that have bases of china, glass, or pottery.

The placement of the lamps is determined by the placement of the furniture. Every use grouping must have its own light. Every chair or work space should be lighted either by its own or a shared lamp. If this plan is followed, the lamps will be spaced evenly throughout the room, and uniform lighting will be achieved. Usually people have too few rather than too many lamps in a room.

The three tests of good accessories should be applied when buying pictures.

Applying the tests for accessories to pictures is somewhat difficult because there are such diversities of opinion about art and such varieties of taste in pictures. Any good book on paintings and any course in art appreciation is helpful in checking or confirming a personal opinion about what is good art.

Test 1: Does the picture serve its function? In order to apply this first test to pictures, we must know what the specific function of a picture is. Some people say it is to tell a story, but books do that better. From a decorating point of view, the basic function for which we use a picture is to decorate a wall. If it does not do this, it fails in its primary function.

If it is very small—a miniature, for instance—it does not decorate but merely spots the wall. If it is too large, it dominates the wall and the room. A mural can do this, but a picture should not.

Test 2: Is the picture beautiful? This second test in pictures is a personal one, and it is in a way a measure of your own appreciation as well as your own interests. Every picture you hang in your home should have personal significance for you. No one should buy or hang a picture simply because it is said to be "good." In addition, it should have an immediate and very powerful personal appeal to its owner. After all, the average living room can take only a few pictures, if they are good-sized, and therefore people should have those pictures which they really enjoy. Good pictures are as much a part of the atmosphere of a home as good music, good books, and good conversation.

Test 3: Does the picture harmonize in color, style, and proportion with the room in which it is hung? If the room is done in soft, blended colors, the pictures should be in those tones. If the room is clear and strong in color, the pictures should follow the same type of color. Thus they will harmonize and become a part of the whole room scheme.

The idea of selecting a picture to suit a certain kind of room has been overemphasized. There is no such thing as a living-room picture, a dining-room picture, or a bedroom picture. A picture that has artistic merit can be used anywhere. A portrait, a landscape, a marine, or a still life—any of these will add great beauty and charm to any room in the house, provided its color and size are harmonious with the room. It is well, of course, to use more formal pictures in rooms of a formal nature, and more informal, gay, casual pictures in informal rooms.

The style of a picture is sometimes distorted by the type of frame. A picture which might harmonize well in style with a simple living room is sometimes made completely inappropriate by being framed in a massive, elaborate gold frame. The wise rule to remember is that a frame is merely a device for hanging. It should never be so important in form or color as to dominate or set the style of the picture. The more delicate or fine the medium used in a picture— such as etching or pen and ink—the lighter and narrower the frame should be. The heavier the medium used in the picture—such as thickly applied oil paint—the heavier the frame can be.

Sometimes people enjoy using framed photographs and snap-

Good and Bad Picture Arrangements

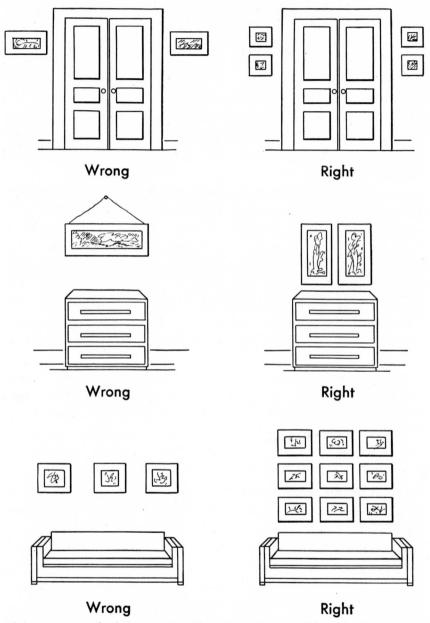

Wrong   Right

Wrong   Right

Wrong   Right

The pictures on the left are not well arranged because they are all horizontal groupings in a perpendicular space. On the right the pictures are placed correctly because they form a perpendicular panel to decorate a perpendicular wall space.

shots to decorate the walls of their homes. Unfortunately, most photographs are of more value as a record than as artistic objects, and therefore they have little value for most guests or even for all of the members of the family. Photographs should be hung in personal rooms, such as a bedroom, a den, or a recreation room. Only photographs of artistic merit and general interest should be used in the living rooms of the house.

Because most photographs are rather small in size for a wall decoration, they should be hung in groups. Those which will be replaced from time to time can be put in loose-back frames so the newer photographs that have more immediate importance can be inserted easily. There are many inexpensive types of temporary frames available. Some are in the form of metal or plastic brackets, which simply hold the picture, mat, and glass together. Very small photographs or snapshots can be massed together on one large mat in the same way that clippings are placed on a bulletin board. This treatment will give importance to a grouping that might otherwise look cluttered.

The importance of the size and shape of a picture is frequently overlooked. First, it must be large enough to be seen and enjoyed from any point in the room and small enough to be in scale with the rest of the room furnishings. Second, its shape must harmonize with the particular wall space on which it hangs. A vertical wall space should be decorated by a vertical picture or by a group of pictures that form a vertical panel. A horizontal wall space must be decorated by a horizontal picture or by a group of pictures that form a horizontal panel. However, it is possible to change the apparent size or shape of even one picture by adding brackets or sconces either below it or on each side of it.

When selecting the pictures for a wall against which furniture has been placed, remember that the space between the top of the piece of furniture and the ceiling should be considered as the size of the wall space. For example, the wall space over a chest should be considered as the width of the chest and the height from the top of the chest to the ceiling rather than as the total size of the wall on which the chest stands. The wall space over a fireplace should be

When placing pictures on a wall above a piece of furniture, the space between the top of the piece of furniture and the ceiling should be considered as the wall space. Here, small pictures placed close together give the effect of one picture, sufficiently large to fill the required space harmoniously.

(COURTESY *The Stylist Magazine*)

considered as the width of the mantel shelf and the height of the wall from the shelf to the ceiling. And the wall space over a sofa should be considered as the width of the sofa and the height from the back of the sofa to the ceiling. The only places where the entire wall space should be considered in the arrangement of pictures are those walls that have no furniture against them. The walls in a hall or the walls on each side of a door or archway are examples of such situations.

Since each wall space is considered separately, every picture in a room may hang at a different height. In consequence, pictures should not be hung from the molding. Few, if any, wires or hooks used to hang the pictures should be in sight. Pictures should be hung as flat against the wall as possible and in relation to the furniture grouping below them. If there is no furniture below it, a picture should be hung as near eye level as is artistically possible, because it was painted at that level and can be seen best from that vantage point.

**The three tests of good accessories should be applied
when buying all other accessories.**

All accessories, no matter how large or small, should meet these
same three tests, or else they should not be used.

Clocks, obviously, must keep time if they are to serve their
function. As an accessory, a clock must be beautiful and must harmonize with the other furnishings. Fortunately, it is now possible to
get electric clocks in all sizes and in all types of cases from the
simple modern to the elaborate grandfather clock.

Mirrors that are large have great functional as well as decorative
value. The chief function of a mirror is to reflect. By reflecting the
room, mirrors increase the apparent size of the room or hall and blot
out wall jogs. They also reflect color and design, and in so doing they
help to balance the furnishings of a room.

An entire wall covered by a mirror is Modern in effect. Therefore mirrors should be used in this way only in a room that is
furnished in Modern. A large, unframed mirror can be used in a
traditional room, however, if it is smaller than the wall space, so that
the margin of wall around it will give the effect of a frame.

Every mirror should be hung flat against the wall to avoid distorted reflections. For the greatest reflecting value, mirrors should
be so placed that the light falls on the person or object to be reflected
rather than on the mirror itself.

Pillows should be designed primarily for use. A ruffled pillow
musses easily. A pillow covered with an embroidered picture or
verse must not be allowed to wrinkle. Therefore pillows of these
types are not functional. A pillow with tufted wool roses or other
decorations that leave an imprint on the cheek that is pressed against
it is also impractical. In fact, the simpler the pillow, the better.
Agreeable texture, resilient, soft stuffing, and good color are the
qualities that make pillows both useful and decorative.

The best shape for a pillow is a simple square or rectangle,
corded or boxed around the edge. If a little more elegance is desired,
a brush fringe can be added instead of the cording, but pillows
should not be decorated.

One good covering for a pillow is the same fabric used on the

COURTESY *The Stylist Magazine*

Large mirrors have functional as well as decorative value. The severely plain lines in this mirror frame are repeated in the lamps and the boxes on top of the chests.

sofa or chair on which the pillow is to be placed. Good homemakers order an extra yard or two of the fabric when they buy their upholstery fabric. In this way a mixed assortment of pillows that is unrelated to the room can be avoided. This extra material can be used not only for the pillow, but also for protectors for the arms and back of a chair or sofa.

Pillows properly planned can also help balance the color scheme of the room. For instance, they can be made of the same material as the draperies and used on a side of the room where there are no windows. They can be made of the upholstery fabric of a chair and used on the opposite side of the room from the chair to balance its color.

A pillow is meant to be used as a headrest or as a support for the back. This immediately rules out the practice of using pillows on the floor, placing them along the top of the back of the sofa, or using them to cover electric outlets.

Screens have great decorative as well as functional value when they are covered with decorative wallpaper or drapery fabric that harmonizes with the
color scheme of the room.

Folding screens should be selected for both use and decoration.
In a small apartment, a screen that shuts off the view of a dinette
or kitchenette from the living room has great functional as well as
decorative value. A screen that will keep light and drafts away from
a bed can add both comfort and beauty to a bedroom. Sometimes a
corner grouping composed of a round table flanked by chairs looks
inadequate. But if a screen, preferably covered with the material
of the draperies, is used as a background, it will add accent, height,
and architectural dignity to the corner grouping.

One of the reasons people have not used screens in the past is
that they were too costly. Nowadays, however, screens are not expensive. Wallboard screens can be bought for about $10 and those
of wood, bamboo, or matting are available for only slightly more.
The wood ones are usually made like a shutter or a latticed door and
can be painted to echo the accent color of the room or to match the

woodwork. Wallboard screens can be painted or papered to match the walls, or they can be covered with the drapery material. They may also be decorated with prints or maps and coated with shellac to protect them from dirt and wear.

Wastebaskets are extremely important accessories from a decorative viewpoint as well as a functional one, because a wastebasket is needed in every room of the home.

Functionally, all that is required of a wastebasket is that it be large enough, conveniently placed, and made of durable material, preferably metal. Decoratively, it must be the right color to blend with the room and the right design to harmonize with other designs in the room. A wastebasket that stands against a patterned wall can be covered with the same wallpaper that is used on the wall, or it can be painted the color of the background and trimmed with bandings in the other colors used in the wallpaper. A wastebasket that stands against a plain wall can be painted in the color of the wall or in some other color that is used in the room. It can also be decorated with a design taken from a drapery fabric or from wallpaper that is used on the ceiling, on an opposite wall, or above a dado.

Ash trays should be selected with enough care to assure that they meet all functional and decorative demands. Often they fail functionally because they are much too small. An overflowing ash tray is not only unattractive, but it is also a real hazard to the finish of a table top.

Ash trays also may fail decoratively if they do not harmonize in style and type with the furnishings of the room. A flower-decked china ash tray is appropriate only in a feminine bedroom. Massive pottery ash trays are proper for a game room, an office, a man's den, or a man's bedroom. Brass and alabaster ash trays are right in an elegant traditional living room. Brass, good pottery, or large glass ash trays fit into a casual, informal living room. For the dining-room table, small ash trays of glass, china, or silver are best.

Vases too often are thought of as decorations in themselves, rather than something to hold flowers. The average family needs several inexpensive vases of different sizes, which are *put away when not in use,* rather than a few expensive ones that never seem to fit the flowers on hand and are forced into double service as decorative pieces when not used to hold flowers. Simple, well-shaped vases can be bought inexpensively. Functionally, they should be large enough to hold sufficient water for the flowers and have a neck large enough to allow the stems of the flowers to spread out.

If you consider vases from this functional point of view, you will never be tempted to spend money for decorative vases that compete for attention that should be given to the flowers.

Maps can be used for wall decoration and frequently have great utility value also. To be useful, they must be accurate and legible. They then become a fascinating and important part of a study, bedroom, library, or living room. Many people think of maps from the utilitarian point of view only, tacking them up casually with no thought of their decorative qualities. Decoratively, however, maps can be very important if they harmonize with the room scheme and are hung with the same thought and care as pictures. They are far less expensive than good pictures of comparable size; they are of keen interest to everyone; and they can be mounted on inexpensive wallboard and then shellacked, thus saving the cost of framing. Maps should be hung according to the same rules as pictures, or they can be used on screens if they are waxed or shellacked for protection.

Doilies were important accessories for many years during and after the Victorian era. Nowadays we realize that the beauty of the wood of a table top should be seen and that covering it is like hiding a talent. In addition, doilies make a room look fussy and cluttered.

Table tops should, however, be protected from scratches. Moleskin, which can be bought in a drugstore, can be cut and pasted on the bottoms of lamp bases, ash trays, or book ends. Felt, which can be bought in an art store, can be used in the same way. The top of a dining-room table can be protected from dampness by using a reflector under vases and potted flowers. This can be left on the table between meals and will double the effectiveness of the centerpiece. Asbestos mats may be used under thin place mats to protect the table from the heat of dishes. When a full-sized tablecloth is used, a table-sized asbestos mat can be used under the cloth.

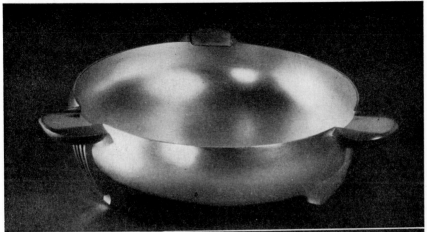

Simplicity of line and a
pride in craftsmanship are
blended to produce these
silver accessories of outstanding beauty.

(COURTESY DAVID-ANDERSON, OSLO,
NORWAY)

Dresser tops can be protected by glass or by a simple tailored
scarf that follows the exact shape of the top. A scarf can be made of
the same material as the draperies or bedspread or of plain linen
decorated with an initial.

Figurines that are well designed make lovely decorative notes
on a table, on a shelf, or in a cabinet with open shelves or glass
doors. However, they must harmonize in spirit with the room in

which they are used. Streamlined, modern figures should be used only in Modern rooms, and fussy, sentimental Victorian figures in Victorian rooms. Dresden-china figures should be used only in a feminine room. Simple, decorative Chinese figures are good in both traditional and Modern rooms.

Book ends, although secondary in importance to the books they support, must be carefully selected to harmonize with the room. Functionally, book ends must be heavy enough to hold books solidly. The metal-spring type of book end that is in one piece and rolls out to adjust to the number of books it holds is appropriate only in Modern rooms. Glass bricks also are good as book ends in a Modern room only. Good-looking pottery book ends that hold plants fit almost anywhere. Brass book ends in simple architectural shapes are appropriate for both traditional and Modern rooms. But if gold is used as the accent in the room, the book ends should be in gold or have a gold trim. If the accent is silver, pewter or silver can be used for the book ends.

Tiles are an interesting decorative motif which have utility as well. They make excellent stands for hot dishes or plants; they can be set into the top of a coffee table; or they can be framed and hung on the wall.

Flowers and green foliage cut from the garden, picked in the country, or bought from a florist are an important part of the decoration of a home. Too often we fail to see the decorative possibilities in the things which we take for granted in the out-of-doors. For example, an attractive decoration for the home in the early spring is a bunch of branches broken from a bush and placed in a simple glass vase. The black stems and the delicate tracery of fine green leaves make an interesting decoration for the room.

A few lovely flowers—such as roses, lilies, or chrysanthemums—surrounded by green leaves, can be floated in a low flat bowl as a decoration on a living-room table or as a centerpiece on a dinner table. Low floral decorations of this sort set off tall candles beautifully. Flowers used as a centerpiece on the dining-room table must be low enough so that the shortest person seated at the table can see over them easily. They must be in a container that is not so

COURTESY CAROLE STUPELL

Green foliage has great decorative value in the home. Here, combined with pottery parrots, philodendron forms a low centerpiece appropriate for a small table. For a large table, it might be mounted on a reflector.

large as to crowd the table but large enough to be in good proportion to the size of the table.

As a rule, we feel we must have more flowers than we actually need for an effective table decoration. A loose bouquet of a few flowers allows each stem, blossom, and leaf to become important. A ball of chicken wire forced into the base of a vase will form an excellent mesh to hold the stems in place and yet allow them to spread out. When flowers are crowded together, they do not show their beauty. Flower arrangements should be large enough to be important but not so large as to dominate the room.

Green plants are the most inexpensive and satisfactory natural decoration for any room. They can be used on mantels, on small tables, on consoles, and on dining tables. They look and grow well in clay pots, in inexpensive pottery holders, or in the most expensive brass or glass containers.

Some grow well in containers of water without soil. They require a minimum of care and they give a maximum of beauty. Sweetpotato vines, with their red stems and green leaves, are beautiful and can be grown in water with no effort. Philodendron and Chinese evergreen grow in water, too, and are good choices for the person who has little time to spend in caring for plants. All these plants need in order to look vigorous and beautiful is to have fresh water occasionally and to have the leaves washed off whenever they look dusty.

One note of warning about containers for plants: Avoid buying the little figures of animals with plants coming out of heads, backs, or ears. They usually are poorly designed and do not allow a fraction of the space for roots that a healthy plant demands.

Artificial flowers are a relatively expensive type of decoration, which in a very short time have a way of looking like last night's corsage—a little dilapidated and sad. Consequently, there is an increasing tendency to discard them in favor of growing greens, which are less expensive and which lend a fresh, alive air to any room they grace.

CHECKING YOUR KNOWLEDGE . . .

1. What are the three tests that all accessories must meet?
2. What test for accessories do most old clocks fail to meet?
3. What test does a sepia print of a good painting fail to meet?
4. Decoratively speaking, what is the function of a picture?
5. What is the most important function of a lamp?
6. How can table tops be protected without using doilies?
7. Would you use glass ash trays in an Early American home? Why, or why not?
8. Which of the following materials for accessories can be used together in one room—wrought iron, coarse pottery, etched glass, fine linen, coarse linen, French figurines, and wooden bowls?
9. If you had a bed of polished mahogany with a velveteen spread, would you choose a polished brass lamp with a stretched-taffeta shade or a wrought-iron lamp with a parchment shade? Why?

USING YOUR KNOWLEDGE . . .

1. Each student might bring an accessory from her own home that meets the three tests listed in the text. Each object should be tagged to explain where it could be used appropriately and why.

2. The students might select from the assembled accessories brought to class in Number 1 the ones that would be appropriate for the homemaking center and arrange them properly according to the rules they have learned. This could be followed by an open house to show the center and to display all the accessories.

3. Invite a member of the garden club to give a demonstration of flower arrangements. Charge a small admission and use the funds to buy accessories for the homemaking center. Divide the money among groups of students, each of which will be responsible for the accessories for one room. Search secondhand stores, dime stores, and rummage sales to find the most appropriate accessories for the money available.

4. Organize a tour to a museum, an art institute, or a good store to see displays of accessories. If this is not practical, get permission to borrow slides or to borrow a few accessories to use in the class while the subject is being studied. Some large museums have a great deal of material that is available on request.

5. Make a file of clippings of good arrangements of pictures, pictures and brackets, pictures and bookshelves, mirrors and pictures, mirrors and plants, and table settings. With the help of that file, plan an unusual arrangement for the wall space above your own bed or desk at home.

6. Make a class list of secondhand shops, auction rooms, and antique shops and of weekly, monthly, or annual rummage sales or auctions in your community. Note the particular type of merchandise usually available in each.

CHAPTER 14: Accessories with Personal Significance

Stripped of its accessories, any room looks as completely impersonal and stereotyped as a station waiting room. It might belong to anyone. Even worse, it looks unlived-in and unloved.

The reason for this is that, aside from the effect produced by the furniture, a room becomes casual or dignified, masculine or feminine, young or old, according to the kind of accessories used in it. It becomes fussy, austere, or inviting according to the quantity and quality of its accessories. The importance of accessories is hard to realize because each object is relatively small. A figurine, a picture, an ash tray, or a pillow may seem to be such an insignificant part of the room that we find it difficult to accept its importance in the total scheme.

Because we do not fully realize this fact, we are apt to continue adding articles we collect as prizes, gifts, or bargains, without considering whether or not they are needed or actually contribute to the tone desired. "Oh, well, it is just a small thing. It can't really matter," is what we think, whether we say so or not. The fact is that it does matter very much, and until we are convinced of this fact our rooms will have all the clutter of a rummage sale.

A very few accessories, each of which has been carefully selected to contribute importantly to the decorative scheme, can make a room express your personality in a charming individual manner that will leave a strong, clear-cut impression.

Once the room is complete, we should never add without subtracting. If a picture is added, another must come down. If a plant

Well-chosen accessories enhance the furniture so as to create the tone and spirit desired in a room. What is the tone of this room? How do the accessories help to create it?

is added, a figurine or other object must be subtracted. We must respect simplicity and space. We must realize that three objects well arranged are more effective than six, because each of the three is set off by space that says, in effect: "This object is a thing of importance and value. It has been separated from others because of that fact. Look at it carefully before going on to look at other things."

Living-room accessories should indicate family interests.

Quite aside from the tests for good accessories which were discussed in the last chapter, no object, no matter how precious, should be used in a room or in a home unless it has personal significance and importance for those who live in that house. For example, a family that is interested in art and has developed a real love for art will enjoy having a piece of statuary or sculpture in its living room. That same piece of statuary or sculpture would be completely out of place and a waste of money, however, in the home of a family which cared nothing for this particular form of art.

Aside from its artistic merit, each accessory in a living room should be an index to the interests and background of the family that lives there. It must also be of some general interest to the friends and guests who might be entertained there.

Animals, such as dogs, horses, or cats, are occasionally a rather important family interest. As a result, well-designed accessories that make this interest obvious would be very appropriate for such families. Pottery or metal animals used as paperweights, book ends, or lamps would please such a family and remind their guests of this special interest.

Music often is an absorbing interest for a family. Lamps made of busts of musicians, a group of steel-engraved portraits massed over the piano, or a framed fragment of an old music manuscript—any of these would be individualized accessories that would lend character and interest to a living room for this type of family.

Travel is a very unifying and stimulating interest for some families. Maps, mounted and used like pictures, globes, and a good atlas would be important, meaningful accessories for them. Detail maps showing trips which they have taken can be mounted on a screen to make an accessory of interest. It would have decorative and informational importance for them and for their friends.

Sports of various types might be the interest of the family and so might be represented in the living room of the house. A really big trophy urn can be made into a beautiful lamp. Smaller figure trophies can be made into book ends. Medals can be mounted on wooden blocks and used for paperweights.

Accessories of this type have meaning and importance, as well as decorative merit. But there is some danger in having too many of any one kind of interest accessory. A room with accessories which express more than one interest will be less monotonous than a room which is entirely dominated by accessories expressing just one interest. With the personality of a room, as with that of a person, a lack of variety tends to be boring.

Bedroom accessories should indicate personal interests.

The accessories in bedrooms can be more personal and individual than those used in the living rooms of a home. For instance, a girl who might be very much interested in foreign dolls could not use such a collection as decoration in the living room of the house. Her father and brothers would be likely to say, "What's the idea— dolls in here where my friends come? They'll call us sissies!" However, she could give her hobby free rein in her own bedroom or workroom. Anyone well enough acquainted with her to be taken into those rooms would be likely to be interested in whatever she found interesting.

Talents are an excellent starting point for individualized accessories. A room that might otherwise have very little distinction can be given personality and individuality by emphasizing a talent or special skill. A girl who is studying music might find the collecting of a series of photographs of leading composers or of interesting old music scores a fascinating side line of her work. If the photographs and scores are framed and hung well, or if the music scores are used to decorate lamp shades, the room will be different from that of any of the other girls.

A girl who has ability as an artist might decorate her room

with equipment for painting. (See illustration on page 312.) A girl who likes to sing might make a collection of her favorite singers, costumed for their most famous operatic roles. Such personalized accessories as these will make a room stimulating to the owner and of real interest to her friends because it helps them to know her better.

Hobbies are very important in the lives of most people. Little children begin by collecting anything they see. As they grow older, the collections are directed by interests. Some girls collect photographs of actors, dancers, or writers. Others collect their autographs. Still others collect recordings, playing cards, travel folders, stamps, cartoons, dog pictures, or perfume bottles. In fact, there seems to be no end of the things that can be collected, some of which develop into worth-while hobbies.

Obviously there are some collections that have more value than others. Only after you have estimated the value of a collection is it wise to spend much time on it, or even to consider it as a possibility for personalizing your room.

There are three tests which might be applied in estimating the value of a hobby.

1) Does the hobby have lasting value? Has the collection any educational or cultural value? Does it lend stimulus to interesting study? Might it be of continuing value in adult life? At least 50 percent of the value of a hobby lies in the kind of hobby selected. The other 50 percent of the value lies in the skill with which it is directed so as to be of lasting value to the hobbyist herself.

2) Does the hobby enrich the person's life by stimulating new interests? The effect and importance of this type of hobby on the lives of people can best be seen in the stories of the lives of a few outstanding people. Grace Moore, the opera star, for example, loved to preserve fruit. It became a hobby that led her far away from the tensions and artificiality of the theater world. It took her to a farm home in Connecticut where she had a garden for raising special delicacies and where she built a specially equipped kitchen for preserving the fruits. Her hobby thus enriched her life by providing enjoyment of something entirely different from her work in the Metropolitan Opera and Hollywood.

Other hobbies have led people directly into an interesting life-

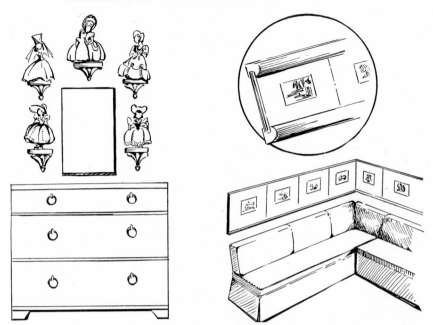

A doll collection, displayed on brackets, might be arranged to form a frame around a mirror. Photographs, prints, or drawings, when mounted and framed between two moldings, form a panel decoration for a day-bed corner.

work. June Platt, whose articles and books on cooking are famous, began with a love of cooking. Fanny Farmer began the same way. Dorothy Draper, the decorator and designer of clothes, began by making doll dresses. In fact, if you take time to look up stories of people's hobbies in the library, you will begin to realize that a good hobby can play a very large part in anyone's life.

3) Does the hobby have decorative value? Many an otherwise drab room becomes interesting and individual when its accessories reflect a hobby.

An easy way to display a hobby or a collection of bulky articles, such as foreign dolls, is to use a hanging bookshelf on which a representative selection can be arranged. Another way is to use a cabinet like a medicine chest without the door. Paint or paper the inside in black, gold, or silver, so the colors in the dolls' costumes will show up effectively.

Some girls who collect smaller articles, such as perfume bottles, buy eight or twelve matching cigar boxes, remove the covers, and

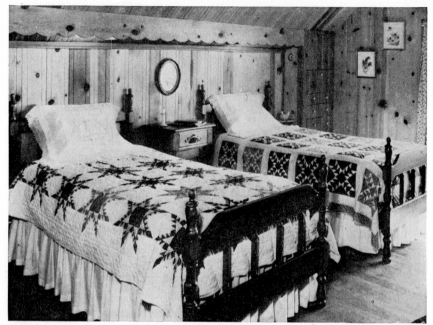

COURTESY *Better Homes and Gardens*

Inherited patchwork quilts, combined with a dust ruffle of white sheeting, make beautiful bedspreads and give a room a distinctive touch of tradition.

glue the boxes together to make a sectional cabinet that will display eight or twelve of their choicest pieces.

If your collection is composed of flat things, like photographs, folders, clippings, or autographs, the individual items can be mounted on uniform pieces of cardboard of the accent color of the room. Two horizontal moldings can be nailed on the wall to form the upper and lower edges of a panel running around the room. The distance between the moldings is dictated by the height of the mounting boards, which then can be slipped between the moldings. In this way the current favorites can always be slipped in to replace the ones that have served their term as decoration. (See drawing on page 293.)

Inherited accessories can individualize a home.

It is very easy to underestimate the decorative value of inherited treasures, simply because they have always been around.

With some ingenuity, old pieces of china and silver can be made into beautiful accessories that give distinction to a room.

(COURTESY *Better Homes and Gardens*)

295

Not until we see an exact duplicate of one of them displayed in a friend's living room or in a glass cabinet in a museum do we think, "Maybe there is some value in that old thing!" After a few such experiences, we begin to look about our homes with more discernment and to recognize our treasures.

Accessories that show skill in needlework are one kind of inherited object that very often seems most unattractive at first glance. For example, an old patchwork quilt or an appliquéd quilt, made by Cousin Sarah when she was just twelve, may look utterly useless and unattractive when it first turns up at the bottom of an old trunk. But closer inspection will show that it has lovely color and beautiful workmanship. Even if it is ragged, there usually are some squares that are good enough to be salvaged and used as decoration for a bedspread. If just one or two squares are intact, they can be framed as pictures or made into small pillows. If there are six or seven, they can be appliquéd on a cornice for a window decoration.

An old sampler that your great-grandmother made when she was a little girl of eight is not at all impressive unless you are smart enough to visualize it as it will be when it is cleaned and pressed and matted widely with a soft color that will enhance its faded designs. Framed and hung over a bed or desk, it could be an interesting center motif for the decorative scheme of a whole room.

The wide embroidered flounce that your father's maiden aunt made and wore to the governor's reception may have a future as a ruffle for a dressing table or, if it is smaller, as trimming for a lamp shade or a frill around a bed pillow.

Accessories that mark old-world connections are another source of individualized accessories. Old china that was brought over from Europe years ago is a fine decorative note in any room. An old sugar bowl or teapot without a lid will make an attractive container for vines or greens of any kind. A quaint old cup and saucer can be used in the same manner. (See illustration on page 295.) An old platter or several old plates hung on a wall can lend distinction to a dining room, a hall, or a kitchen.

A carved clock from Switzerland without its mechanism will have decorative as well as utilitarian importance if it is equipped with electric works and hung on the wall in the home of one of the descendants of the Swiss people who brought it over.

An old picture frame brought across the ocean with loving care many, many years ago can have new life and importance if it is polished, fitted with a plate-glass mirror, and hung over a dressing table or in a hall. (See illustration at right.)

Accessories that mark sectional interests are another type of inherited treasure which can be used to personalize a home. Confederate money may be useless in the bank, but it can have real value decoratively if it is mounted and used under glass for a tray or a table top. Even small pieces of the woven coverlets that were the pride and joy of the women of the cold New England colonies make interesting wall decorations when framed and hung in the homes of their descendants.

Old oil lamps or vases that were the important decorative notes in many a living room or bedroom of bygone days can be weighted and wired to light the bedrooms of the present day. An old statue or doll can be made into an unusual lamp

COURTESY *Popular Home*

Old picture frames can be used to frame mirrors that will harmonize well with antique furniture, braided rugs, and needle-point pillows. Old picture frames may also be used for shadow boxes. (See illustration on page 313.)

of great decorative value. First it must be attached to a base. Then the electric wire should be run through a metal pipe that is bent to conform inconspicuously to the back of the figure and to hold the shaded light directly above it. Thus a soft light is cast down on the figure, spotlighting it into decorative importance.

These individualized accessories, drawn from inheritance, from interests, and from hobbies, will make a room or a home utterly different and distinctive.

CHECKING YOUR KNOWLEDGE . . .

1. What interests in your family would be a good starting point for living-room accessories? How could you use them?
2. What talents or hobbies of your own could you use as a starting point for your bedroom accessories? How could you use them?
3. What are three tests of a good hobby?
4. Compare the collecting of playing cards with that of stamp collecting as a worth-while hobby from the point of view of the tests in this chapter.
5. How could the collecting of pictures of movie stars be channeled into a worth-while hobby?
6. What sectional or foreign inheritance would give you the start for an interesting decorative accessory?

USING YOUR KNOWLEDGE . . .

1. Ask your mother or father to tell you what they know about your family history, and list unusual talents or interests represented among some of your ancestors.
2. Tell in detail how you might use one of these talents or interests as a decorative climax in your own room.
3. Select one hobby—your own or one you would like to adopt—and plan a proper system of display that would fit into your own room. Look up materials you would need and figure costs. Bring supplies to class and carry out your plans, getting help if necessary from the boys in the shop class.
4. Arrange a display of student hobbies. Write up the story of each. Tell how it started, what it has cost, and what it has led to in contacts, widened interests, and influence on life plans.

5. Tell about a novel, a play, a short story, or a movie in which a hobby played an important part in the lives of the characters.

6. Find out from your reading the hobbies of some well-known people in our political, social, or artistic world. (For example, Winston Churchill paints pictures.)

7. Select one outstanding man or woman in your community who has developed a hobby. Interview him. Write up a story and ask him to arrange a display of the hobby in your school for some special occasion.

CHAPTER 15: Accessories You Can Make for Your Room

During the Victorian era embroidery, crocheting, and other types of needlework were responsible for a clutter of accessories completely lacking in beauty. As a result, since 1900 handicrafts of this type have fallen into temporary disrepute. Despite that fact, there still are many women who spend their leisure time putting fussy embroidery on sheets and pillowcases that would be far smarter if left plain.

Nowadays, however, a new type of handicraft is coming into favor—handmade accessories that are useful and personalized. These accessories not only fit perfectly into a personalized room scheme of decorating—which is the trend in decorating today—but they also fill a definite need. As a result, people are beginning to make things again. Well-designed lingerie cases that exactly fit a special dresser drawer, repeat a special color scheme, and hold just the right amount of lingerie; closet boxes that are uniform in color and design and that are the right size for hats, shoes, and accessories; lamp shades that add personalized decoration to a room; pillows and mats; finger-tip towels and napkins; and decorative articles like samplers and chair seats—these are the modern versions of handicraft that help to make a room personal and beautiful and that are worth the time and effort necessary to produce them.

If you enjoy making things, you will be interested in the suggestions in this chapter for making articles to add charm to your own room or to a future home. Some of the things you make may be kept for many years. Some of them will only serve you for a short time. But all of them will add charm and personality to your bedroom, and making something creative and useful for your room will give you confidence.

Handmade lingerie cases can be practical and decorative.

There are two types of lingerie cases: (1) the folding type like those used for lingerie in department stores, and (2) the envelope style that is especially useful for traveling.

The folding type is very simple to make. All you need is a piece of material about 24 × 30 inches in size and a smaller one 12 × 15 inches. This smaller piece should be sewed into the center of the large piece as if it were an oblong patch pocket on an apron. Into this pocket slip a heavy piece of cardboard, measuring 11¼ × 14¼ inches. This will form the stiff base on which slips, nightgowns, or panties can be piled; the rest of the large square is folded around them. In this way it is possible to keep each type of lingerie separate from the others, and the drawers of your dresser will be as neat as the lingerie shelves in a ready-to-wear shop.

These cases can be made of chintz or gingham to harmonize with your room scheme or of Indian Head in striking colors to contrast with it. They can be made of quilted satin or lovely linen. No matter what material you select, these cases will add to the decorative effect of your room when you open the dresser drawers, and they will make it easy to put your hand on whatever you want without a moment's hesitation. (See drawings on page 302.)

The envelope type of case is unequaled for traveling comfort. If they are made up in different sizes and shapes, they will accommodate every type of accessory and clothing. The easiest way to visualize the pattern is to slit open the two sides of an unsealed envelope. You will notice that when opened out flat the envelope forms a long oblong, with the corners of one end cut off to form a point. In making a fabric envelope, follow that pattern exactly, in all different sizes. The sides should be sewed together exactly where you slit the paper envelope when making the pattern. (See drawings on page 302.)

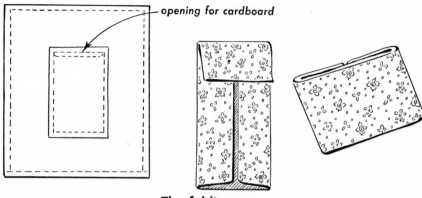

The folding type

Cut and hem an oblong piece of material. Now cut a second, smaller, oblong, and sew it in the center of the large oblong, leaving the top open for inserting a piece of cardboard. This will serve as a base for the folded lingerie when it is placed in the case. The large piece of material should then be folded over to cover and protect the lingerie.

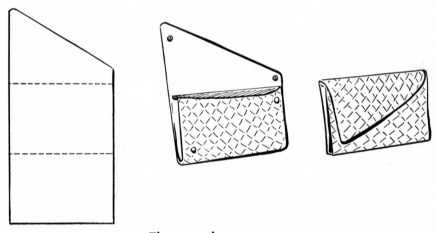

The envelope type

First, estimate the size of the finished envelope desired. Double that size and add a flap to the oblong before cutting the shape out of the material. Fold, and sew the sides together. Hem the flap and the opening and add snaps.

If the fabric is quilted onto outing flannel and then lined, the envelope will have more body and be a much more elegant one than it would be if it were made of a single thickness of fabric. A heavy frog made of cordings of the material can be used to close the envelope, and an initial on the cover will be a final note of individuality.

If you make shoecases to match, you will be completely equipped for really smart vacation traveling.

Handmade closet boxes give individuality to a closet.

Closet boxes for hats, shoes, and other bulky accessories make your closet decorative and individual. They also simplify the work of keeping your closet in order because there will be an obvious place for everything.

Start by visiting shoe stores, millinery shops, and drugstores. They will be glad to sell sturdy boxes in which their merchandise was shipped. The price should be very reasonable. Even these sturdy ones should, however, be reinforced at the edges before they are covered. Gummed fabric tape, which can be bought in a stationery or hardware store, is the best thing to use for reinforcement and should make it possible for the box to stand a great deal of wear.

Whether you use wallpaper or fabric in covering them will depend on the decorative scheme of your room. If the wallpaper is the accent in your room, it would be smart to get more of it and cover the boxes with it. If you have used chintz or cretonne for draperies or a chair covering, your logical selection will be this fabric, and it can be pasted on in exactly the same way as the paper. If your room is quite plain, you may wish to cover the boxes with a wallpaper which is dramatically decorative and which includes the colors of the room. It would make each opening of the closet door a pleasure.

The actual method of cutting and applying the covering is diagrammed on page 304. Follow it carefully, being sure to use a thin, even coating of wallpaper paste or rubber cement. Press all edges down very firmly. After the paste is thoroughly dry, add good-sized decorative labels. Then coat the boxes with wax or shellac to make them easy to clean.

How to Cover a Hat Box

Reinforce the corners of a sturdy hat box with gummed tape. Cover with wall-paper that matches your closet or bedroom color scheme, and, if you wish, add a decorative label.

Personalized lamp shades add individuality to bedrooms.

The tone of your room should determine the general type of the lamp shades used. Parchment-paper lamp shades are especially good for the casual, informal type of room in which the curtains are made of gingham, chintz, muslin, or cretonne. Embroidered fabric and ribbon shades are proper in the more feminine room. They harmonize with ruffled curtains, taffeta draperies, or draw-curtains of sateen or Multicord.

A very casual type of shade, made of heavy linen crash, raffia, or homespun, is a good addition to the room that has an outdoor feeling or that has Venetian blinds or bamboo shades with wooden cornices instead of draperies.

A *personalized parchment shade,* covered with the autographs and comments of your friends, makes an entertaining novelty that you will enjoy during your high school and college days. Get water-color paper from an art shop. Draw the outline of the shade on it according to the diagrams on page 306. Get a set of colored crayons or colored inks and start collecting signatures. When you have all you want, make up the shade, following the construction plan on page 306. Put it on your lamp and shellac it. The only materials you need in addition to the paper are the wire rings and the gummed paper tape, called "passe partout," which you can get in a stationery shop. This shade will not have permanent value, but you will enjoy seeing your friends' names and greetings when you light your lamp at night. You will also have a pattern for making a more conservative shade when you are ready for it.

Novelty shades made of raffia can be woven on any wire frame. The raffia shade will harmonize beautifully with any informal or outdoor setting. The natural tan of the raffia would be especially effective for a shade on a planter lamp, with the green vines acting as a foil.

Handmade pillows add comfort and beauty to a room.

Pillows which try too hard to be unusual are like people who try too hard to be funny; they are, as a rule, miserable failures. A pillow should have comfort and utility as its main concern. It may be decorative as well, but that quality is of secondary importance.

The shape and size of a pillow are important. If it is too small, it is a nuisance. If it is too large, it is clumsy. And if it is an odd shape, it is marked as the work of an amateur.

A pillow 18 inches square is a good medium size that is useful and appropriate on chairs and sofas. A rectangular pillow, 14 × 18 inches, is sometimes particularly harmonious when used as a bolster against the arms of a deep sofa.

The covering for a pillow can be selected from a wide range of styles and types, but you might test your selection by asking yourself, "Does it feel good to the touch?" If it does, you can then consider, "Does it harmonize with the rest of the room in color and style?"

Embroidery or ruffles are not good for pillows. Embroidery creates a raised pattern that is not comfortable. Ruffles also are not comfortable, and they become mussed with even a little use. Pillows are made to be leaned against and should be soft and comfortable. (See pages 278 and 279.)

Handmade mats are useful indoors and out.

When many of your friends come over, there is usually a dearth of chairs, especially if they choose to stay in your bedroom, as they often do. The answer is pillow mats which you can hand out lavishly and which, incidentally, are fun to make.

They can be made round, oblong, or square, and should har-

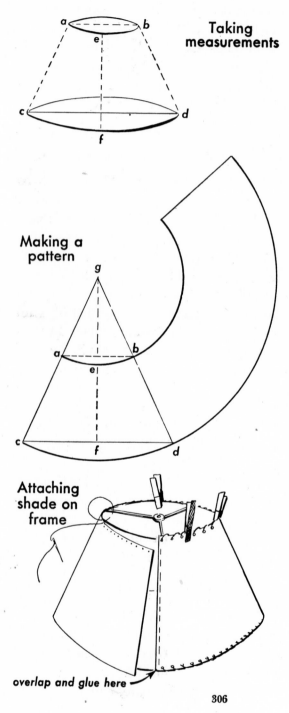

Taking measurements

Measure the diameter of the top wire circle (*a–b*), the diameter of the bottom wire circle (*c–d*), and the slant height desired for the shade (*e–f*).

Making a pattern

Mark off *a–b, c–d,* and *e–f* on straight horizontal and perpendicular lines as shown. Extend *e–f* and connect points *c–a* and *d–b*. Extend these last two lines until they meet on center line, giving point *g*. Now *g–c* or *g–d* is the diameter for drawing bottom of shade, and *g–a* or *g–b* is the diameter for drawing top of shade.

Attaching shade on frame

Glue or sew parchment to frame, using clothespins during process to keep shade intact. Overlap ends ⅛ inch and glue.

overlap and glue here

a Lamp Shade

Add passe partout to cover wire and stitches, to reinforce, and to decorate both top and bottom edges of the shade.

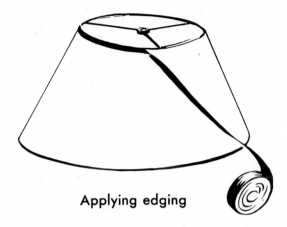

Applying edging

For finishing, use clear shellac inside and out. When dry, rub with burnt umber for antiqued effect if desired.

Giving shade a surface finish

If shades are to be personalized with signatures of friends, they should be written or painted on before the shellac is applied.

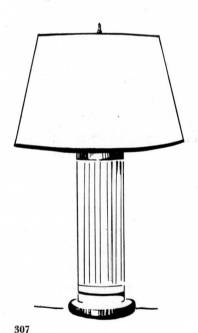

307

monize in color with your room. If you are expecting to take them away to school, you might make them of felt in the school colors. A backing of oilcloth or a water-repellent fabric used on both sides will make them easy to clean as well as practical. They should be stuffed with a layer of cotton for comfort.

Handmade finger-tip napkins and towels can be useful now and later.

Finger-tip napkins and towels are easy to make and small enough to finish at one sitting, yet their effect is important. Handmade towels add a note of elegance to the bathroom, and handmade napkins make even the most casual refreshments take on importance. Both the napkins and the towels make attractive shower gifts for brides or housewarming gifts for career girls setting up an apartment.

Finger-tip napkins can be made in an infinite variety of styles. If they are made of coarse brilliantly colored cotton, they will make the snacks you serve in your room gay and festive. If they are made of fine white linen, they can be beautifully elegant, a fitting start for a hope chest. The following suggestions will give you some ideas for different kinds of napkins you can make, but you will want to vary them to suit your type.

1) Fringed napkins of brightly colored cotton can be smartly plain or decorated in a gay, whimsical style. Each napkin can be different in color and each can be decorated with a different design. One can be decorated with a cross-stitched map of some lake where you spent a wonderful two weeks. Another can be a stylized caricature of a favorite boy or girl friend, complete with halo and nickname. These, like the signature lamp shade, have no permanent or artistic value, but you will enjoy them for the time being.

First, decide on the size you want to make the napkins. A square 6 × 6 inches or an oblong 4 × 6 inches is a good size. In making fringed napkins, allow an extra 2 inches to each dimension so that the fringe on all sides can be 1 inch wide. Stitch around the center rectangle several times with a sewing machine to form a firm heading at the top of the fringe. Then ravel the threads up to the point of the stitching. Next, add the decoration. If the design is to be done in an outline stitch, draw the design on paper and trace it onto the napkin by using carbon paper. If it is to be done in a cross-stitch, baste the scrim onto the napkins and follow a design from a cross-stitch pattern booklet, varying it to suit yourself.

2) Hemstitched napkins are more conservative than the fringed ones. They are usually made of linen and can be lace-edged or monogrammed for decoration.

3) Rolled-hem napkins made of coarse linen can be decorated with a crocheted edging that will make them look like Italian imports.

Finger-tip towels, or the slightly larger guest size, can have much the same variety as the finger-tip napkins. They can be "pretty" with a lace edging, "elegant" with an initial and hemstitching, or "rich" with a scalloped embroidered edging and an initial. The accepted sizes vary, but towels 9 × 12 inches are usually considered the standard size.

The small size of finger-tip towels and finger-tip napkins makes them easy to carry around in a purse, so they can be worked on at any time and in any place.

Handmade luncheon cloths should be dainty.

The size of card tables is one thing that changes very little. As a rule, both the folding and the rigid variety can be counted on to be between 30 and 32 inches square. For that reason you can plan linen luncheon cloths, with matching napkins, knowing that they will fit now and in the future.

The same variety in style can be used for luncheon cloths as was suggested for the finger-tip towels and napkins. But since more material and more work are involved, it might be well to be a little more conservative in the choice of design. Embroidered initials and hemstitching are always good forms of decoration for luncheon cloths and will be the sort of thing you will use with pride as long as the linen lasts.

Modern samplers make a new kind of memory book.

In olden days our great-grandmothers designed samplers to show a sample of their skill in needlework and, indirectly, to record

COURTESY *The American Home*

Samplers are made after the fashion of those in which our great-grandmothers showed their skill in needlework. This one, made in 1942, is designed around the Biblical story of Noah's Ark. The top line reads: "And the rain was upon the earth 40 days and 40 nights." How did the designer of this sampler use the story of Noah's Ark to good advantage here? Samplers may be made with modern themes pertaining to interests, school life, home, or family.

something of their family background and the vital statistics about family members. It might be fun to adapt the sampler idea by making a modern version that would be a decorative memory book of different phases of your life.

A *school sampler,* for instance, could list entertaining things about your school life. The design could include the year of your graduation, your name, the town, the subjects you took, and the teachers who taught them. The picture in the middle of the sampler could be the doorway of your school with the name of it in cross-stitch above or below it.

A *family sampler* could list facts about your home life. The picture on it could be your own home doorway with your street address below it. The design could also include names of your family, your birth date, special occasions in your life, your friends, and your pets. This last—your pets—could be done in pictures. Cross-stitch books will furnish amusing designs of dogs, cats, birds, and fish.

Hobby and interest samplers could show special vacations that meant a great deal to you. Special hobbies or interests, such as swimming, boating, fishing, or riding, furnish excellent visual material for samplers. This type would be of interest to your friends and furnish decoration for your walls.

Needle point creates heirlooms for the future.

Needle point is the most permanent form of needlework if good wool is used. For that reason the designs should be copied from the traditional ones in books or museums.

For some time it was thought that needle point demanded black backgrounds. But that idea was merely the result of the Victorian influence. Actually, any color can be used for background—anything from creamy toast color or apple green to navy blue or cinnamon brown.

So, if you decide to do needle point, make the background of your favorite color. It will probably be the color thread of your home or room, and consequently the needle point will become an integral part of it and will show off to the very best advantage. Be sure to get a large piece of scrim so that it will fit the seat of any chair you may select for it later on.

Shadow boxes add a touch of Victorianism.

Shadow boxes, which are miniature hanging cabinets, are a type of accessory which has come to us from the Victorian era. They

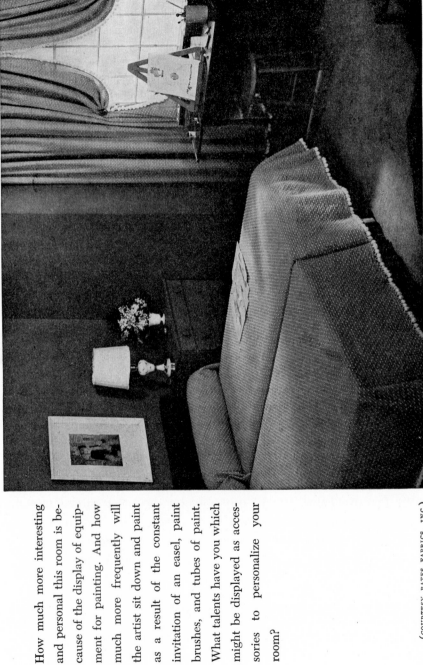

How much more interesting and personal this room is because of the display of equipment for painting. And how much more frequently will the artist sit down and paint as a result of the constant invitation of an easel, paint brushes, and tubes of paint. What talents have you which might be displayed as accessories to personalize your room?

COURTESY SAMUEL L. DINKELSPIEL

Old picture frames can be used to make a shadow box for displaying hobby collections. (See directions below.)

can be made by attaching a box onto the back of a frame for displaying choice small objects of art, still-life groupings, miniature collections, or small flower arrangements. They can be very lovely or a meaningless jumble, depending on whether or not they are handled with restraint. A few objects arranged artistically can be shown off effectively in a shadow box. But if this simplicity is violated, the result becomes a clutter that is anything but attractive.

CHECKING YOUR KNOWLEDGE . . .

1. What are the two types of lingerie cases?
2. What are the steps in making closet boxes?
3. Which of the personalized lamp shades would be appropriate in your own room? Why?
4. What is a good size for pillows?

5. What kinds of finger-tip napkins would you like to make for immediate use? For the future?

6. What is a good size for finger-tip towels?

7. What information would you put on a school sampler?

8. Is it good form to use color for the background of needle point?

USING YOUR KNOWLEDGE . . .

1. Plan a series of dresser-drawer cases for your lingerie and accessories. Determine the yardage and select material that would be especially practical, inexpensive, and attractive. Figure the cost and make at least one.

2. Make one good-looking closet box that would harmonize with your room scheme, covering it with wallpaper or fabric and labeling it attractively.

3. Look up different alphabets in the art room of the library, and select a style of initial for your own use on underwear, household linen, and silver. Figure out the proper-sized letter for tea napkins, finger-tip towels, card-table covers, slips, and silver place service.

4. Make a lamp shade of parchment paper, following the diagrams on page 306. See how humorously attractive you can make it by collecting signatures and cartoons for it.

5. Make a lamp shade of raffia for a lamp in your room. Keep track of your expenses so you can report the total cost.

6. Design a sampler that would be a historic record of your grade school days and one that would be a record of your high school days. Use squared paper, allowing four cross-stitches per square of paper.

SECTION FIVE: Management of the Home

CHAPTER 16: Saving Time and Energy

You have probably heard your mother say many times: "I don't understand where my time goes. I work constantly and I've bought all kinds of things to save work, but the house is always upset."

You, yourself, have probably said: "I want to help Mother by doing my share, but I can't even keep my own room in order. I work most of the time while I'm at home, but I never seem to finish all the things that I should do."

Life seems to have become so complicated that everyone feels this sort of pressure. There are four remedies for this situation: (1) the selection of home furnishings which will simplify housekeeping, yet which will not sacrifice beauty; (2) the planning of closet and storage space to make it possible to find things and put things away quickly and easily; (3) the systematized arrangement of work areas in kitchens, which will save steps and motions; and (4) the use of fatigue-saving equipment to conserve energy.

Home furnishings can be selected to simplify housework.

Unfortunately, the time spent on housework is not checked by a stop watch or measured by a time clock. Consequently, women tend to minimize the "few minutes" it takes to do one detail after another. They do not realize that, added together, these "few minutes" spent on unimportant details add up to precious hours. Many of those hours could be saved by selecting home furnishings that require a minimum of attention and care, and which would, consequently, simplify housework materially.

Window curtains that are easy to keep clean will simplify house-work and save time. Following are examples of such types of curtains.

1) Heavy curtains or net curtains that can be hung up damp or put through an ironer will reduce the usual amount of time and work spent in laundering curtains.

Nylon and homespun fabrics require no ironing. Sateen, cotton taffeta, muslin, Glosheen, antique satin, broadcloth, and linen curtains can be washed and ironed easily if they are made without ruffles and if they are made with French pleats that are not sewed in. There are several types of tapes which are sewed flat on the heading to form French pleats and which flatten out completely for easy ironing. One of these tapes is slotted so that the French pleats are formed by sliding the rod through the slots. Another tape has eyelets through which a wire pin is inserted to draw the curtain together in a French-pleat type of gather. A third is equipped with draw cords which pull up after the curtain is ironed to form a French pleat. Any one of these devices makes it possible to put a curtain through an ironer in a fraction of the time required to iron by hand one that has the usual permanently sewed French pleats.

2) Curtains with a permanently finished surface, such as permanently glazed chintz or a plastic-coated fabric, can be shaken free of dirt or wiped off with a damp cloth. The time saved by the elimination of the whole process of washing and ironing would be considerable during the life of the curtain.

3) Eliminating curtains entirely is a third way to save housekeeping time. Windows in bathrooms, kitchens, recreation rooms, and dinettes look decoratively smart when framed with a well-designed wooden cornice or treated with inside shutters. Turn to the illustrations on page 225 to see how privacy can be achieved and light controlled with this type of treatment.

Slipcovers that do not require ironing are also timesavers. If the material of a slipcover is made of softly twisted fibers, it can be put back on the furniture while it is partially damp. It will dry smoothly, and no ironing will be required. The time thus saved may mean that the ironing can be finished by noon instead of dragging on into the middle of the afternoon.

Bedspreads that can be cared for easily save a great deal of energy and housekeeping time. Divided bedspreads, composed of a dust ruffle and a coverlet, require only a fraction of the care of a one-piece bedspread. They are easy to remove and fold at night and equally easy to unfold and place on the bed in the morning. The coverlet can be washed or cleaned separately from the dust ruffle. This saving of energy and time is important to a woman who is doing all her own work.

Covers to protect furnishings speed housekeeping and are great timesavers. These protectors, however, should not detract from the beauty or the simplicity of the room, nor should they ever give the impression that the furniture is being saved for company and is not being enjoyed by the most important people in the world—the family for whom the house exists. Plastic covers for chairs and lamps, antimacassars on chairs and sofas, doilies on tables or chests, or any other kind of obvious protectors are not good artistically and say quite frankly, "These furnishings are too fragile or too good for ordinary family use."

Covers on backs and arms of chairs made of the same material as the upholstery are in an entirely different class. They are inconspicuous and can be kept on at all times. They take the brunt of the wear and they reduce the number of complete cleaning jobs necessary for the chair itself. It is wise to order an extra yard or two of fabric for this purpose whenever furniture is bought. The manufacturer usually has it on hand.

Tooled leather mats under lamps or other accessories protect table tops inconspicuously and can be wiped off easily and quickly.

Mirror reflectors for the center of the dining-room table will protect the surface of the table from the dampness of porous vases or plant containers, yet they add beauty and can be kept bright and sparkling with very little effort.

Throw rugs can be used to protect carpeting in doorways, under piano pedals, or in front of a fireplace. They should be made of the same carpeting they cover so that they will be scarcely noticeable. These can be taken up and cleaned quickly and easily.

The use of a few important accessories, rather than many unimportant ones, will save a great deal of housekeeping time. One

Bad

Good

Contrasting upholstery protectors (antimacassars) are fussy and Victorian in appearance. Protectors for back and arms of chairs and sofas in material that matches the upholstery fabric do not detract from the beauty of the piece of furniture nor the fabric in which it is covered.

good-sized plant costs no more than five or six small ones, yet it is five times as easy to care for and is decoratively more effective.

If the collecting of miniatures is a hobby of one of the members of the family, the collection should be housed in dustproof cases. Collections of larger items should be kept in cabinets or stored in boxes. They should be brought out only occasionally for special enjoyment and should not be displayed where they must be cared for constantly.

Plain, well-made silk or rayon lamp shades can be whisked up and down in warm, soapy water and hung out to dry, whereas fussy ones decorated with ruffles or garlands of flowers take considerable time to denude before washing and to redecorate after they are dry. Parchment-paper lamp shades can be wiped off with a cloth which has been dipped in warm, soapy water and wrung out, and parchment-skin shades can be cleaned with a soft eraser.

Individual place mats for meals will save time and work. Many place mats, such as those made of plastics, cork, metal, or heavily surfaced fabrics, can be washed off with a damp cloth; others require laundering. Laundering a soiled place mat, however, is much less work than laundering a whole tablecloth that is soiled only in

When too many accessories are displayed on a mantel, none of them is given emphasis, and dusting becomes more of a problem.

With a few well-chosen accessories, each becomes important, and less work is required to keep the mantel clean.

COURTESY THE GORHAM CO.

Place mats are neat and attractive for any meal, and they are much easier to launder than a large tablecloth.

one spot. Thus, higher standards of cleanliness can be maintained and hours of time will be saved by the frequent use of place mats.

Storage and closet space can be planned to save time.

Space for storing things of all kinds—such as cleaning equipment, supplies, hobby equipment, and clothes—is as important to the smooth running of a home as are the equipment, supplies, and clothes themselves. Many homes seem disorderly because of inadequate, poorly planned storage space, rather than poor housekeeping. Ample storage space not only encourages and teaches orderliness, but it also increases the speed of straightening rooms and of doing housework.

Look at your own room this afternoon when you go home from school. Look at your closet and the drawers of your dresser. Are they in good order? Is it easy for you to find things and put them away properly? If your answer is "yes," you are one of the fortunates who have enough storage space. If your closet and dresser drawers are not in order, it is quite probable that you do not have enough space to make orderliness possible, and that you need to plan more storage space for your room.

Look at the rest of the house. Bulging closets are not a sign of bad housekeeping. They are a sign that one closet is trying to do the work of three or four.

As a result of research in the field of home-storage needs, storage closets, cabinets, and boxes are now obtainable to meet every storage need. Department stores and mail-order houses now carry a complete line of inexpensive containers made of wallboard and heavy cardboard which can be painted or papered to match any room in which they are used.

When people own their own homes, built-in closets and cabinets are advisable because they not only add real value to the property but also save housekeeping time. There are many places where unused rectangles and triangles of floor space can be turned into closets and wardrobes without in the least destroying the beauty of the rooms. (See drawings on pages 324 and 325.)

The following list of different types of closets for rooms other than the kitchen will suggest additional storage space in your own home that will save time and energy and at the same time encourage orderliness.

Closets for household equipment should be planned to hold complete equipment for doing a certain type of household job. For example, one closet might contain all the equipment needed for cleaning the living rooms of the house. Another might have equipment for electrical repair work. Another might contain all the equipment for silver polishing, for laundering, for packing lunches, or for canning. If these closets are kept well stocked with the necessary items, the work connected with the particular household job can be accomplished quickly and efficiently.

Closets for supplies should have shelves that are carefully planned as to width and height to fit the specific materials they are to hold. A bathroom supply closet, a linen closet, or a medicine chest

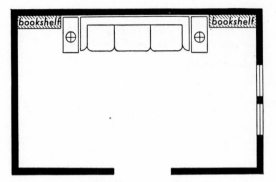

In a living room

Unused corners can be made more attractive and useful by building in bookcases that have storage cabinets beneath them to hold records, game equipment, etc.

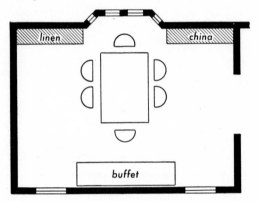

In a dining room

Linen and china closets, built into each side of a shallow bay window, will help to accentuate the window as well as adding storage space.

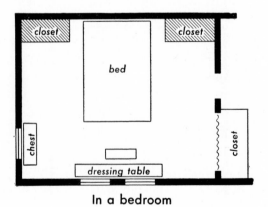

In a bedroom

Wardrobe closets on each side of a bed provide space for clothes and improve the appearance of the furniture arrangement in the room.

324

Storage Space in a Home

Useless recessed areas on each side of a fireplace can be used for built-in storage cabinets or bookshelves. Such cabinets or shelves can be made in a variety of combinations and built from floor to ceiling.

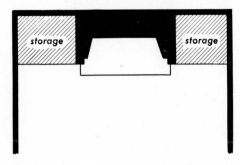

In a living room with fireplace

A shallow closet with sliding doors can be built into the space at one side of the entrance to the vestibule. Such a closet is convenient for hanging the coats of guests.

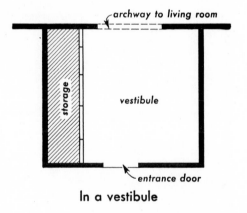

In a vestibule

Corner closets for holding a variety of equipment can be built on stair landings without detracting from the appearance or taking up traffic space needed on the landing.

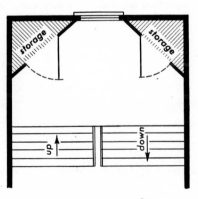

On a stair landing

COURTESY NEW YORK STATE COLLEGE OF
HOME ECONOMICS AT CORNELL UNIVERSITY

Closets for household equipment should be planned to hold complete equipment for certain kinds of work. This closet for cleaning equipment is well arranged so that each article is easily accessible.

A cabinet built especially for kitchen utensils will save time and energy and make for neatness in the kitchen.

COURTESY NEW YORK STATE COLLEGE OF
HOME ECONOMICS AT CORNELL UNIVERSITY

A specially built cabinet to hold everyday dishes makes it easier to set the table or put away the dishes for the three meals a day. Note how many dishes can be packed into a small space when the shelves are low and shallow.

are examples of this kind of specialized supply closet. This grouping of supplies makes it easier to know when some item is running low and also to avoid duplicate buying of articles.

Closets for hobby equipment are important in simplifying housework and also in encouraging the pursuit of a hobby. Many

If the shelves in a closet are planned to take care of specific items, the home-maker can find needed supplies easily, put things away quickly, and know at all times what her stock is of all items.

(EWING GALLOWAY)

times the fun of following a hobby is lost in the work of getting things out or putting them away after a relatively short period of use. As a result, what might have become a fascinating interest is gradually dropped. Having a special closet for keeping the equipment used in following a hobby will add to its pleasure and will encourage the hobbyist to do his part in helping to keep the house in order.

Closets to hold sports equipment should also be a part of every home, because participation in sports is important for the health, happiness, and normal living of every member of the family. The space beneath the basement stairs will hold a great deal of bulky, unwieldy sports equipment if it is sealed off into carefully planned compartments. Some people find that a closet in the garage is ideal for storing large pieces of sports equipment. The equipment then is no longer a problem in the house and in the housekeeping activities.

Closets for clothes that are ample and carefully planned can hasten the job of straightening up a bedroom. When storage is inadequate, each item of clothing to be put away presents a fresh and often irritating question, "Where can I put this?" But when there

A series of cupboards under the stairs on the first or second floor will take care of much cumbersome equipment which never seems to have a place, but which must be kept somewhere.

(COURTESY ARMSTRONG CORK COMPANY)

is adequate storage and a spot has been planned for each type of clothing, things can be put away without conscious effort in a fraction of the time formerly spent in looking for a place to put them.

It is surprising to realize that 20 inches is ample depth for a wardrobe closet. Look around your bedroom for a space of that depth where a wardrobe could be built. Then use your present closet for storage of accessories and out-of-season clothes. Turn to page 58 to see how a wardrobe can be built into a small space without detracting from the appearance or living space of the room.

Work areas can be arranged to save steps.

The daily round of work in the home can run smoothly on a minimum of time and with a minimum of steps and motions, or it can be a time-consuming mix-up of confused backtracking and duplicated effort. The difference depends upon the placement of equipment and the arrangement of the work areas. Such planning is even more important for getting work done quickly than the speed of the worker. A conscious effort to hurry builds up tensions that produce accidents rather than efficiency. The old saying "Haste makes waste" is still true.

Instead of trying to hurry, an effort should be made in advance to analyze steps and movements and from that analysis to determine a plan or arrangement that will be more advantageous for saving time and effort.

Check yourself and your mother, or have someone else chart the steps each of you takes, in doing any one job—such as washing the dishes, setting the table, or clearing the table. Do the same for the process of daily cleaning or dusting. You will be surprised at the number of unnecessary steps you have taken that might be eliminated.

Analyzing work areas in the kitchen is a good way to begin to try to save time. There are certain general principles of storage and work-space arrangement which have been worked out as the most efficient. Nickell and Dorsey [1] say that kitchens can be divided roughly into three large unit groups: (1) the refrigerator and preparation center, (2) the range and serving center, and (3) the sink and dishwashing center. These three can and must be interchanged to fit the different situations which exist in every home. Yet if the kitchen is planned around these basic units, a well-organized kitchen will be assured.

The refrigerator and preparation center includes an adequate work-space counter next to the refrigerator and a good cupboard space above the counter. Work counters must be 24 inches wide for comfortable and advantageous use in cooking preparation, and cupboards above them should not be more than 12 inches deep. An 18-inch space between counter and overhanging cupboards is sufficient for the work space. Adjacent cupboard space must be sufficient to hold the following equipment: sugar, flour, spices, flavorings, and other staple supplies, as well as mixing bowls, pans, knives, spoons, small utensils, and cookbooks.

The range and serving center must have the same type of adequate counter space and cupboard space as described above, but it

[1] Nickell, Paulena, and Jean Muir Dorsey, *Management in Family Living,* John Wiley & Sons, Inc., New York, Second Edition, 1950.

A Step-saving U Kitchen

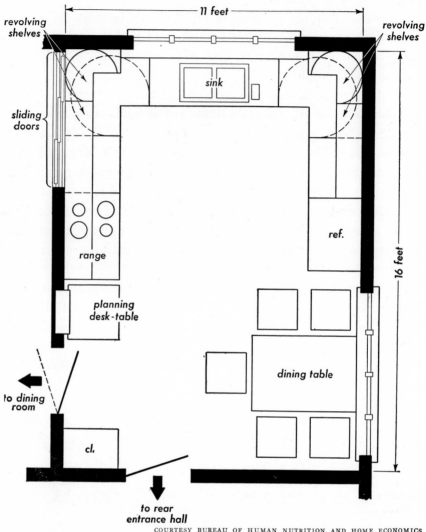

COURTESY BUREAU OF HUMAN NUTRITION AND HOME ECONOMICS

Maximum convenience for the homemaker at her work is the aim of this step-saving kitchen, designed in the housing and household equipment laboratories of the Bureau of Human Nutrition and Home Economics of the U.S. Department of Agriculture. The unbroken U shape was chosen for arranging equipment because it forms a compact dead-end work center through which household traffic cannot pass. It also allows the dining corner to be planned and decorated as a separate center. The dining corner may be used for a baby's play pen by pushing the dining table to one side when not in use.

COURTESY BUREAU OF HUMAN NUTRITION AND HOME ECONOMICS

Here is a photograph of the kitchen plan shown on the opposite page. As shown on the plan, the three key pieces of equipment are brought within easy reach of each other—sink at center of U, refrigerator and range at ends. The U-shaped work area, complete within itself, may be adapted to a small kitchen that does not have space for desk and dinette areas.

must be next to the range. The following equipment must be stored near this center: skillets, lids, ladles, forks, spoons, seasonings, roaster, pressure cooker, bread, cake, cookies, ready-to-eat cereals, china, silver, linen, trays, and flower containers.

The sink and dishwashing center also needs a counter space, preferably one on each side of the sink, and cupboard space adjacent to it that is adequate to hold dishwashing equipment—such as dish towels, dishcloths, soap flakes, washing powder, and scouring pads—and equipment for preparing food at the sink—such as kettles, saucepans, strainers, coffeepot, and coffee.

In a well-planned kitchen, the centers are so compactly placed that one work space will serve two or three purposes.

Suggestions for handy storing of kettles, trays, and other equipment are shown on page 327, but the basis of arrangement must follow the personal work pattern of the woman who uses the kitchen.

Check your kitchen at home and see whether it is conveniently arranged for the way in which you and your mother work.

Fatigue-savers conserve energy.

There are four specific fatigue-savers in housework that can make a tremendous difference in the effect of work on a home-maker: (1) the right kind of lighting, to prevent eye fatigue; (2) the proper height for work counters, to reduce body fatigue; (3) well-designed seating equipment, to make it easier to relax muscles while working; and (4) the use of laborsaving devices.

Proper lighting, to prevent eye fatigue, is lighting of adequate intensity that does not glare. "Adequate intensity" is measured in foot-candles. A foot-candle is the amount of light cast by one standard candle on a surface held perpendicular to its rays and at a distance of 1 foot from the candle. On a sunny day outdoors, the light measures 10,000 foot-candles of light—a light that is too blinding to read by. A shady spot under a tree has 1,000 foot-candles of light and is much better for reading. Indoors, near a window, on a day without strong sunlight, there are 2,000 foot-candles of light. Such a light is excellent for reading.

The amount of light that is adequate to prevent fatigue is determined by the type of work being done. Turn to Chart 14 on page 269 for an analysis of your light needs.

The only accurate way to determine the amount of light at any point in a room, and therefore to check the efficiency of the lighting you are using, is to use a light meter, which may be borrowed from an electric company service department or from a photographic supply house. Any other method of trying to gauge the amount of light is mere guesswork. The number of watts of a bulb is not a true measure, because the type of shade used, the design of the fixture, the color of the walls, rugs, and ceiling, and the amount of light each of these reflects or absorbs all add to or subtract from the power of a bulb. Accurate analysis will make it possible for you to prevent unnecessary eye fatigue.

The type of lighting selected—whether fluorescent or incandescent—is a matter of personal choice. However, the kind of lighting should not be selected because of the efficiency alone. The effect

Proper lighting over sink and range prevents eye-strain, and thus fatigue, for the homemaker.

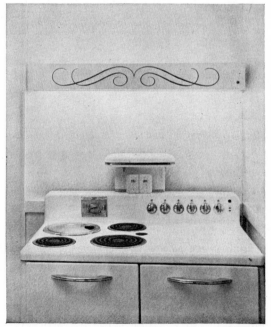

Watching television is not supposed to be hard on the eyes if the room is properly lighted. A dark room is too much of a contrast. On the other hand, the lights should not be too bright, should not fall directly on the screen, and should not be reflected in the screen. To check this, test possible reflection on set when not in use. Lamps should be placed at the sides of the room, as shown here. Opaque shades on lamps are preferable. It is a good idea to lighten dark background walls by a concealed bulb in back of set. This has been done here by the use of a planter lamp placed on top of the set. Adults should sit 8 to 12 feet away from screen. Children should be a bit nearer. It is also better, if possible, to sit directly in front of the screen.

of artificial light should be carefully tested on the appearance of the people and on the color of the furnishings. Color is very important in a home, and artificial light should not and need not distort it in any way. (See also pages 268 and 270 in Chapter 13.)

Proper counter heights, to reduce general fatigue, is a somewhat personal matter because it depends on the height of the worker. Interesting studies have been made on the best work-surface height according to the height of the worker, and these should be consulted when kitchens are being built or remodeled. A counter is the

Proper counter heights for kitchen work surfaces prevent fatigue. The proper height depends on the height of the worker. Check with standards given on these pages and tell why this counter is the correct height for this woman.

(COURTESY OREGON STATE COLLEGE)

correct height if a worker, standing erect and not bending her knees, can place her hands, palms down, on the top of the counter, bending her arms only slightly. In general, counters 34 inches high are about right for a person of average height. Good posture is an important factor in the length of time it is possible to work without fatigue.

Proper seating equipment, to encourage a woman to relax while working, is another fatigue-saver. A well-designed chair will save a great deal of energy by making it possible for a woman to work as well when seated as when standing. A good chair or stool permits the worker to sit with both feet resting on the floor or on a footrest in such a way that the edge of the seat does not press on the legs. The seat should be approximately 15 inches square and should slope backward slightly, so the worker can sit back easily. A chair or stool with a back high enough to support the small of the back is the most restful.

Laborsaving devices used to be considered an extravagance when servants were cheap and numerous and a homemaker's time was not valued highly. Nowadays, when all help is expensive and

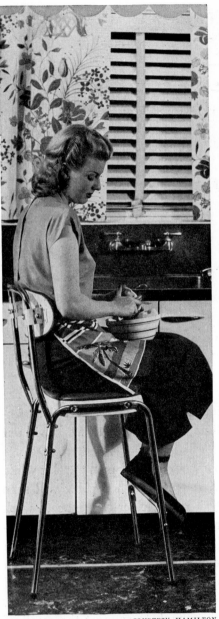

COURTESY HAMILTON
MANUFACTURING CORP.

A well-designed chair for the kitchen will save a great deal of the homemaker's energy. Why is this a well-designed chair? (See page 337.)

when so many women work part- or full-time outside the home, laborsaving devices are looked upon as a necessity. Even those women who do not work outside the home find laborsaving devices a necessity if they do their own work and try to carry on such additional activities as church work, charitable work, and social activities. Consequently, the question becomes *which* of the laborsaving devices to buy rather than *whether* to buy.

Most couples consider a washing machine of some kind a necessity. Another great saver of time and energy is an electric iron that can be heated instantly and adjusted quickly for different types of fabrics. A refrigerator which permits once-a-week shopping, even for perishables; a vacuum cleaner to keep rugs, carpets, draperies, and upholstery clean; an electric clock which doesn't require winding or setting; an electric toaster, which frees the housekeeper to set the table or prepare the other food while the toast is being made; an automatic coffee-maker which only needs to be plugged in—all these are necessary time- and energy-savers.

While laborsaving equipment helps to reduce the working time and energy of the homemaker, a family should consider its needs and habits before buying any large piece of equipment. (See pages 337–341 for some factors to consider in making decisions.)

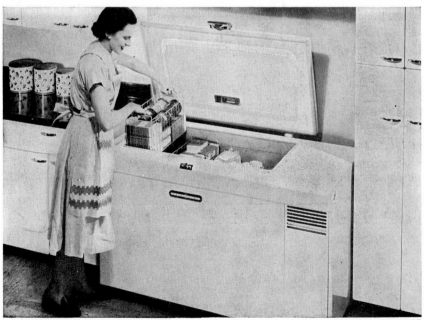

Chart 15: Wattage Required for Various Electric Appliances Used in the Home

Appliance	Wattage required
Clock	2
Coffee-maker . . .	500
Dishwasher	500
Electric blanket . .	200
Electric roaster . . .	1,650
Fan	75 to 100
Food freezer . . .	350 to 450
Food mixer	100
Garbage disposal unit .	500
Grill	100
Heater	800 to 1,200
Heating pad . . .	60
Iron	800 to 1,000
Ironer	1,650
Radio	100
Range	7,000 to 14,000
Razor	10
Refrigerator . . .	300
Sewing machine . .	75
Sun lamp	400
Television	500
Toaster	550 to 1,000
Vacuum cleaner . .	400
Waffle iron	1,000
Washing machine with spinner	375 to 1,200
Washing machine with wringer	375 to 400

A girl who likes to cook can save herself hours of time and energy as well as money if she has an electric mixer. A girl who likes to sew can make an electric sewing machine pay for itself in a short time. A couple that works all day will find an electric roaster, which turns on or off automatically, a help in saving time and energy. A couple should analyze their needs and their habits carefully. Then they should decide which of the laborsaving devices helps them the most. The cost of such equipment is small when compared with the time and energy saved by its use.

How to use electric devices without blowing a fuse is something that should be studied carefully when electrical equipment is purchased, because many houses and apartments were built when electric laborsaving devices were few in number. It is a good idea to call the home service department of the local electric company and ask them to analyze the wiring to be sure it will not be overloaded by your new equipment. (See Chart 15.) A slight increase in the amount of power made available may save a large fire loss.

Good management can be learned through study and experience.

During high school days your responsibilities at home vary considerably with the season. From September to June most of your time is filled by school or school activities. Yet, actually, the most effective way to learn good management is to put it into practice in your own home.

During the school year home projects must be kept to a minimum. Yet by applying the principles of efficient management of time, you will not only be able to keep your own room as it should be, but you may also be able to assume your share of family duties, despite the fact that your time is limited.

After you have studied the best method of cleaning, work out a schedule for keeping your room clean, and keep an accurate record of the time consumed by each job. Gradually you will find that you can reduce the time of each job by following the suggestions made in this chapter. Habits of efficiency worked out now for one room will be an excellent starting point for efficient organization of the total housework job when you have a home of your own.

During the summer vacation you can expand your activities as far as your ability, your sense of responsibility, your family needs, and your interests dictate. Some girls, even in their middle teens, are still expecting a watchful mother to say, "Now make your bed before you go downtown," or "Straighten up your room before Helen comes." In other words, some girls take no responsibility and so can be given none in matters of handling money, selecting their own furnishings, or making personal decisions about dates and social affairs.

The majority of girls, however, are self-reliant and eager for the freedom that comes with greater responsibility and maturity. Most girls actually work at growing up. To them the matter of personal time-management will come as a short cut in that process, because it is the logical foundation for achieving real independence.

CHECKING YOUR KNOWLEDGE . . .

1. Show how the careful selection of curtains, slipcovers, bedspreads, and protective covers can save housekeeping time.
2. Why does adequate storage space save housekeeping time? Refer specifically to closets for household equipment, for supplies, for hobbies, for sports equipment, and for clothes.
3. What three work centers of a kitchen can be arranged to save work time?
4. What four different types of fatigue-savers do we have?
5. What is considered adequate light for three activities in the home? What is the unit of light measurement and what device have we for checking the efficiency of any lighting?
6. What is considered adequate light for (*a*) housework, (*b*) conversation, and (*c*) reading?

USING YOUR KNOWLEDGE . . .

1. Work out three laborsaving changes you could suggest in the furnishings of your home right now. Figure out how much they would cost.
2. As a class, make a floor plan of the home economics laboratory and then plan a rearrangement that would be more efficient. Get prices from carpenters and compare them with prices on stock cupboards of metal and wood.

3. Check the lighting in eight seating or work areas in your home. Is it adequate by present-day standards? If not, how could it be improved?

4. Invite the head of the industrial arts department for boys to give a demonstration of repairing ordinary electrical equipment, making an extension cord, rewiring a lamp, and replacing a fuse. Each girl may bring at least one article to class to be repaired after the demonstration under the supervision of the industrial arts teachers.

5. Make a tentative schedule of the time you have available for helping at home. Check the time necessary for the specific jobs you are now responsible for. Figure out what additional work you might do if you planned your jobs ahead and made them a matter of routine.

6. What long-time projects could you do on week ends? Estimate the time necessary for each and figure how they could be worked into a week-end schedule.

7. Check your working time on one job over a period of two weeks, changing routine and placement of equipment used for it frequently as you see opportunities to save time. See how much time you can save on that one job without consciously hurrying.

8. Ask the head of the home service department of your local electric company or department store to give the class a demonstration of laborsaving devices now available. Follow it with a class discussion on original cost, expense of installation, and cost of operation compared with time and labor saved.

CHAPTER 17: Upkeep of the Home

Twenty-five years ago "upkeep of the home" included spring and fall house cleanings—activities that upset the whole family. It was a time of soap and water, rug beaters, and curtain stretchers, supplemented by the painter who came in to administer "another coat of ivory" because it "blended with everything." It was a time of total confusion from the front door to the back. No corner, however small, escaped.

Today "upkeep of the home" means quite a different thing, because the rooms of the home are kept clean all of the time and cleaning can be done so unobtrusively from room to room that no one is disturbed. Even the arrival of painters and paper hangers is less of an ordeal if careful planning is done in advance. The main problem in redecorating today lies in the selection of the paint color or the wallpaper, because nowadays we know both the dangers and the joys of color and we shun the safe, dull security of "another coat of ivory," unless we are using it as a background for the color in the furnishings.

Allowing time for careful selection of colors for the walls is, however, a small price to pay for the very real psychological lift that comes to the whole family as a result of redecorating a room. In fact, the result is as stimulating to every member as a new dress is to a girl. Just as a shop or a restaurant occasionally changes a color or makes improvements to keep up with new trends, to attract new business, and to hold the old, so houses need these occasional changes or improvements that will make the family "home con-

This is the way house cleaning used to be! But modern equipment and new methods of keeping house have eliminated the headaches of the old way when the whole household was upset every spring and fall with "house cleaning."

scious." Upkeep for the home therefore includes much more than cleanliness or unchipped paint. It includes the creating of beauty and readjustments to keep up with the changing interests and tastes of the family. No home is ever "finished" unless the people in it die. Living people change, and their homes must change with them if their homes are to fit their new interests, habits, needs, and standards.

Ceilings, walls, and woodwork need periodic cleaning.

Ceilings, walls, and woodwork need thorough cleaning periodically. How or when they should be cleaned depends entirely on the amount of dirt in the air and the type of heating plant in the house. If the walls are subjected to much dirt, this fact should be taken into account at the time of decorating. The use of extra coats of paint, an extra hard-finish paint, or washable wallpaper will make cleaning an easier job and prolong the time until redecorating is needed.

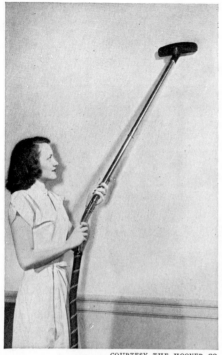

Except in soft-coal areas, walls may be kept clean by dusting them with a vacuum cleaner attachment to prevent them from becoming dirty.

Wallpaper cleaning methods depend on whether or not the wallpaper is washable. The most expensive washable wallpaper has a heavy, waterproof, plastic surfacing which is guaranteed to last for the life of the paper. The less expensive, so-called "washable," papers can be washed lightly two or three times, but eventually they lose their waterproof quality and must be cleaned with a wallpaper cleaner.

Nonwashable papers are of two types—the very expensive imported or hand-blocked papers and the very cheap domestic papers. Both of these can be cleaned with one of several commercial preparations, most of which are puttylike substances that erase the dirt. Any nonwashable paper can be made waterproof by coating it with a colorless shellac or wax. This coating will not affect the colors in the paper, but it may turn a pure white background slightly cream color. It will, however, protect the wallpaper quite satisfactorily and allow it to be washed for some time. Expensive imported papers are frequently treated in this way.

Paint cleaning can be done effectively by the use of solvents dissolved in water, provided the paint itself is washable.

There are some very inexpensive water-soluble paints of the calcimine type that are not washable. They usually come in powder form to be mixed with water. Paints of this type have to be dusted or cleaned like wallpaper.

There is, however, a type of water-soluble paint that is washable. It comes in paste form and is thinned with water to paint consistency. This paint has a rubber emulsion base which makes it washable to a certain extent.

Ordinary dull or flat oil paint, which is the most practical paint for the large surfaces of walls and ceilings, does not have a hard finish and so will take only a few washings with a strong solution of washing compound. However, if three coats have been used — the accepted standard for paint jobs over new plaster—the number of possible washings is greatly increased.

As a final aid to easy cleaning, some people add a protective coat of colorless wax or shellac to window sills, doors, and bannisters. This

EWING GALLOWAY

Soiled places on woodwork should be washed with one of many good solvents. Therefore, the paint selected for the woodwork should be a kind that will take frequent washings without having to be renewed each year.

protective shellac, added to the hard-enamel surface, produces a finish that is almost impervious to moisture and dirt.

Ceilings, walls, and woodwork need occasional redecorating.

Occasional redecorating of ceilings, walls, and woodwork is part of the normal upkeep of a house. The best job of redecorating is done when all old wallpaper has been removed and all old paint has been thoroughly washed. It is sometimes considered a justifiable economy, in cases of temporary occupancy, to paint or wallpaper over old wallpaper, but actually it is a very small and temporary economy when one considers the extra time and labor that must be expended the next time the room is redecorated. In addition, some communities prohibit by law the application of new paint or wallpaper over old, and many landlords prohibit it by special stipulation in the lease.

The advantages of wallpaper must be weighed against the advantages of paint in redecorating. The first advantage is the fact that a heavy, rough-textured wallpaper will hide cracks or uneven plaster better than paint. Moreover, the design of a wallpaper may add an important decorative note to a room which might otherwise be nondescript. In fact, wallpaper can establish the color scheme for the room.

There are some wallpapers and decorative borders on the market now with a backing of glue which only needs wetting for application. This type of paper is a great help to an amateur to whom the even spreading of paste may be a problem. However, the selection of patterns is so much wider in the regular wallpapers that most people prefer to use this type, even if they have to learn how to apply the paste.

When buying wallpaper, remember that the cost of the paper itself is a small fraction of the total cost of the job if it is being done professionally. The labor is the expensive factor. Consequently, it is wise to buy the best paper available so that it will last as long as possible and thus make redecorating a more infrequent expense.

In considering wallpaper, it should be remembered that wallpaper comes in both patterned and plain colors. Therefore, if plain walls are desired, it does not necessarily mean that paint must be used. Neither is it necessary to paper the whole room simply because some paper is used in it. One wall, the wall above a dado, or a ceiling may be papered, and the rest can be painted.

The advantages of paint in redecorating are many. For areas that take heavy wear, such as the walls of halls and stairways, for rooms where there is a great deal of steam or dampness, such as bathrooms or kitchens, or for rooms that must be redecorated frequently, paint is the best choice. It is obvious that paint can meet all these situations more effectively and more inexpensively than wallpaper.

There is an enamel on the market which has no sheen but which produces the same hard, durable surface as the shiny enamel. It is considerably more expensive than flat paint, but it is being used instead of flat paint for walls in institutions, such as hospitals, because it will stand so many more washings than flat paint and because it is almost odorless, even while being applied.

A dull-finish enamel is the most popular paint for woodwork in homes. Its hard finish will take many washings with strong washing solutions, in addition to the lighter, more gentle daily or weekly washings.

Another advantage of paint in redecorating is that it is an adaptable medium for harmonizing the colors in a room, since it can easily be mixed to match the color of the draperies or other furnishings. It is wise, however, to have it mixed professionally even if the applying of it is to be an amateur job. Most paint shops have a paint-mixing service for which they charge a few cents extra per gallon—a charge which is an actual economy because most amateurs waste considerable paint when they try to mix it themselves.

For an inexpensive, easy, amateur job, water-soluble paints are the best selection. The cheapest is the powder form of calcimine which is mixed with water. A slightly more expensive water-soluble paint is the type which comes in paste form and which is thinned with water to paint consistency. Both these paints spread easily and can be touched up invisibly within the first twenty-four hours. Both can be applied with a brush or with the paint rollers which are such a help to the amateur painter.

If, however, the painting is being done by professionals, it is advisable to use the best paint available. Remember that the largest cost of the job is in the labor, and a good paint will increase the life of the job considerably.

Redecorated backgrounds can add great charm to rooms.

It is possible to give a great deal of charm and personality to a room by redecorating it—whether wallpaper or paint is used. Therefore, it is important to analyze walls, woodwork, and ceilings very carefully before deciding how to treat them. By using a dado, by accenting a wall, parts of a wall, a ceiling, or woodwork, or by using some other unusual method of decorating, a whole room can be given new beauty. The following are a few of the possibilities.

Accentuated walls heighten the dramatic effect of a room. Dark walls are particularly effective to show off well-designed woodwork if the woodwork is painted in a light contrasting neutral. The ceiling can be painted to match either the dark walls or the light woodwork. It is best, however, to match woodwork and ceiling if the room needs light. (See drawing on page 351.)

A single wall can be accentuated by being painted with a contrasting color or papered with a striking wallpaper. The important point in creating such an accent is to select the right wall. It can be a long unbroken wall, on which some important piece of furniture is centered. It can be a window wall on which a bay window is centered or a pair of windows is evenly placed. It can also be an inside wall in which a doorway or an archway is centered. In any case, it must be a wall with some special interest, because throwing it into relief by the use of a contrasting value or hue of paint or a wallpaper which contrasts with the other three walls gives its proportions and architectural features great importance. The placement of furniture against accented walls must be carefully planned because the accented wall and the furniture against it will be the focal point of the room.

When paint is used to create an accented wall, the remaining three walls must be painted the same color as the woodwork, if the woodwork is painted. If the woodwork is natural, the three remaining walls and ceiling should be alike.

When wallpaper is used to create an accented wall, the remaining walls and the ceiling must be papered or painted in a plain color that matches or harmonizes with the background of the wallpaper. These plain surfaces will increase the decorative importance of the accented wall.

The upper part of all the walls of a room can be accentuated if a dado is used. A dado can be created by applying a wooden chair rail or by using a wallpaper border, both of which will divide the

Dark walls help to emphasize light woodwork and blond furniture. Only a very large room should have all four walls and ceiling dark. In most rooms one or two dark walls are sufficient to accent, and then they need to be offset by light woodwork and ceiling.

walls of the room horizontally. Once that is done, an important wallpaper or a striking color in paint can be used above the banding to make the room more dramatic. This is the only way in which a scenic paper should be used in a room. Dark colors might be oppressive if used over an entire wall, but they are comfortably enjoyable with a lighter color below the dado rail for relief. Strongly patterned papers are also enjoyable when set off by a plain area below the dado rail.

A small bathroom can be completely rejuvenated by the use of a plain dado with wallpaper on the wall above it and on the ceiling.

Accentuated pattern decoration, such as wallpaper borders or cut-out wallpaper motifs, if well designed, may be used effectively against a plain wall, as was mentioned briefly in Chapter 3. The borders can be used around windows, around doors, above a dado, on screens, and on ceilings. The cut-out motifs can be scattered over

In redecorating a room, motifs cut from wallpaper or chintz might be pasted on the ceiling or woodwork to give the room a new look.

walls, on the ceiling, below a dado, or in closets. (For illustrations, see above and page 57.)

A small amount of patterned wallpaper will give a home a pleasant accent, but too much patterned wallpaper will make the walls of a house too important and demanding. Adjoining rooms can be papered with the same paper if the paper is plain or has a textured effect. Adjoining rooms should not be papered in different patterns. If one room has a patterned wallpaper, plain paper or paint must be used in the adjoining rooms. Thus the rooms done in plain paper or paint will set off and heighten the effect of the one that is done in patterned wallpaper.

An *accentuated ceiling* is an effective variation of the usual procedure in handling backgrounds. No ceiling, however, should be given decorative importance unless it is unbroken by gables or jogs or unless the room is 8 feet high or more.

The use of patterned wallpaper on the ceiling is one way to give a ceiling decorative importance. However, the paper selected should be in a geometric or stylized design that is equally attractive from all points of view. A paper with a design that must be seen from one position only should never be used. For added dramatic effect, the ceiling wallpaper can be used in the closets of the room, on a screen, on wastebaskets, or on lamp shades, to repeat the color and pattern and to contrast with the plain walls of the room.

The use of paint that contrasts strongly in value or hue with the walls is another way of creating a decoratively important ceiling. It can be painted to match the color of the rug or to match the color of the draperies, if they are different from the walls.

Unusual decorating treatments require unusual care.

The moment a decorating plan departs from the trite safety of ivory walls or softly blended wallpaper patterns that "harmonize with everything" it is necessary to be more careful in avoiding pitfalls. Knowing about these pitfalls will make it possible to have unusual decorative effects without falling prey to the overdone, the garish, or the cocktail-lounge type of decorating which ruins the beauty in some rooms.

An *unusual color* may be used successfully, provided the following fact is recognized: Color intensifies and darkens when used in large areas. Many people, who—after having used cream or ivory for many years—suddenly decide to have walls painted with a color, make the mistake of selecting a color that is too strong. They do not realize that it is absolutely necessary to select a color that looks considerably grayer and duller on a small sample than the color they really desire, because the total effect of the color will be stronger and darker on the walls of the room. If two coats of paint are used, the color selected should be used as an undercoat, so that the total effect can be judged in time to modify the paint of the final coat before it is applied. (For more information about the effect of color over large areas, see pages 20 and 37 in Chapter 2.)

An unusual paper may be used successfully if it is remembered that the total effect of pattern, like color, intensifies with area, and that its effect cannot be properly determined from the sample in the wallpaper book. If the paper is in stock in the store, several strips of it should be hung side by side before a final decision is made. If the paper must be specially ordered, it should be checked in this same way when it arrives and before it is trimmed. Then, if the pattern is too strong, the paper can be returned, but no firm will take back paper after it has been trimmed.

In ordering wallpaper it should be kept in mind that wallpaper sometimes is made in narrower or wider rolls than the regular size. In some cases, the length is adjusted so that the total area of the roll of paper is the same as that of paper in the normal width. Some papers come in what is known as "double rolls" or "triple rolls," which contain twice or three times the length of paper in a regular single roll. If the wallpaper chosen happens to come in these larger rolls, the areas to be covered can be estimated in the ordinary way— that is, in terms of single-roll lengths—and the number of lengths required can then be divided by either two or three, as the case may be, to find out how many double or triple rolls to order.

Review Chapters 2, 3, and 4 for more information about pattern and its effect on the size of a room.

An unusual room can be most successfully decorated if the factors that make it unusual are analyzed carefully and taken into consideration in the planning.

For instance, in decorating a gabled room, people are apt to ignore its gables and treat it like an ordinary rectangular room. Consequently, they find it very difficult to know where to stop the wall color or wallpaper and where to begin the ceiling treatment. This whole problem would not arise if it was recognized that walls and ceiling blend into each other in such a room and as a result must be treated with the same color of paint or the same wallpaper. If paper is used, it should be one that has a small, allover pattern with no line of growth. If the color or pattern of the paper is rather strong and it seems as though such a treatment will give the room too much pattern, it might be well to use a dado. The lower part of the wall should be painted the background color that appears in the paper.

When a room with an alcove or bay is being decorated, it must be decided whether the room would look better if the alcove or bay is made a part of the room by means of similar decorating, thereby increasing the size of the room, or whether it is to be decorated as an accent, thus appearing to be separated from the room. If the room is small, it would be wiser to unify the two by decorating them in exactly the same way. If the room is large enough, the bay or alcove can be decorated with a paint or wallpaper in an entirely different color from that of the room to create an attractive decorative accent.

Floor coverings need periodic attention.

Floors and floor coverings should be carefully and periodically cleaned, repaired, and renewed. The wrong care or lack of care can ruin the appearance and shorten the life of a floor surface or floor covering; a neglected floor can give a whole room a run-down appearance that even the finest draperies and furniture cannot counteract.

Wooden floors need constant care and protection to show off their true beauty. One of the best protections is a coating of wax which can be washed off and renewed periodically. But even this care does not always prevent the appearance of bare spots where hard wear has worn off surface finish. These spots can be restained if care is used in removing all surface coating and in blending the edges of the stain. After the stain has dried thoroughly, shellac should be brushed on lightly. Then, when the spot is again dry, the entire surface should be varnished or shellacked. If the floor is in bad condition, the entire floor should be stripped and refinished. If the floor has been neglected, it may be necessary to sand it down to the raw wood before any refinishing is done.

Linoleum, rubber tile, and asphalt tile all will take harder wear and will demand less care than wooden floors. Washing and rewaxing occasionally is the only regular care which is necessary. There are several different types of plastic coatings on the market that are not slippery. Whether they will eventually prove injurious to the floor covering is still unknown.

Upkeep of these floor coverings is mainly a matter of watching for signs of cracking. The moment a crack appears, linoleum should be recemented so that water will not seep underneath and rot the back—thus increasing the damage. In the case of rubber or asphalt tile, cracked or worn tiles can be replaced without touching the rest of the floor surface.

Carpeting and rugs must be cleaned regularly. How thoroughly this must be done depends on the amount of dirt tracked onto them. Some women use a sweeper for daily cleaning and a vacuum once a week. Occasionally it is necessary to supplement this regular cleaning with a more thorough process, such as washing or dry-cleaning.

It is very true that any rug becomes dirty faster after it has once been cleaned. The reason for this is that each washing or dry-cleaning removes some of the natural oils from the yarn and makes the rug more susceptible to dirt. However, it is obviously impossible to ignore the fact that rugs need cleaning after a certain amount of wear. The question, therefore, is not whether to clean them but how to clean them.

Any straight-pile rug can be washed on the floor. This type of thorough cleaning will put new beauty and resilience into the rug fibers. The rug will feel deeper underfoot, and it will look like new. It is occasionally necessary to resize a rug after washing. Stiffening is necessary to keep the rug from wrinkling and to give it more body.

If the rug has a twist weave, washing or shampooing is not always advisable. The water may uncurl the yarn, just as shampooing removes a wave which has been set in straight hair. There are a few types of twist rugs which are advertised as washable. This point should be checked with the dealer before a purchase is made. The difference in cost of dry-cleaning and shampooing is considerable.

Another method of prolonging the life of rugs is to turn them periodically so as to equalize the wear. This method, of course, can only be used with rectangular shaped rugs. Stair carpeting should be shifted every year or two. Usually it is laid with the ends turned under about 9 inches, which is generally sufficient to allow the part of the rug that was first used on the riser, and therefore not stepped on, to be moved up onto the tread. The part of the carpeting that has been walked on will have a respite, and the wear will be evened. If the steps are unusually wide, the turn-up will have to be correspondingly greater.

If the same kind of rug or carpeting has been bought for several rooms and has become worn in some places in each room, the best parts of two rugs or carpets may be combined to make one good one, provided they are in either a plain color or have an allover pattern which can be evenly matched at the new seams. This is especially easy if 27-inch carpeting has been bought originally.

Household fabrics should be given the same care as clothes.

The regular and periodic care given fabrics for a house should be much the same as that given to clothes. As with clothes, airing, brushing, pressing, washing, or cleaning these fabrics will renew their appearance and lengthen their period of usefulness.

Curtains can be freshened or cleaned in several ways. Sometimes a light allover brushing and the pressing of hems will restore them temporarily if they are not soiled enough to require a more thorough cleaning. Heavy draperies, whether lined or unlined, may be cleaned with a vacuum-cleaner attachment without removing them from the rods. Draperies and curtains that are made of washable fabrics may be washed at home in the automatic washer. If the drapery panels are wide, a padded table top can be used to advantage as an ironing board. If draperies or curtains must be dry-cleaned, they should be sent to the cleaners. Trying to clean large draperies or curtains at home with a cleaning fluid is both dangerous and unsatisfactory.

Nylon net curtains wash easily and need not be ironed if they are hung up to dry with care. Other nylon fabrics, such as gauze, or the heavier nylon fabrics usually look better if hems and headings at least are pressed carefully with a cool iron.

Net curtains, such as marquisette or celanese, are like a sheer

Upholstered pieces of furniture should be gone over with the vacuum attachment or brushed with a soft brush each time the frame is dusted.

white blouse—they must be immaculately clean at all times. They should be washed regularly, and if they have no ruffles, they can be put through an ironer or stretched on a stretcher.

Slipcovers may be cleaned by washing or dry-cleaning. The process which is to be used should be decided at the time of the selection of material, because slipcovers are far too expensive for experimenting. If they are to be washed, the material used should be guaranteed to be preshrunk and washable. If the slipcover is dark and so used that cleaning need not be frequent, it may be an economy to plan on dry-cleaning and to use a less expensive material that does not have these guarantees. For a more complete discussion of washable slipcovers that need not be ironed, see Chapter 16.

Upholstered furniture should be brushed thoroughly with a soft-bristled brush or gone over with the vacuum-cleaner attachment each time the frame is dusted. Occasionally it should be thoroughly cleaned with a soap solution. A brush of medium stiffness should be used for applying the soapsuds. Only a small area should be worked on at one time, and the applications should overlap with one another to avoid any water marks. An effort should be made to finish one section at a time, such as an arm, the back, or a side. The suds should be brushed on and wiped off immediately with a soft

EWING. GALLOWAY

Stains or spots on furniture should be removed as soon as possible after they are discovered. After they have set for several hours or a day they are harder to take out.

cloth which has been dipped in clear, warm water and wrung out. The whole piece should be dried as rapidly as possible by placing it near a heat outlet or an electric fan or by putting it in the sun or wind. The material should not be roughened by being brushed too vigorously. In fact, any material with long yarn which lies loosely on the surface or delicate materials, such as satins, should not be brushed at all. Instead, a cloth should be used to apply the soap and water.

Upholstery usually shows wear first on the arms. It is sometimes possible to save a complete re-upholstery job by patching with material from some concealed spot. One side of a reversible cushion or the back of a sofa that stands against a wall may furnish plenty of material for repair or for protectors to cover the worn spots.

Chairs that have slip seats can be re-upholstered in a very short time. The chair should be turned upside down on a table, and the four corner screws that hold the seat in place should be unscrewed. The seat will then drop out, so the old cover can be taken off and the new cover tacked firmly over the square frame. The frame should then be placed upside down on the table, the chair frame put over it in position, and the four screws replaced.

Spot removal is an important part of upkeep in a home, because accidents will happen! Carpets, upholstery, bedspreads, and slip-covers all are bound to be spotted at one time or another.

It is helpful to know the cause of the spot and as much as possible about the fabric to be cleaned—whether its colors are fast, whether it has been preshrunk, and whether it contains filling. This sort of information should be written down at the time of purchase so it will be on hand when the emergency arises.

Speed of removal is important, because spots that have been allowed to set are difficult to remove. Of course if the accident occurs when guests are present—as it often does—it is obviously impossible to do anything about the removal until the guests leave.

Information appears frequently about new methods of spot removal, so it might be wise to keep an up-to-the minute file of clippings for reference.

Window upkeep includes care of shades and blinds.

Some women feel that window care includes only the washing of the window and the cleaning or washing of the curtains. A good upkeep program, however, should also include a careful check of the shades or blinds and any necessary cleaning or refurbishing of them. Worn or sagging shades or blinds give the whole house a neglected appearance on both the outside and the inside.

Cleaning shades and blinds must be done carefully if the result is to be good. If the shades are made of washable cloth and are fairly new, they can be laid flat on a table and washed. Unfortunately, window-shade cloth, like washable wallpaper, loses much of its washability with age and exposure to sun. So, if the shade is old, it may be better to use wallpaper cleaner, even if the shade is supposed to be washable. Fingerprints on the slat hem of a shade can be removed with art gum between general cleanings.

Venetian blinds, like a series of narrow shelves, must be dusted regularly. Metal or well-finished wooden blinds can be wiped off

Keeping windows clean is important, but window upkeep also includes a check of shades or blinds, curtains or draperies.

(COURTESY DU PONT COMPANY)

occasionally with a damp cloth, but all blinds need a thorough cleaning occasionally. Some blinds have slats that can be removed and scrubbed separately, which makes the job of thorough cleaning much easier. Some blinds have plastic-coated tapes that can be wiped clean.

Split bamboo blinds can be brushed and dusted frequently, but they should be scrubbed with soap and water for a thorough job of cleaning.

Repairing shades and blinds can be done in several ways. New material for window shades can be put on old rollers at a minimum of expense. The new shades may not exactly match the other old shades in the house that do not need replacing, but if the color is approximately the same, they will do. However, all the shades in a room or in a group of windows must be identical.

If a change of color scheme in a particular room necessitates a shade color that is completely different from those used in the rest of the house, shade cloth of two colors—one on the inside and the other on the outside of the shade—should be used. Such shade cloth

The appearance of the outside of a home, as well as the inside, is greatly affected by the condition of the windows and the window hangings.

makes it possible to have the outside color the same for all shades in the house, while the inside colors are different to harmonize with the color schemes used in the various rooms of the house.

Blinds should be checked for broken tapes, cords, and slats. Replacing these is imperative, even if it is expensive.

CHECKING YOUR KNOWLEDGE . . .

1. What is the modern method of house cleaning which most women use nowadays?
2. What methods can be used for thorough cleaning of (*a*) a painted wall and (*b*) a papered wall?
3. What are the advantages of redecorating a room with (*a*) wallpaper and (*b*) paint?
4. How can paint or wallpaper be used (*a*) to accent a wall, (*b*) to unify a gabled room, and (*c*) to accent a ceiling that is rectangular?
5. What is the effect of strong colors and strong patterns when used over large areas? How can this effect be guarded against?
6. Describe a room of unusual shape and tell how you would treat it in redecorating.
7. Describe the care necessary for different types of floor coverings and wooden floors.
8. Describe the care necessary for curtains, slipcovers, and upholstered furniture.

USING YOUR KNOWLEDGE . . .

1. Plan a redecorating scheme for two rooms in your own home. Then give a reason for each of your decisions.
2. List ways of cleaning, protecting, or repairing the furnishings in your own home that might help to lengthen their time of usefulness.
3. Have the class make plans to renew one of the rooms in a model house or in the school. Divide the responsibilities of cleaning, redecorating, and repairing among class members. Discuss plans and procedures carefully, estimate costs, and submit your plans to the principal for approval before proceeding with the actual work.

CHAPTER 18: Management of Money

It is not possible to say that a certain amount, or even a certain proportion, of income should be spent for the different types of living expenses. One girl may spend a large proportion of her allowance for movies, sundaes, and candy. Another may spend more on books and magazines. Still another may not spend much for any of these things but will use most of her allowance or earnings for clothes. Some families believe that a car is a necessity but that owning their own home is an extravagance. Others, with the same income, feel that they do not need a car but that owning their own home is an absolute essential.

To a certain extent this sort of variation will always exist because of people's individual differences. However, there is one basic principle of money management that should guide everyone's spending: The money to be spent for basic living needs and for luxuries must be so planned as to fit within the income available if there is to be happiness in the present and security about the future. The obvious way to manage this is to have a budget.

Suppose you decide that you want to buy some new things for your bedroom or redecorate it next year. Your first reaction may be that you can't afford it until you have a full-time job. Actually, if you take an inventory of the money you spent last year and what you have for it, you may find that you frittered away much more money than you realize. In fact, you are likely to discover that the amount was not much less than the amount you need to change your room into the kind of room of which you have always dreamed. Just how much do you really want a lovely room? Perhaps if you are willing

COURTESY ALEXANDER SMITH & SONS CARPET COMPANY

Families that enjoy being together in the home or entertaining friends there will want to spend more money for home furnishings than they do for interests outside of the home.

to forego a few of your present expenditures, you could have it. Think it over carefully. This chapter may help you to figure out a way.

First, analyze how you spent your money last year.

Many girls have the idea that it is not necessary to budget their money until after they are married. Some feel that budgeting does not apply to them now because their incomes as school girls are so small. Very few girls, however, are really satisfied with what they get for the amount of money they have to spend.

Handling money in a way that will make you happy does not happen without planning. It is a habit that you build into your life exactly as you form habits of brushing your teeth or standing properly. The time to begin establishing the habit of managing, or budgeting, your money is the present. Actually, the smaller the

Reviewing last year's income—however small—may bring some doubts to your mind as to what you really got out of your money.

(CHARLES PHELPS CUSHING)

income, the more carefully it must be spent if it is to produce happiness.

By reviewing last year's income you can discover whether you are getting the best results from your spending. Just what money did you receive last year? Did you get an allowance, gifts of money, or a salary for part-time or short-time jobs? Put them all down as completely as you can remember and find the total. The amount may surprise you.

Once you have totaled your income and subtracted any amount or money you may have saved, you can see the total amount you spent during the year.

By reviewing last year's expenditures you can determine some of your probable expenses for the coming year. Of course you cannot possibly remember everything you bought and the cost of it, but you can make a fairly accurate list. Memory, estimates, and such records as a diary, a school calendar, or even your school yearbook will help a great deal.

You will find it easier, in making your estimate, to divide a sheet of paper horizontally, according to months, and vertically, according to general expense items. The following are expense items every girl in school is likely to have:

School supplies	Movies and other entertainment
Transportation	
Lunches	Gifts
Clothes and accessories	Snacks and drinks
Cosmetics	Hobbies
Books, papers, and magazines	Club fees

By evaluating last year's expenditures you may find ways of economizing. If you had realized at the beginning of the year that you would have as much money to deal with as you did, would you have spent it as you did? In other words, did you get the things you wanted last year? Did you buy things that were basically important to you? Or did you spend your money in driblets for unimportant things simply because your money came to you in such small sums?

Next, plan how you want to spend your money next year.

No two years of life will ever be exactly the same, even during your school years. Each will bring its new interests, its new needs, and its new responsibilities. For instance, this coming year, as a result of studying home furnishings, you may want to refurnish your room.

A well-planned personalized budget should take into account this sort of change in the demands on your income. In fact, one of the main reasons for budgeting is to help you meet just this sort of big, new expense.

Estimating next year's income is the place to begin in planning next year's budget. If you expect to be in school, estimate your income on the basis of your allowance and the amount you think you can earn on part-time jobs during the winter and summer. Base that estimate on last year's income, but add to it if you can see ways in which you can increase it. It may be possible that you can increase your allowance by taking over some job that is now done by someone outside the family and for which family money is spent. It may be possible that you can increase the money you earn outside by getting a regular part-time job helping in a shop, an office, or a

Part-time work in the home furnishings department of a store or taking care of children are both good ways to earn extra money and at the same time prepare yourself to be a good mother and an efficient homemaker.

home. Baby-sitting is an ideal part-time job for a high school girl. A job in the yard-goods, drapery, home furnishings, or housewares department of a store will be tremendously valuable not only in wages but in the knowledge gained. Jobs in summer camps are a wonderful way to get a vacation free and earn a little income in addition. Week-end jobs and summer work in stores sometimes lead directly into full-time employment when you finish school. In fact, part-time work is a splendid opportunity for you to try out many different types of work, and in so doing to know more accurately the type of work you wish to do after you finish your schooling.

But even without this added advantage, the immediate advantage of earning your own money is obvious. Life is far more satisfying for the girl who begins planning and managing her own money while she is in high school. She can decide what she wants to buy or what she wants to spend and work toward it, whereas the girl who lives on an allowance only—spending all of it each week, without one thought toward the future—can simply hope that a kind father will have saved enough money to give her what she wants above her allowance. She can never plan for it. Even if she gets it, it is a gift and in no way a personal achievement.

If you are graduating from high school and will be employed full time, find out what is the usual salary in the field in which you intend to work. You can get this information through your guidance counselor, through friends who are working, or from an employment agency.

Estimating next year's expenditures is the next step in making out a budget for the coming year. The thing that is so easy to forget is that you can only spend your money once. Yet it is perfectly obvious, when you stop to think, that unless your income is increased, your expenses will have to be cut somewhere to allow for large purchases. It is comforting to remember that saving for a big project need not be done in one lump. If you organize a play-reading group to take the place of some of your movies, you might be able to cut down the amount you spend on movies by a couple of dollars a month without noticing the loss. In that way you will have saved $20 to $25 from that source alone in one year. Keep this sort of small

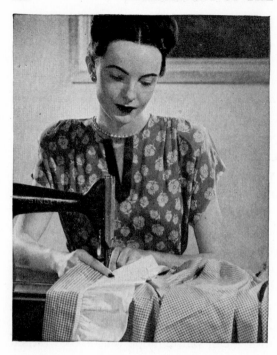

If you can make your own curtains, slipcovers, spreads, and pillows, you will have more money to spend on furniture and accessories for your room.

(COURTESY SINGER SEWING CENTERS)

economy in mind as you make a list of your probable expenses. The way to begin is, again, to rule off a sheet of paper, in the same way you did in reviewing last year's expenses. List the months horizontally and the expenses vertically. Analyze last year's expenses and decide which of those must be continued, which can be reduced, and which, if any, can be dropped. Then consider what new things you want to add for the coming year. If you are interested in redecorating your room or buying new things for it, the following pages will give you some concrete suggestions about figuring the cost and method of budgeting for furnishing your own room or an apartment.

List the minimum furnishings needed for your bedroom.

In planning to furnish your room, list the minimum furnishings that you must have or the things that you wish to replace. Until that is done, you cannot figure costs. In making your list, do not fall into the trap of buying what others are buying. Make sure your list is based on your own specific needs and not on current style or custom. For specific help in making this list, turn back to the discussion on pages 119–122 in Chapter 7 and list the furnishings you should have.

Next, decide which of these you can supply by remodeling things you already have. Only after you have done this should you list the things you must buy. Section Three will help you to decide what your needs are for curtains, bedspread, slipcovers, and floor coverings.

When this list is complete, you are ready to start shopping for information about costs of furnishings.

Know what the minimum furnishings are for an apartment.

The experience you gain in budgeting to refurnish your bedroom will be of value to you later when you furnish an apartment. The same principles of taking an inventory, planning, and budgeting your money apply to the furnishing of a few rooms as well as to one. Since you may be furnishing an apartment for yourself, with another girl, or with a husband within the next two or three years, a brief consideration of the essential items needed to furnish it may be of help to you.

There are so many things to buy for an apartment that it is especially important to cut the list down to the minimum essentials for the first year. It is far easier to close your eyes to certain furnishing lacks than it is to close your eyes to unpaid bills.

What actually constitutes essentials is much the same for most people, because everyone must sleep, eat, store clothes, and have a place to sit down, work, and read. Everyone also needs a certain provision for privacy and quiet. To fulfill these needs, the following items are necessary.

For sleeping, good springs and a good mattress are absolute essentials. Whether you buy these for a double bed, a three-quarter bed, or twin beds is a personal matter. Any of them can be mounted on legs and used without a bedstead for the first year to save money. Good pillows, ample bed linen, and good bedding are also necessities for comfort and good sleep.

For eating, a range and a refrigerator—if they are not furnished —and a table and chairs are the necessities. The table can be a game table which matches the living-room furniture so it can be used there

The minimum essentials for an apartment include a table for eating, good light for reading, a place to sleep, and chairs for sitting. Storage space for dishes, linens, clothing, books, etc., are also essential according to the possessions and habits of the occupants.

also, or it can be a drop-leaf extension table that is used in the living room or hall when not in service for meals. Even a pair of semi-circular console tables can be put together to form a table for the first few months.

For storing clothes, a chest with as many separate drawers as possible is the first requirement. Dressers, which have fewer drawers than a chest, and dressing tables, which have almost no storage space, cost a great deal and take up about the same amount of room. Therefore, they should not be included on the essential list for the first year's purchases.

For sitting, a studio couch offers the maximum accommodation for the minimum cost. It also furnishes extra sleeping space for an occasional guest. Upholstered host and hostess chairs, which are less expensive than living-room upholstered chairs, can be used with it to make a conversation group that has beauty and distinction. If beautifully designed, comfortable wooden-backed dining-room chairs have been purchased, two of them can be used in the living room. The carved wooden back would be a pleasing contrast to the upholstery of the studio couch or sofa.

For working and reading, it is necessary to have at least two good lamps. If table lamps are bought, they will require tables that are chair-arm height. They should be at least 28 inches tall to give good general light for the rest of the room. If floor lamps are bought, they should be low ones to ensure comfortable use with a studio couch or a low lounge chair.

For privacy, window curtains must be bought. In a small apartment all the curtains may be alike, so there will be a quantity of the same curtain material that can be used later on to curtain a bigger room with more windows. In all probability, if the curtains are well selected, they will last through at least one moving, and a motley assortment of pairs of curtains are likely to be found useless in a new place with different window arrangements.

For quiet, rugs or carpets are of primary importance. Some couples have good luck in buying rugs or carpets secondhand. Others get around the high cost of wool rugs and carpets by using grass matting. Still others buy felt floor coverings (see page 253)

It takes time, planning, and energy to complete the finishing touches and add the necessary accessories for a charming and comfortable room or apartment.

which come in a wide range of colors and which can be used as pads under better rugs later on.

Supplementary furniture can be bought in the following years for added comfort and beauty. For example, if the bed for the first year has consisted of a mattress mounted on legs, the bedstead or headboard can be added the second year. If folding chairs were used in the dinette, permanent ones can be bought the second year. A good comfortable lounge chair can replace one of the host and hostess chairs. A coffee table, a third lamp for the bedroom, and a second chest—all can come into the second year's budget, if plans are made for it in a wise program of allotting money.

Shop before you buy furnishings.

Your next job is to take the list of minimum furnishings for your room or an apartment and start shopping—not to buy, but to get information. Do not depend on your memory. Get a notebook and keep careful and accurate notations of prices and stores so that you can be sure you are dealing with facts.

Check the price range of each item first. You will find that there is a wide difference in cost on each item and that it will be wise to make a notation as to quality after each price. Then, when you have all the information, you can review it completely.

Check the decorative range at the same time you check the price and quality. You may discover that the use of a certain color as a dominant will save considerable money on the carpets and draperies. Put this information down so it will be ready for you when you do your final deciding.

Formulate a three-column chart covering all the essential items you will need. In the first column list the minimum price at which each item can be bought. In the second column list the middle price, and in the third column list the top price.

There will be some items, such as mattresses, which you will wish to be of very good quality, and there will be others that you will know you can save money on. Review Chapter 6 on furniture buying to refresh your memory on these points.

One helpful way to estimate proportionate costs of furniture was worked out very carefully by Leon Pescheret for the President's

Chart 16: Furnishing Budget on the Unit System *

Three-room apartment	Relative unit value	Number of units in apartment
Living room and dining room:		
Bookcase (unfinished)	1½	1½
Curtains (2 windows)	½ (each)	1
Easy chair (2)	1 (each)	2
Large table	2	2
Rug	1	1
Side chairs (3)	½ (each)	1½
Small table (unfinished) . . .	¼	¼
Sofa	3	3
Total units		12¼
Bedroom:		
Chest (unfinished)	1½	1½
Curtains (2 windows)	½ (each)	1
Double bed	1	1
Mattress, spring, pillows . . .	1½	1½
Mirror	¾	¾
Rugs	¾	¾
Side chair (unfinished) . . .	¼	¼
Total units		6¾
Kitchen:		
Glass and china	1	1
Kitchen equipment	1	1
Linen (complete apartment) . .	1	1
Total units		3
Accessories:		
Blankets	1	1
Lamps (2)	¼ (each)	½
Pillows (2)	¼ (each)	½
Vases and pictures	1	1
		3

* Leon Pescheret's Estimate of Proportions and Costs of Furniture.

Conference on Home Building and Home Ownership in 1932. (See Chart 16.) Because this table was prepared in terms of relative unit value, it is just as useful today as it was the day it was created. Also, it is just as useful for figuring prices at low costs as for high. For instance, suppose the value of a unit, established by dividing the entire furnishing budget by the number of units needed, is $20. According to the chart, a side chair or dining chair would cost one half a unit, or $10, and a sofa would cost three units, or $60. If, on the other hand, the amount per unit is $40, the same proportion would work. A side chair would cost $20, and the sofa $120.

Another good thing about the chart is that the whole chart or any part of it can be used equally well. For instance, if just a few of the items listed under living room, bedroom, or kitchen are needed, the relative unit value as listed on the chart would still keep the buying in the proper scale. The amount of money spent on side chairs would still be in proper proportion to the cost of the sofa.

Fit total cost of furnishings into your income.

Only after all of the information about costs is at hand and all the decisions about relative values are made is it time to begin to add the total cost of furnishing a room or an apartment. It is at this point that savings are so important. The use of these savings for purchases that may be used for many years is absolutely justifiable and proper. Strenuous economy can sometimes make it possible to buy the minimum essentials for a bedroom out of one year's income, but it is quite probable that savings or a loan would be necessary to help in the buying of minimum essentials for a small apartment.

Total your costs so that you know exactly what expense you must meet to have the things you have tentatively selected. If the

---

Method of using Chart 16:
   A. Deduct all units already obtained or not desired from number of units to be bought.
   B. List remaining total number of units to be bought . . _____
   C. List total budget for furnishings . . . . $_____
   D. Divide C by B for budget allowance for each unit . . $_____

cost is too high, decide how much you must cut and where econo-
mies are possible. Take into consideration such factors as the Janu-
ary white sales, the August furniture sales, and the end-of-the-year
clearances. Plan to do as much painting, sewing, and refinishing as
possible yourself.

Divide your total by 52, the number of weeks in a year. Figure
exactly how much you must save each week. In that way you will
know whether it is possible for you to swing the project in one year,
or whether you must allow two years' savings for the expenditures.
In other words, compare the total cost with your total income so
that you will know what is possible. Never make a single purchase
before you have done this preliminary planning.

Be careful where, when, and how you buy.

Shrewd buying is an art that is learned rather than inspired.
It comes with study and comparison and is an important part of the
wise use of money. No one ever has so much money that buying can
be done without concern for due return for every dollar spent. In
fact, people with a great deal of money are frequently more careful
in spending it than those who have far less.

Where to buy is an important consideration in furniture buying.
Many people have a relative or friend through whom they can get
a card to a wholesaler. This is really not as fortunate as most people
think. In the first place, retail customers generally enter a wholesale
house feeling apologetic. The salesman who is unlucky enough to
have to serve them would rather wait on a furniture buyer with an
"open to buy" of thousands of dollars than help retail customers
who have only a few hundred dollars to spend. Consequently, the
salesman is impatient and the customers continue to feel apologetic.
The salesman is not interested in pleasing them. In fact, he hopes
that they will not be pleased and will never come back. And they,
realizing this, make decisions quickly without taking time to weigh
and consider. Thus, any saving on individual pieces of furniture is
outweighed by the mistakes made in a quick selection.

The place for retail customers to buy is in a retail store. There
the salesmen want to please them. The management wants their
continuing patronage, and so he will help them if they make an

error in judgment. Retail customers in a retail store feel free to browse around for weeks, if they wish to, before doing any buying. (For more detailed information on furniture selection, see Chapter 6.)

When to buy is a vital question. If you want to buy furniture on sale, buy merchandise that has been in the store for some time and then has been reduced. In that kind of sale the merchandise is standard, and the store itself is taking a cut on the profit.

By contrast, merchandise that is announced as "Special Purchase Sale Merchandise" may have been bought to sell at the lower figure. The manufacturer has turned out a product that he and, in turn, the retailer can sell for less than the usual price and still make a profit. Basic quality, as a rule, is not present in this type of merchandise.

How to buy is a problem which can be easily solved in one word, and that is *slowly*. Furniture bought slowly will give never-ending pleasure. Hastily bought, casually selected furniture has a way of haunting its possessors the rest of their lives. Very few people can afford to toss out pieces of furniture that they do not like, because furniture is too costly. And, by some twist of fate, such furniture never seems to break or wear out. It seems to last on and on, having to be dusted, sat on, or looked at forever.

CHECKING YOUR KNOWLEDGE . . .

1. What are the first two steps in planning to manage money?
2. What forward-looking plans must be made in managing money?
3. What sources of income are possible during school days?
4. What are the steps in buying home furnishings?
5. List the essentials in furnishing a first apartment.
6. Name three basic principles of good buying.

USING YOUR KNOWLEDGE . . .

1. Review your own expenses for the past twelve months and average them to see just what your weekly expenses were.
2. Review your income for the past twelve months, keeping careful track of money earned as against money supplied by an allowance or gifts.

3. Work out a tentative estimate of your expenses for the coming twelve months, taking full account of changes in your interests and needs.

4. Get detailed information about the costs to refurnish or improve your own room. Decide how much you could afford to do this coming year by readjusting your budget.

5. Make a survey of the cost of furnishing a bedroom in mahogany and in maple, in Modern and in traditional.

6. Using Leon Pescheret's scale (Chart 16), work out a unit analysis of the pieces of furniture you now have in your room, or the furniture you would like to have if you were refurnishing your bedroom. Divide them into minimum essentials for the first year's buying and the pieces to be added in the second year's buying.

7. For future reference, plan the apartment you would like to have after you marry. Figure the proportionate units according to the Pescheret chart.

SECTION SIX: *Plans for the Home*

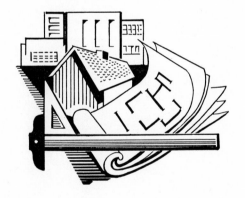

CHAPTER 19: Selecting a Place to Live

Many a bride and groom, their heads in a blissful whirl, have decided on an apartment or a house because of some relatively unimportant detail, such as the tile in the bathroom, the wrought-iron grille over the front door, or the wallpaper in the dining room.

Actually, none of these details are important enough to be considered when a home is being selected, nor do they have any bearing on living comfort. They may be pleasant dividends, but they should not be the deciding factors. Colored tile and wrought-iron grilles are small comfort if the apartment is cold in winter and hot in summer or if it has temperamental plumbing.

The decision of where to live should be made on the basis of practical living needs and desires. Shall we rent or buy? Do we want to live in the country or the city? How important is the neighborhood to our living? Do we want to live in an apartment or a house? Is the place provided with the comforts of living? Will it be large enough for us? Will it serve our pattern of living and our individual interests?

A home selected on the basis of these points will give continuing happiness, and so this chapter is devoted to a discussion of these basic factors.

Whether to rent or to buy should be decided first.

The major question to be decided by everyone who is establishing a home is whether to rent or to buy. The answer to this question is not merely a matter of money, because since World War II it has been fairly easy to arrange for the financing of a home. There are many more important questions involved, so perhaps the only way to consider the matter properly is to list the pros and cons of each. The pros and cons of buying are listed in Chapter 20, and those of renting are listed below. Only after weighing the values of both can people decide which is the better arrangement for them.

The advantages of renting may vary for different couples or families at different periods in their lives. But there are two definite advantages in renting over buying which generally hold true.

1) The freedom to move when it is necessary or desirable is probably the greatest advantage in renting. Some people are in a line of work that prevents them from settling down permanently in any one place. Many young men, for instance, are shifted from one part of the country to another in the early years of their careers in order to learn all the branches of the business. The length of their stay in any one place is unpredictable, and the flexibility of renting a home, which permits them to move at the end of a short period, suits this type of life much better than buying a home.

2) The possibility of economy is a second advantage of renting. Those who rent can plan their expenses more closely than can those who own their own homes. Owners are faced with the necessity of being ready to finance unexpected repairs, increased taxes, or special assessments on their property. More than that, the day-by-day living cost is actually less for renters, because they are not building an investment as are people who are purchasing a home.

The disadvantages of renting may depend upon a person's temperament and his desire for stability. Most people feel a joy in the possession of a home of their own, no matter how much more work or money may be entailed in the upkeep of it. Even aside from this, however, there are disadvantages to renting which many people do not realize until after they have experienced them.

1) Insecurity is the main disadvantage of renting. There is always the possibility of being forced to move or of finding that it is advisable to make a change in residence. Consequently, there is less feeling of permanency in the making of friends or in participating in community activities.

The freedom to move when it is necessary or desirable is the greatest advantage in renting over owning a home.

2) Impersonality of background in the apartment or house is a smaller but sometimes irritating disadvantage of renting. The colors used for the walls, the kinds of shelves and closets, the types of lighting fixtures may all have been selected according to the taste of the landlord and his ideas of what some future tenant might like. The individuality which most people wish to have in their homes is thus harder to achieve in a rented home.

3) The terms of a lease may be a definite disadvantage. They should be studied carefully before the lease is signed. Whether or not the rent covers heating and utilities, for example, is a matter that should be checked. Some apartment rentals include these items. Who is responsible for redecoration and repairs and whether care of lawn and window cleaning are included in the rent should also be understood before the lease is signed. As a rule, none of these items is included in the rental of an apartment or of a multiple-family dwelling. The tenant's right of occupancy in case of sale of the property is another point to be watched in a lease. Some land-

lords prohibit subleasing, and some do not allow a tenant to break a lease in case of a change in business. Leases should be read carefully and understood thoroughly before they are signed.

The kind of community should be considered.

After the question of buying or renting is settled, location should be carefully investigated. The question of location used to be determined by the geographical location of the man's place of work. Nowadays, since good transportation for commuting is generally available and many people drive to and from their work, the question of location can be determined entirely on the basis of personal preference.

Rural or suburban living is the natural choice for people who like the restfulness of the suburbs or country, for people who enjoy long walks and picnics, and for those who want to garden or are interested in the study of birds, flowers, stars, and scenic beauties. For the person who likes pets and who enjoys riding, hunting, or outdoor sports, a home away from the city pavements may be worth any inconveniences that are likely to be a part of suburban or rural living.

City living is the natural choice for people who like activity, who enjoy shopping and the theater, who are stimulated by crowds, and who want excitement and close neighbors. The people who want the bus to stop at the corner and who enjoy frequent callers probably should live in the city, even if their work forces them to commute to the country daily.

The cost of each type of living is about the same. What might be saved in rent by living in the country is generally spent for extra transportation to and from town. What might be saved in commercial entertainment is likely to be spent on equipment for sports or gardens.

The important thing to remember is that both types of living are possible for everyone, regardless of income. The neighborhood or the location of the man's job need no longer be a determining factor in the location of the home selected.

The neighborhood and the neighbors should be investigated before a final selection is made. One of the main reasons for this

Suburban living is the choice of more and more people as cities become crowded and better transportation makes it unnecessary to live close to the place of work.

careful investigation is that the neighborhood is one of the logical sources of friends. Even when people have an established circle of friends outside of the neighborhood, it is difficult to ignore the people nearby, whether in the city or the country. It is also bad psychologically to feel either inferior or superior to them. Wise people establish their home where it will bring them in natural contact with the kinds of people they would like to know and associate with.

Accessibility to stores, transportation, schools, and churches should be investigated before a location is chosen.

Is the transportation good and is it dependable for going to and from work? Sometimes people purposely want to live far away from town in order to discourage certain relatives from making frequent calls; but if the husband or wife must be on the job at seven in the morning, a long ride to work may be more of a hardship than the frequent visits of undesirable relatives.

Nearness to schools is an absolute essential for children and in many cases for young adults. A young husband or wife often continues to take courses after marriage. Or it may be that adult classes and other activities at the school are the focal point of the community, so that being nearby would be an advantage.

Closeness to a church is important to most people. A church is one of the best sources for meeting congenial people. Living near a church of the family's faith will make it easier for the members of the family to attend services, meetings, and social affairs.

The various types of dwellings should be considered.

In past years when a couple married they moved directly into a house or lived with parents until they could find or afford a house of their own to live in. Now there are many types of dwellings from which to choose, especially in the more metropolitan areas. Before deciding on a place to live, every young couple or family should consider the kinds of dwelling places available and weigh the advantages and disadvantages of each for their particular needs, their financial situation, and the kind of living which they wish to have.

Hotel apartments, which are available in cities, probably offer the easiest type of living. They are, as a rule, partially or completely furnished and provided with services similar to those in a hotel. This type of living is expensive, but if the wife is working or the couple have many outside interests, a hotel apartment may be satisfactory for a while.

Small apartments in medium-sized buildings usually offer more individualized living than is possible in apartment hotels or large buildings. This is important to some people.

On the other hand, large apartment buildings, both publicly and privately owned, often have the advantages of laundry service, maid service, and commissaries, as well as organized social activities, such as dramatic clubs, dancing clubs, and study clubs.

Remodeled apartments that are comfortable and attractive are available in most cities and towns. Many old houses and buildings have been completely remodeled into small, modern apartments.

Large-scale housing projects have made a new kind of living for many people in cities who like the convenience and facilities that such a community within a community offers them at a price within their incomes.

Smart, cosmopolitan city living in large apartments or cooperative apartment buildings is the choice of many people in large cities who could afford their own homes but who prefer to be "in town" and like the services and conveniences that such living offers.

(DON MORGAN FROM FREDERIC LEWIS)

Sometimes these apartments do not have the privacy or security of apartments in large apartment buildings, but they very often have a more homelike atmosphere, and they may be less expensive.

Flats or duplex apartments offer far more privacy than the usual multiple-living arrangement of an apartment house. However, most flats have two or three bedrooms and are expensive to furnish and heat for a small family. Generally, also, in a flat the tenant assumes more responsibility for upkeep than is the case in an apartment.

Houses of all sizes are also available to those who wish to rent. Their advantages of privacy, independence, and freedom are obvious. These advantages, however, are balanced by responsibilities for care and upkeep of walks, lawn, heating, and the seasonal changes from storm windows to screens in some climates.

Factors that assure living comfort should be checked.

There are certain points to check for general living comfort before renting an apartment, a flat, or a house. Even a desperate desire to have a home should not make a couple lose sight of certain basic needs.

Heat for cold weather is a basic need. A previous tenant or other tenants in the building may give information as to whether the radiation or the heating plant is adequate for comfort. In the case of a flat or a house where the tenant is paying the heating bill, it is a good idea to call the fuel company and check on the cost of heating for the last two or three years.

Ventilation for hot weather is important. A check on the position of doors and windows and an additional check on insulation if the apartment is on the top floor will help to indicate whether the rooms would be bearable during hot summer months.

Quiet—or the absence of too much noise from traffic, nearby recreation centers, or people in adjoining apartments—should be investigated. Many people can adjust themselves to noises in time, but some people cannot. People who do not become accustomed to noises easily should investigate these possible irritations when selecting a home.

Building upkeep is important to those renting an apartment. It shows itself in the condition of halls, walks, laundry, and service rooms. Their state of cleanliness indicates the type of service to be expected and the type of tenants in the other apartments.

Light is important if members of the family spend time at home during the day. In families where all the members are employed, a sunless apartment which permits them to sleep late on week-end mornings may be an advantage. In other families, where some members are at home a great deal of the time, choosing an apartment that has no sun in any of the rooms would be a mistake.

The size of the family should be considered.

How well an apartment or house fits the size of the family has a great deal to do with the comfort of living. The housing shortage during and following World War II that forced people to live with relatives or in cramped quarters proved that space which allowed for privacy was necessary to happiness. Too many people living in quarters that are too small is likely to produce strained relationships. But one or two people living in quarters that are too large is

The interests and needs of the family should be carefully considered before selecting a place to live. For instance, if each member of the family needs some work space for his activities, a home with a basement, an attic, or a garage may be a requirement.

(COURTESY *Popular Home*)

equally ill-advised. A large house is an unnecessary expense as well as an unnecessary burden to manage and keep up when time and household help are at a premium.

Between these two extremes is a point at which people are happiest, housekeeping is easiest, and expenses are in proper proportion.

Space that is psychologically adequate allows people to have enough room to follow their private interests without irritating or interfering with others. Of course every room should be used sufficiently to justify the expense of furnishing, cleaning, heating, and lighting. There should be enough space so that each person can have privacy—and this means children as well as adults.

Space that is physically adequate for living comfort is claimed by many experts to consist of a home with one more room than the number of people in the family—for instance, a four-room apartment for three people. Of course, there is no formula that fits every situation. Especially generous storage space will make a house comfortable for a family for whom the same number of rooms, without generous storage space, would be utterly inadequate.

The only effective way to plan proper space for a home is to have a very clear-cut idea of the individual needs of each member of the family, as well as to consider the size of the family. Space is at once the most important and the most expensive requirement of people.

The interests of the family should be considered.

In evaluating possible places to live, a couple should consider whether the apartment or house fits their particular interests. Most people never find a place that completely satisfies them on every score. Life just does not offer that kind of heaven as a rule. Therefore, most people must be satisfied with the selection of a home that most nearly meets their needs. Once that selection is made, they are wise if they close their eyes to the deficiencies until they are in a position to change them. No one should expect perfection, but anyone, by persistent effort, can approach it.

Booklovers should have enough wall space for plenty of bookcases. Of course, bookshelves can be built in or unfinished shelves

COURTESY ARMSTRONG CORK COMPANY

When possible, closets and cabinets should be planned for the needs of the individuals who are to use them. How would a closet for a man's clothes differ from one for a woman's? How does a child's closet differ from that of an adult's?

COURTESY *Popular Home*

can be bought and painted the color of the woodwork, but in either case ample wall space is necessary.

Music-lovers should have adequate space for a piano or a phonograph. When renting an apartment, they should also check whether the building is insulated sufficiently to make the playing of recordings or practicing possible without bringing down the wrath of every neighboring mother who has a napping child. In addition, the apartment-house rulings about music should be checked before signing a lease.

Amateur photographers should have a darkroom where they can develop their pictures, as well as a place where they can show them and store them. An extra storage closet, large enough to convert into a darkroom, will take care of the former, and a series of frames with removable backs plus adequate filing space will satisfy the latter.

Active adolescents who enjoy games, dancing, and music should live in a house, if possible, where they can have these things without bothering people in neighboring apartments. If apartment living is necessary, folding card tables and chairs and a folding table top that will fit on the dining-room table for games will help to make an apartment meet these needs of teen-agers.

The amount of closet space should be considered.

The whole subject of closet space and its importance for comfortable living was covered in Chapter 16. The only reason for mentioning it again in this chapter is that any discussion of the selection of a home is incomplete if closet space is not considered. Therefore, turn back to Chapter 16 and review the section on closets in order to complete the list of basic factors to consider before selecting a place to live.

CHECKING YOUR KNOWLEDGE . . .

1. What are the advantages of renting? What are the disadvantages?
2. What are the practical points to consider in determining the location of a home?
3. What are the psychological points to consider in determining the location of a home?

4. What types of living quarters are available to those who rent? What are the advantages of each?

5. What general factors in living comfort should be checked before renting a house or an apartment?

6. How does the size of a home affect (*a*) living comfort and (*b*) living costs?

7. In what ways do the special interests and talents of the family affect the selection of a home?

USING YOUR KNOWLEDGE . . .

1. Divide the class into groups and have each group investigate a different type of housing. Each student should interview at least two families who live in the type of house which her group is considering—one who likes it and one who does not. Careful notes should be taken on their reactions, and then the findings should be pooled in the small group.

2. Present the findings of each group in Number 1 by means of a panel composed of one girl from each group. The others can prepare an exhibit of pictures of the different types of housing. Invite another class, a few interested teachers, or some parents to hear the discussion.

3. Select a locale you would like to live in and list the reasons.

4. Draw a floor plan of two rooms in your house. Mark off existing storage space in blue crayon. With green crayon, draw in possible placement of new wardrobe, storage, and cabinet space. Take sizes from advertisements of portable cupboards and wardrobes in magazines, newspapers, or mail-order catalogues. List all costs.

5. Invite a young couple who live in the country and a couple who live in the city—preferably former students—to discuss the reasons for their selection of location before the class. After the talks have been given, invite questions from the class addressed to one or the other of the couples.

6. Talk with three couples who rent apartments and find out what their rents cover. Ask questions regarding the conditions under which they rent, such as occupancy rights in case of sale, subletting rights, rules of conduct, etc.

CHAPTER 20: Buying or Building a Home

The possibility of buying or building a home is not nearly so out of reach for most people as it used to be. Since World War II, government loans, inexpensive prefabricated houses, and the prevalence of large-scale home-building projects have put home ownership within the grasp of many people who formerly could only dream of it. Consequently, it is advisable for everyone to know the main factors involved in buying or building a home so that they can make the best decision when the time arrives for making a choice.

To the many important factors, listed in Chapter 19, which should be considered in renting a home must be added quite a few new ones for those people who are going to buy or build. Future liabilities—such as taxes, zoning laws, and repairs—must be carefully investigated. Personal expectations, both financial and social, must be anticipated as far as possible before a home is purchased or built.

If a house that will need considerable remodeling is being purchased, definite costs for the work and material involved should be figured as part of the purchase price.

If a new house is being built, there is the matter of costs and financing, plus the added concern of selecting or formulating—with the help of an architect—a plan that will meet present and future needs.

Owning a home involves far greater responsibilities than renting, and therefore far greater care should be taken to consider all the aspects before a home is bought or built.

The advantages and disadvantages of home ownership should be considered before buying.

The question of whether to buy property presents itself to most families in days of a housing shortage when rented places are hard to find. Many people who would not consider buying a home at any other time are forced into buying in order to have a place to live. In normal times, however, it is possible to weigh the advantages and disadvantages and make a decision according to what is found to be more advantageous for the family.

The advantages of owning a home may seem obvious to those who have always lived in a home that was owned by the family. But to many people, who have always lived in a rented apartment or house, the advantages may not be known or may not be so apparent.

1) Security that comes with the possession of a home is perhaps the most important reason of all for owning. It has psychological importance that far outweighs any material importance. Knowing that you can live in your home as long as you like makes you feel a part of the community and of its institutions. Good citizenship comes more easily as a result.

2) Family solidarity is another result of owning a home. The interests which develop for every member of the family around such things as the planting of shrubbery, gardening, remodeling, and redecorating make the family a closer unit. The home thus becomes a physical magnet that supplements the psychological ties that family life cultivates, and authorities on marriage and family life consider it an important factor in stabilizing and making a success of marriage.

3) Respect for and an understanding of the value of property develop from home ownership. A boy is anxious to beautify a lawn if it belongs to his family, whereas if it belongs to a mythical landlord, it is difficult for him to take the same interest.

4) The financial benefits that accrue from owning a home are another advantage in buying. Regular savings are induced by the payments on the house. The payments not only force the building up of an investment, but the plan provides a means of saving. In

In the past, country living was available only to the farmer, the retired man, and the wealthy.

Today, because of better transportation, new methods of construction, and new means for financing the ownership of a home, the joys of country living are within the reach of many.

normal times the usual improvement of a neighborhood and the year-by-year improvement of the property will make the investment pay off more than a normal rate of interest at the time of resale. Moreover, in an emergency a house can be offered as security on a loan or mortgage.

The disadvantages of owning a home, as a rule, do not seem important compared to the advantages. Only those who are forced to move frequently and those who have neither the time nor the inclination to accept responsibility feel that the disadvantages of home ownership are great.

1) The concentration of a large part of the family income on shelter may prove to be a disadvantage to some. Home ownership forces the investment of money in the home which might otherwise be available for recreation, education, or cultural pursuits. The building up of an investment is in itself good, but if it has to be done by sacrificing too many other immediate needs or pleasures of the family, it may be unwise.

2) Unpredictable expenses are another disadvantage of home ownership for many people. If the roof leaks, if something happens to the plumbing or the heating, or if the taxes are raised, there must be money on hand to take care of it. Some people cannot adjust their incomes to take care of such unexpected costs.

3) Increased responsibility is a third disadvantage of home ownership. Upkeep on property involves a great deal of hard work, either on the part of the owner or of the men he hires. Even if it is financially possible to hire help, there is the responsibility for their safety and welfare which must be assumed by the employer.

4) The possibility of loss is a fourth disadvantage. A change in the economic condition of the family may make a quick sale at a loss necessary. Economic conditions of the country or of the community may automatically reduce the value of the property. These reductions might equalize themselves over a period of years, but if it should be necessary to sell during a low period, there is a real loss of money.

Many of these disadvantages can, however, be somewhat minimized if care is taken to consider them when the purchase is made.

**The possible liabilities on property
should be checked before buying.**

Buying a home is a long-term proposition and, as such, should
be carefully investigated from all points of view. Not only should
the present situation be known, but probable future trends should
be estimated.

Taxes are legal liabilities that should be investigated before a
house is purchased. If the neighborhood is new, inquiry should be
made about special assessments that are apt to be made for utilities,
street pavement, and sidewalks.

Zoning laws are a factor in future property value. Any property
under consideration should be protected from the encroachment of
industrial plants, taverns, apartment houses, or rooming houses, all
of which lower property values. On the other hand, if the property
is bought as an investment to be turned into a combination home
and income-producer, the zoning laws should be checked to be sure
that whatever is planned is permissible.

General condition of vital equipment is another important item
to check. A prospective owner should be sure that the furnace, the
hot water system, the roof, the screens, the storm windows, the
plumbing, and the insulation are in good condition. Such equipment represents large expenditures, and its condition should be considered carefully when the value of the property is being estimated.

Personal expectations should be considered in buying.

A family considering the purchase of a house should try to
look into the future as far as it is possible, so as to anticipate such
things as an increase or decrease in the size of the family living at
home, the need of additional work space, and the probable increase
or decrease in income in the years ahead.

The size of the family living at home is seldom static. It is wise,
therefore, to consider the probability of children leaving home to
go to school or to establish homes of their own, as well as the possibility of elderly parents joining the family circle. Well-planned
homes are able to meet these changes comfortably.

The possibility of need for additional space for work or hobbies is another consideration of great importance. Many parents add to the family income by doing work at home. Many young people develop hobbies in home workshops that have led to important vocations later on. Many grownups have found satisfaction and considerable financial return in the development of a hobby. Space is necessary for all these pursuits.

The financial expectations of the family should be taken into account. To buy a house that will be outgrown economically in a few years is as unwise as it is to buy a house that is far beyond the normal expectations of the family income. Couples are smart to look at their income and their probable earning power in an objective way. Only on that basis can they estimate what they can expect in the way of increases or reductions of income in the years to come. Because buying or building a home is a long-term investment, people should weigh their expectations as honestly as possible and allow for them. A home should be so carefully selected that it will fit the family needs for some years to come.

Remodeling instead of building has advantages and disadvantages.

The remodeling of a house has both advantages and disadvantages over building a new house. All of these should be known and weighed as far as possible before work is begun.

The advantages of remodeling over building a new house are many and varied. The most obvious is economic. As a rule, the cost of buying and remodeling a house is less than the cost of building a new house. But this is only part of the important advantages of remodeling.

1) Dealing with the known is the first advantage in remodeling. If a room is too narrow for effective placement of furniture and it is decided to remove the wall between the room and a hall so as to enlarge it, it is possible to estimate the exact cost and final size of the remodeled room. The contractor or architect should be consulted to be sure the wall carries no weight and has no heating pipes or electric wiring to interfere.

If a room is too dark and it is decided to add a window, it is

BEFORE

Sometimes it is less expensive and safer to remodel an old house than to buy a new one or build.

AFTER

easy to anticipate the view and what can be done with the furniture around it, because all of it can be seen rather than merely imagined.

2) The possibility for more individuality in the home is another advantage in remodeling. Materials and styles of other times have a charm that cannot be incorporated into a new house except at tremendous cost. Even the general plan of a house created at a time when labor and space were less expensive will have a distinction and a spaciousness that are quite different from the houses which are built today.

3) The possibility of stretching a remodeling job over a period of time is another advantage. Bills that come in from month to month can be met with income. Remodeling is therefore easier to handle than a total building job which must be met and financed at one time.

4) The advantage of having a beautiful setting of trees and shrubbery full grown, such as that shown on page 403, is one that weighs heavily with people who love the outdoors. Many will trade a new house for that sort of charm and feel they have profited, regardless of the economic or financial advantages.

The disadvantages of remodeling fall into several classifications. They may be financial, architectural, or purely psychological. All are important, and all should be weighed carefully before the decision to remodel is made.

1) The possibility of an emergency is fairly great in remodeling. Plumbing which seemed good may prove to be unsound when a new bathroom is added. Wiring that functioned perfectly may not meet building codes when opened up for changes. Plaster that seemed secure may crack and fall with change of weight of walls. It is this type of emergency which must be expected in remodeling.

2) The final cost in remodeling is usually uncertain. This is often due to the fact that there is no contractor or architect on the job and the bids are made in a more or less unbusinesslike manner to the owner himself who has had very little experience in such matters. The wording of a contract may fool a layman and leave him with a far larger bill than he expected.

3) The fact that the purchase price and remodeling costs are paid at different times sometimes blinds people to the fact that the total investment is out of proportion. Many people who would refuse to buy a $25,000 house in a certain locality because it obviously could not be resold at that price, will pay $15,000 and gradually invest $10,000 in remodeling. To check this, an architect or contractor should estimate remodeling costs before the house is purchased.

4) Some old houses do not lend themselves to remodeling. Regardless of infinite care and expense, they may never be well heated, they may never be attractive architecturally, or they may never be really convenient for modern living. A good contractor will see this fact in advance, and his opinion should be respected.

Building a home has many advantages but also some disadvantages.

Building a home is usually considered one of the greatest joys that can come to a family. Yet there are many factors that make it a precarious as well as an interesting project.

The advantages of building, as a rule, far outweigh the disadvantages for most people who love a home and are discriminating in their requirements.

1) The possibility of a perfect background for family life as the family wishes to live is probably the biggest advantage in building. Every family probably hopes eventually to have a house that is planned for them alone, and if a wise architect is employed, it will be. His training and knowledge will produce a beautiful house and a completely individualized one as well. He can, with the family's help, produce a home that fits them like a glove.

2) The educational value of building is undeniable. Every step of the planning and building opens up a new field of interest for every member of the family. Decisions about the slope of the roof, the size of the windows, the curve of the walk, the kind of wood, tile, or brick are all interesting projects to be worked out.

3) The increased interest and pride in the home that comes from a feeling of personal creation is important in family life. Each

The plans for a new home are of interest to each member of the family, and watching a house develop as it is being built is a real experience for the children as well as the parents.

member of the family feels a sense of personal responsibility for the results of decisions in which he had a voice.

The disadvantages of building under normal conditions are far outweighed by the advantages. In time of shortages, however, there are apt to be such great delays in getting labor and materials that many people hesitate to try to build a house.

1) The uncertainty of final cost is one of the big disadvantages of building. This is especially true in time of inflation, when labor is high and contracts are let on time and material. Under these conditions, the amount of the final bill is anyone's guess. In normal times, when bids are made, the owner himself often creates a rise in cost by his extra demands. Because it is his first experience, he is unable to visualize blueprints and is constantly demanding changes once the building is under way. This need not be so, but avoiding it takes a great deal of self-control on the part of the owner and some detailed study and planning of the prints.

2) The difficulty of financing a building is obvious because of the possibility of changing costs. The book *Mr. Blandings Builds*

His Dream House is a vivid lesson in the financial pitfalls of building and one that is repeated whenever there is a lack of businesslike decision on the part of either the architect or the client.

Architecture should be analyzed before buying or building.

Before any house is bought or plans are accepted for building or remodeling, the architecture should be analyzed for its beauty and its authenticity. Not only is the architecture of a house important esthetically, but also it is important in determining the resale value of the property. A beautifully designed house will sell in any market. A poorly designed house sells slowly, even when houses are scarce.

Good line and proportion are major requirements in evaluating a house that is to be bought or built. Some houses that are good in basic plan fail miserably because they are clumsy in line and ungainly in proportion. The relation of the height to the width and depth and the relation of window sizes to house size are vitally important. The line of the roof can ruin the whole effect of the house and subtract thousands of dollars from its value.

It is sometimes possible to improve the effect of a house with shutters and landscaping or by the removal or addition of a porch. However, the best way to ensure pleasing architecture is to employ a trained architect—one who is an artist and who innately knows good lines, balance, and proportion. If his services cannot be afforded all through the building of the home, he should be hired at least for the original designs. He will charge a flat fee for this— a fee that will depend on the size of the house, the community, and his standing as an architect.

It is also well to realize that it is very unwise to hire an architect and then try to dictate his work. A good architect will incorporate all the personal needs and likes of his clients into his plans. But he will do a very much better job if he is allowed freedom to create, once those needs and likes are stated. The client's job is to make plain his needs at the beginning.

Authenticity of style is another point that must be considered. However, almost any architectural style used nowadays has been sifted through the fine screen of twentieth-century demands for safety, ease of cleaning, economy of heating, simplicity, and comfort. The stairs are not nearly so steep in present-day Cape Cod houses as in those of early days. Ceilings are not so high nor windows so deeply recessed in present-day Mediterranean houses. Moldings are simpler and rooms are smaller in the twentieth-century version of Georgian houses. A good architect simplifies but never distorts period individuality.

The placement of the house on the lot should have careful consideration. The shape of the lot will have a definite bearing on the shape of the house. Its placement may be somewhat determined by zoning laws, but as a rule there is enough flexibility within them to enable a good architect to create a feeling of privacy and an appearance of individuality. He will see to it that windows have the best outlook and that there is space for recreation, garden, and lawn. The ability to locate a house advantageously on a lot is an important part of an architect's training and is one of the many advantages of his services.

Traffic lanes should be checked in any new home.

By the time people arrive at the point of buying, remodeling, or building their own homes, it becomes important to select or plan room arrangements that most nearly suit personal and family needs.

In order to visualize the effect of room arrangement on the livability of a home, turn to the house plans for good and poor traffic lanes on pages 410 and 411. Pretend that you are living in the houses diagrammed. Make a tracing of the plans, and then mark off the line of march you would follow if you were managing that house for a day or week. You will find that on the plans marked "good" you would use a minimum of time and energy to accomplish the maximum amount of work, whereas you would retrace your steps and waste endless time to accomplish a minimum of work in the houses planned according to the layout marked "poor."

Another point to notice is whether it is possible to get from one room to another without going through intermediate rooms. Extra traffic through rooms is hard on carpets, disturbs privacy, adds to housekeeping work, and means that the basic plan is poor.

The daily round of meals and housework can be quickly plotted. Notice whether the doors are well placed or whether the addition of a door would save steps. Notice whether there is an easy place to serve the noon lunch. Check the placement of coat closets to see if they are easily accessible from the front and back doors. Notice whether there is a utility closet large enough to hold a vacuum cleaner, and whether there is a clothes chute which will save carrying soiled linen to the laundry.

Special occasions and the presence of guests should be thought of in connection with traffic lanes. Women guests are perfectly willing to trek through the house to remove their wraps in a bedroom, but men cannot be bothered. The ideal house allows for this situation. It has a coat closet and a bedroom that can be reached by guests without the interruption of conversation in the living room. These needs should be analyzed carefully before making any decisions to buy a house or to accept blueprints.

Furniture arrangement should be planned as early as possible.

Furniture arrangement for a home should be planned before a house is bought or a blueprint accepted. Room sizes, wall spaces, and window placements should be such as to allow for the use of the furniture already owned or to be bought. This should be done accurately, according to the method suggested in Chapter 8. Sometimes the moving of a doorway or window just 6 inches while the house is being planned will make it possible to use a sofa or a secretary which might otherwise have to be discarded. The importance of planning the arrangement of furniture before the blueprints are accepted cannot be stressed too much. Changes after construction of the house has begun cause the cost of building to mount unbelievably.

People who are buying a house may find that some of their furniture cannot be used without costly remodeling of the house. In such a case, the loss of furniture may be far outweighed by other advantages in owning the house.

Placement of outlets for electricity should be planned for each

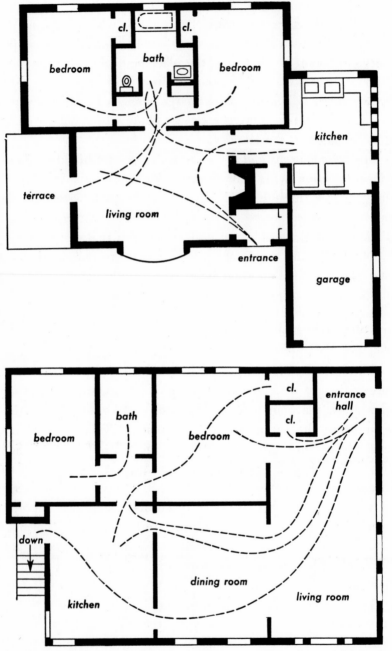

Poorly designed house plans, such as these, necessitate long and circuitous traffic lanes through the rooms of the house.

House Plans that Make for *Good* Traffic Lanes

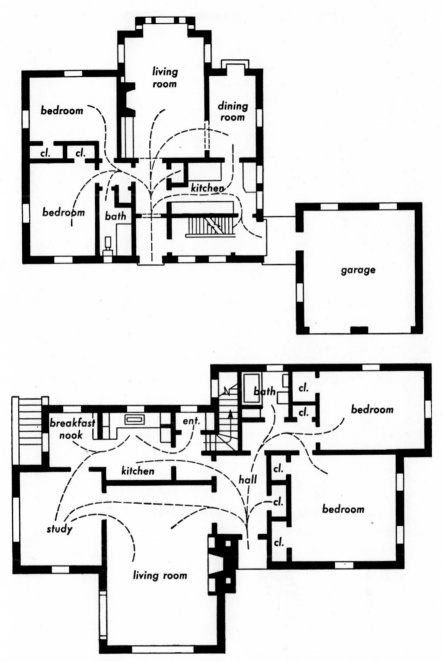

Well-designed house plans allow short, direct traffic lanes that do not cut through the main part of rooms.

The doorway of a home is a tangible expression of welcome and hospitality. Consequently, it should be beautiful and individual.

412

furniture grouping, rather than being scattered about a room in a hit-or-miss fashion. Most rooms do not need a center light. Bedrooms, living rooms, and sunrooms all look better with lamps. Even a hall, if it is wide enough to hold a table, will look far more inviting and homelike with a lamp that has a low light. It is important, however, to have at least one lamp in each room that is controlled by a wall switch at the door so that a light can be turned on before entering a room.

When remodeling or building, all the changes possible should be made while the blueprints are being made. Then it should be remembered that the perfect house has never been built. Everyone makes concessions of some kind.

But once the work is done and the last carpenters, painters, plumbers, and electricians have packed up their tools and gone, no small disappointments should be allowed to shadow the big joy of possessing a home. That joy should add something to life every time the key slips into the lock and opens the door of HOME. Never take it for granted! Enjoy it and make it beautiful—inside and out— a worthy setting for a happy family life.

CHECKING YOUR KNOWLEDGE . . .

1. What are the advantages and disadvantages of (a) buying, (b) remodeling, and (c) building a home?
2. What are the possible future liabilities of property?
3. What personal expectations should be anticipated in buying a home?
4. What is the importance of good architecture?
5. What are traffic lanes and in what way are they important to living comfort?
6. Why is it important to check furniture arrangement in buying, remodeling, or building?

USING YOUR KNOWLEDGE .

1. Ask a real estate man what it would cost to buy a small house that would be suitable for a young couple. Find out how long it would take to pay for it if you put into it just a little more than the average house rent each month. Find out what percentage is usually required as a down payment on such a purchase.

2. Hunt up a piece of property which would be absolutely appropriate for your family right now and find out how much it would cost.

3. List the advantages and disadvantages of the property in which you now live. If you are renting, find out the value of the property and what the monthly payments would have to be to buy it. List the effects that owning it would have on the family.

4. Have a discussion group made up of as many of the following people as are available: an outstanding architect, a member of a housing commission, a manufacturer of prefabricated houses, the head of a bank specializing in house loans, and a man who has remodeled his own home into apartments. Ask each to present what he believes is the important contribution toward living made by his organization, his profession, or his work. Hold the meeting in the evening and invite parents.

5. Use squared paper to draw a plan of your own home or a home you know very well. Trace the traffic lanes on it in red crayon.

6. Find a small house in your community with fairly usual room sizes. Draw its plan on squared paper and indicate possible furniture arrangements.

7. Clip pictures of four different types of houses. Mount them and label the styles below them. Check your favorite and tell why you prefer it.

Glossary

(The words listed below are defined only as they are used in connection with home decoration.)

Absolute balance: The balance produced by the placing of identical pieces of furniture and/or accessories opposite each other within a group or as separate groups; also called formal balance.

Abstract design: A design consisting of geometric patterns, random lines, or free forms rather than realistic forms.

Accent color: A color that is stronger and more intense than the dominant color used.

Accessories: Pictures, lamps, book ends, smoking equipment, and small objects of art.

Afterimage: A temporary visual impression following the removal of an object from the area of sight. The afterimage of a strong color is the complement of that color—for example, the afterimage of red is green.

Alabaster: A smooth, fine-grained, milk-white stone used for ornaments, statuary, and lamp bases.

Analogous color scheme: A scheme made up of colors that lie side by side on the color wheel—*e.g.*, yellow, yellow-green, and green.

Antimacassar: A cover to protect the back and arms of a chair or sofa. Originally, antimacassars were made of lace and used to protect a chair back from the Macassar hair oil used by men in the Victorian days.

Antique: Any piece of furniture or work of art that is at least one hundred years old.

Antiquing: A toning, or finishing, process used on furniture, woodwork, or objects of art to give them an appearance of age.

Apartment: A suite, or set, of rooms in a hotel, house, or large building that is a complete dwelling.

415

Appliqué: A form of decoration in which materials have been cut out and sewed, embroidered, or pasted on other materials.

Apron: The strip of wood directly under a window sill. Also, the facing of a chair or table connecting the top with the legs.

Asphalt tile: A square-block, heavy-duty, waterproof floor covering, the important or distinctive ingredient of which is asphalt.

Axminster: A kind of carpet weave.

Bamboo: Hollow woody stems from a treelike tropical plant used for furniture and picture frames. Bamboo blinds and draw-curtains are made from bamboo which has been split into narrow lengthwise strips.

Baseboard: The board at the foot of a wall, running flush with the floor.

Beige: A warm, light tan color.

Bleaching: The process of removing all or part of the color from a piece of wood or fabric.

Block printing: A method of printing by hand in which a design is stamped on paper or fabric from engraved blocks, as distinguished from machine printing with rollers.

Bolster: A long cushion, often cylindrical, placed at the head of a bed when it is made up.

Borax furniture: The name used in the trade for furniture of undesirable design and of inferior construction.

Box spring: A bedspring made of coil springs that have been incased in a thin layer of padding and covered with ticking.

Boxed cushions: Cushions having a squared shape formed by inserted side pieces.

Bracket: A wall shelf or set of shelves, supported by a bracing arm, used to hold ornaments.

Braided rug: A rug of any size or shape made of braided strips of material sewed together. Originally, all braided rugs were handmade and were always either circular or oval shape.

Break front: A piece of furniture with a break in the continuity of the principal surface. Specifically, a tall cabinet-bookcase combination divided into three perpendicular sections, the center section of which is deeper and projects several inches in front of the shallower side sections.

Bridge lamp: A floor lamp with an arm to hold the light directly over a table or a lounge chair.

Broadloom carpeting: Carpeting of any quality, weave, or type which is woven in standard rug widths on looms from 3 to 18 feet wide.

Brush fringe: A short, thick cotton fringe, which is inexpensive and can be used in place of cording in seams on pillows, slipcovers, upholstery, and curtains.

Buckram: A plain, strong jute cloth, stiffened with flour paste, china clay, and glue, that is used to stiffen curtain headings and lambrequins.

Buffet: A sideboard.

Burlap: A plain, inexpensive fabric made of coarse jute yarns that is sometimes used to cover screens and for makeshift curtains.

Burnt sienna: A deep red-brown pigment which is mixed with white to produce flesh tints.

Burnt umber: A very dark brown oil pigment used to mellow or soften colors.

Calcimine: An inexpensive, easily applied wash consisting of glue, whiting, and water, to which pigment may be added—for walls and ceilings.

Candelabra: A branched candlestick that holds several candles.

Canopy: The fabric draping over a four-poster bed, dressing table, or seat of honor.

Card table: A table used for playing games, usually 30 to 33 inches square.

Carpeting: A floor covering made up of 27-inch strips sewed together, as distinguished from rugs which are woven in room sizes.

Case furniture: All chests and cabinets, as distinguished from chairs and tables.

Casement cloth: A fairly opaque, undecorated drapery fabric.

Casement curtains: Unlined, somewhat heavy curtains that hang next to the glass and are used primarily to give privacy or to control light.

Casement windows: Hinged windows that open out (outswinging) or in (inswinging) like a door.

Center of interest: See *Focal point.*

Ceramic tile: A tile made of clay which has been baked to give it a hard surface and which is used for floors, walls, and counter tops, as well as for decorative accents architecturally.

Chair rail: The molding that separates a dado from the upper part of a wall.

Chaise longue: The French term for a long-seated chair.

Chesterfield: A large overstuffed sofa, straight-lined and masculine in style.

Chinese lacquer: A furniture finish of red, deep green, black, or cream enamel varnish with Chinese decorations.

Chintz: A fine cotton fabric, usually glazed, and either plain or decorated with a delicate printed design. From the Hindu, meaning "many colors."

Chroma. See *Intensity.*

Cloisonné: An enameled surface decoration in which the design is formed and outlined by wires secured to a metal base.

Coffee table: Any low table used for serving refreshments or to hold magazines, objects of art, or smoking equipment.

Color scheme: A systematic arrangement of colors on the color wheel which can be applied for use.

Color thread: One color repeated in all the rooms of a home in such a way as to produce unity and harmony in the whole.

Color wheel: A circular arrangement of colors, based on the spectrum, that classifies colors conveniently for use.

Commode: A chest of drawers.

Complementary color scheme: A scheme made up of colors that lie opposite each other on the color wheel—*e.g.,* blue and orange.

Console: A large shelf hung against the wall and often used as a table. A console table is a table designed to stand against the wall.

Contemporary: Of the same time or period.

Contrasting color scheme: A color scheme which includes, either singly or fused together, all of the primary colors of the spectrum (complementary, split complementary, and triad color schemes).

Conventionalized design: A design inspired by a naturalistic or realistic form which has been simplified or varied to improve its decorative value or increase its possible decorative use—*e.g.,* as in an allover pattern for fabric or wallpaper.

Conversational groupings: Furniture arrangements planned to encourage conversation, the most satisfactory of which are a semicircle, a U shape, and a square.

Cool colors: Colors that have a predominance of blue, such as green-blue, blue, violet-blue, etc.

Corded seam: A seam in which a cording has been sewed to give it accent and rigidity.

Cornice: A wide board used across the top of a window in place of a valance. A cornice may also be made of metal.

Coved ceiling: A ceiling that curves to meet the wall.

Cretonne: A strong, unglazed cotton fabric with a bold design, usually printed on one side only.

Crewel embroidery: A kind of embroidery, usually done in wool yarn on a natural linen or cotton drill.

Dado: The lower part of a wall when it is decorated differently from the upper section. A dado is usually separated from the upper part of the wall by a molding called a chair rail.

Damask: A one-color fabric into which a design has been woven, as in a linen tablecloth.

Davenport: A large upholstered sofa.

Day bed: A narrow bed that can be used as a couch during the day.

Découpage: A method of decorating furniture with cut-out paper designs pasted flat and covered with colorless shellac.

Diameter: The length of a straight line that bisects a circle.

Dominant color: A color used in greater quantity than all other colors in a room; for variety it may be used in different values and intensities.

Dormer window: A vertical window set in a gable that has been built out from a sloping roof to contain it.

Double-hung sash windows: Windows that are divided into two horizontal sections, both of which slide up and down.

Dovetailing: A method of joining two pieces of wood at right angles by cutting the edges in alternating wedgelike shapes that lock together.

Dowel: A headless pin of wood or metal used to hold two pieces of wood together.

Draperies: Heavy curtains used to decorate or cover a window.

Draw-curtains: Curtains that can be drawn across the window to give privacy and to control light.

Duplex: A two-family dwelling, whether divided vertically or horizontally. A duplex apartment is a one-family apartment with rooms on two levels.

Dutch curtains: A pair of curtains made of four panels, each slightly longer than one-half the window length; two are hung from the top of the window and two from the center.

Eggshell finish: A slightly glossy finish similar to that of an eggshell.

Enamel: A hard-surfaced, shiny paint used where greatest wear is anticipated.

End table: A small table about chair-arm height placed next to a chair or sofa.

Etching: A print made from a copper plate upon which a drawing or design has been etched out of the copper with acid.

Extension rod: A standard rod which can be extended to fit windows of different sizes.

Figurine: A small ornamental figure or statuette of pottery, metal, wood, or stone.

Filet lace: A lace produced by embroidering a pattern on net, usually with embroidery thread that is similar to the thread of the net.

Finger-tip napkins: Small napkins used when light refreshments are served.

Flat: A dwelling that occupies a complete floor or part of a floor in a small building. Sometimes called an apartment.

Flat finish: A dull finish, or a finish without gloss.

Flounce: A pleated or gathered piece of fabric sewed to a bedspread, slipcover, or dressing-table skirt.

Focal point: The center of interest in a room toward which attention naturally turns. The focal point may be built around an architectural interest—such as a bay window or a fireplace—or it may be only a grouping of furniture sufficiently interesting to be the center of attention in the room.

Foot-candle: The amount of light cast by one standard candle on a surface held perpendicular to its rays and at a distance of 1 foot from the candle.

Formal balance: See *Absolute balance.*

French doors: Doors that are composed of small panes of glass.

French pleat: A large pleat composed of three small pinch pleats sewed together. French pleats are used especially at the top of draw-curtains and draw-draperies to give even distribution of fullness when they are drawn closed.

Fusion: The blending, or mixing together, of different colors of paint on wet paper.

Gabled ceiling: A slanted ceiling in a room directly below a gabled, or slanted, roof.

Geometric pattern: An abstract design created by using such exact forms as the square, circle, oval, or diamond shape, or by the use of exact combinations of lines, such as in plaids, checks, and stripes.

Glass curtains: Curtains that hang next to the window glass.

Grass cloth: A wall covering made of fine grass glued and pressed onto paper; also, a wallpaper that imitates this texture.

Grayed color: A color that is muted or softened by adding a small amount of its complementary color or by adding a neutralizer, such as black.

Hassock: See *Ottoman.*

Highboy: A tall chest of drawers mounted on legs.

Hollywood bed: A bed consisting of box springs on four or six legs and an innerspring mattress. A Hollywood bed may or may not have a headboard.

Homespun: A coarse, heavy fabric suitable for men's and boys' rooms, recreation rooms, or informal rooms where oak or maple furniture is used.

Hooked rug: A handmade rug formed by hooking strips of cloth or yarn through a canvas backing to form a kind of pile. Hooked rugs that look handmade are now made by machinery.

Host and hostess chairs: Straight-backed upholstered chairs which can be used in dining rooms or living rooms.

Hue: The name of a color, such as red, yellow, blue, orange, yellow-orange, blue-green, etc.

Informal balance: See *Occult balance.*

Inlay: Anything set into a solid surface for adornment; also, the surface it forms.

Intensity: The brightness or dullness, strength or weakness of a color.

Interchangeable: Any article that can be used harmoniously in more than one room.

Intermediate colors: Those colors produced by the mixing of equal parts of a secondary color with one of the primary colors which it contains—*i.e.*, yellow-orange, yellow-green, red-orange, blue-green, etc.

Jaspé: French term meaning streaked or striped.

Kneehole desk: A flat table-top desk supported by two piers of drawers at the sides so as to allow a center opening to accommodate the knees of the writer.

Lacquer: A tough, durable liquid varnish sprayed or painted on wood and metal to give it a high gloss.

Lambrequin: A shaped piece of fabric that has been stiffened with buckram and hung from a shelf or used at the top of a window in place of a valance or cornice.

Linoleum: A flexible, hard-surfaced floor covering that resists moisture.

Love seat: A settee which seats two people.

Lowboy: A table-height chest of drawers supported on four legs.

Mantel: The projecting shelf surmounting a fireplace.

Marbleize: A process of graining or veining a surface in imitation of marble.

Mercerize: A treatment given to cotton yarn for the purpose of making it stronger and more lustrous.

Middle value: A value halfway between black and white or halfway between the darkest shade and the lightest tint of a color.

Mitered corners: Corners formed by the joining of two pieces on a line bisecting the angle of junction, as in a picture frame.

Moleskin: A heavily napped fabric which can be pasted on the bottom of objects to prevent their scratching the surface of a piece of furniture on which they are placed.

Monochromatic color scheme: A one-color scheme in which one hue is used in different values and intensities.

Mortise-and-tenon joint: A joint for holding together two heavy pieces of wood or metal by making a hole (mortise) in one and fitting a block (tenon) on the other into it tightly.

Motif: The unit or central figure in a design.

Mullions: The vertical bars between windowpanes.

Multiple-purpose furniture: Any piece of furniture which may be used to serve more than one function.

Mural: A large picture or design painted directly on a wall or applied to a wall like wallpaper.

Muslin: A strong, plain cotton material used in both bleached and un-bleached form. "In muslin" is the term applied to upholstered furni-ture sold without upholstery and therefore covered only in muslin.

Muted: Softened, or grayed.

Natural-wood finish: A finish of wax or colorless shellac that does not change the original color of the wood.

Naturalistic design: See *Realistic design.*

Needle point: A form of embroidery on canvas or scrim executed with a blunt needle.

Neutralized colors: Colors which have been so grayed that they have no perceptible hue, such as beige, tan, or brown.

Neutrals: Black, white, and all values of gray.

Nubby fabric: A fabric which is woven from yarn with small knobs or lumps to create a rough surface.

Occasional chair: A light open-arm chair that can be moved easily from one group to another for different occasions.

Occult balance: The balancing of unlike things, such as that of two chairs with one sofa. Also referred to as informal balance.

Opaque fabric: Any closely woven material that obscures light and view.

Ottoman: A big, stuffed, upholstered footstool about the height of a chair seat. An ottoman without legs is also called a hassock.

Panel: An area on furniture, doors, walls, or ceiling set off, usually by a frame, from the surrounding area by being raised above it or lowered below it.

Parchment: The skin of a young calf, sheep, or goat, which is used for expensive tailored lamp shades.

Parchment paper: A heavy, semitranslucent paper, imitating parchment, which is used in making inexpensive lamp shades.

Passe partout: A paper tape, gummed on one side, that is used to edge lamp shades and to hold picture and glass together when no frame is used.

Patchwork: A kind of needlework in which pieces of cloth (patches) of different colors and sizes are sewed together, usually into a pattern or design, such as on a patchwork quilt.

Pedestal table: A table which has its top supported by a center column.

Pediment: An architectural cresting, used on top of cabinets, that may be triangular, segmented, or scrolled in shape.

Petit point: A fine embroidery done on canvas or net with very small satin stitches or cross-stitches.

Pewter: An alloy of tin and lead resembling silver in color but duller in finish.

Piecrust table: A table with a fluted edge resembling a piecrust.

Pier mirror: A large, tall mirror.

Pilaster: A rectangular or half-round pillar or column placed against a wall, a piece of furniture, or any other surface.

Pile: Soft, fine hairlike nap, which is present in some fabrics (velvet) and many soft floor coverings.

Pillow sham: A decorative cover for a bed pillow which is separate from the bedspread but made of the same material.

Piping: A narrow edging applied to draperies, slipcovers, and bedspreads.

Planter lamp: A lamp with a base that is a container for growing plants.

Plywood: Wood made of thin sheets of veneer glued together with the grains of the layers usually at right angles one to another.

Primary colors: The three basic colors—red, yellow, and blue—which cannot be made by mixing other colors.

Priming coat: The first coating of paint, varnish, or sizing laid on a surface to be painted.

Print: Any fabric on which a design or pattern has been stamped (by hand or machine) as distinguished from patterned fabrics into which the design has been woven.

Quilting: The process of sewing layers of fabrics together, with a padding between, in which the stitches form a pleasing pattern or design.

Raw sienna: A yellow-brown pigment used in mixing grayed warm colors.

Raw umber: A dark gray-brown pigment used in mixing grayed, softened colors.

Realistic design: A design composed of recognizable objects from the world around us.

Register: A grilled opening in the floor or wall of a room allowing for passage of warm or cool air into or out of the room.

Related color scheme: A monochromatic or analogous color scheme.

Riser: The upright piece of wood that connects the treads of a stairway.

Rug: A heavy fabric floor covering, woven in room sizes, as distinguished from a carpet which is woven in strips and sewed or cut to room size. Hard floor coverings in room sizes are often referred to as rugs.

Rush seat: A seat made of twisted rushes.

Sampler: A piece of needlework with embroidered letters or verses.

Sash: The frame in a window or door into which panes of glass are set.

Sateen: A cotton fabric resembling satin.

Scale: Relative dimensions or proportions.

Scatter rugs: Small rugs that are scattered about in a room.

Scenic paper: A wallpaper portraying landscapes.

Sconce: Originally, a wall bracket with branches for holding candles. Now, any lighting fixture which is attached to a wall.

Scrim: A light, coarse cotton or linen netlike fabric, with some sizing, used as a base for needle point. When made of fine fibers and not sized, scrim is used for curtains.

Secondary colors: Those colors which are formed by mixing equal parts of any two of the primary colors together—*i.e.*, green, orange, and violet.

Secretary: A slant-top desk with bookshelves above it.

Sectional sofa: A sofa consisting of two or more parts, each of which may be used separately or together in various arrangements.

Selvage: The edge of a woven fabric.

Sepia print: A photographic reproduction in tints and shades of rich brown instead of the usual black, white, and grays.

Settee: A small sofa, about twice the width of a chair, with low arms and back; settees are frequently upholstered.

Shades: The darker, or below middle, values of a color.

Shadow box: Originally a shallow inclosing case with a glass front in which a framed painting was set for protection. Currently, a shallow open case to hold a still-life grouping of objects which, theoretically, has the beauty of a painting. Shadow boxes are usually hung on the wall as are paintings.

Sheer fabric: Any fabric that can be seen through.

Shellac: A refined varnish.

Side chair: An armless straight chair.

Silhouette: The outline or shadow of an object.

Sill: The horizontal board at the base of a door or window.

Sizing: A gelatinous solution used for the glazing or stiffening of fabrics and wallpapers.

Slipcover: A removable cover for furniture.

Sofa: A long seat with a back and raised side arms.

Spectrum: The colors formed when a beam of white light passes through a prism and is divided into its prismatic colors, as in the rainbow, which is a natural spectrum.

Split complementary color scheme: A color scheme made up of any one color in combination with the two colors on either side of its complement on the color wheel—*e.g.*, yellow, red-violet, and blue-violet.

Stair well: The open compartment, or space, extending vertically through a building where stairs are placed.

Stenciling: Decorating a surface with a painted design by means of painting over a piece of cardboard out of which the design has been cut.

Still life: A grouping of small inanimate objects (fruit, flowers, food, vases, etc.) assembled for artistic effect. Also, a painting or photograph of such a grouping.

Strip carpeting: Carpeting of any quality, weave, or type that is 27 inches wide.

Studio couch: An upholstered, backless couch that can be made into a double bed.

Stylized design: See *Conventionalized design.*

Swag: Originally a decoration in wood, metal, china, etc., of festooned draperies, garlands of leaves, or wreaths of flowers. Now, a festooned fabric valance hung over the top of a window.

Swing arm: A hinged curtain rod, fixed to the wall at one end so that it can be moved out. Swing arms are used to hang curtains on in-swinging casement windows so the curtains may be pushed back when the window is opened. A swing arm on a dresser or bureau is a wooden support which holds the mirror.

Terrazzo: A kind of flooring made of small chips of marble set irregularly in cement and polished.

Texture: The characteristics and surface effect of a fabric produced by the weaving.

Ticking: Any firmly woven cotton or linen cloth used for making ticks (coverings on mattresses and pillows).

Tile: A flat piece of pottery which has been fired to give it a hard surface.

Tints: The lighter, or above middle, values of a color.

Toile: The French word for fabric.

Toile de Jouy: French term for a fabric printed with a realistic design on cotton or linen.

Tôle: French word for decorated, painted tin accessories.

Tooled leather: Leather which has been decorated with an embossed pattern. Sometimes the pattern is gilded or colored to make an object more decorative.

Traffic lanes: The paths ordinarily created by people in the normal process of living or walking about in a building or house.

Traverse rod: A curtain rod arranged with pulleys for drawing curtains.

Tread: The upper, horizontal part of a step on which the foot is placed.

Triad color scheme: A color scheme composed of three colors equidistant from one another on the color wheel—*e.g.,* red, yellow, and blue; green, violet, and orange.

Unfinished furniture: Furniture which is complete in form but not in surface—unpainted, unvarnished, and undecorated.

Upholstered furniture: Furniture to which some fabric, padding, or springs have been added for increased beauty and comfort.

Upholstery fabric: Any fabric which is heavy or durable enough to be used in the covering of furniture.

Use grouping: A grouping of furniture for a special purpose, such as eating, studying, or talking.

Valance: A horizontal banding of pleated or gathered material which is used at the top of a window.

Value: The lightness or darkness of a color.

Varnish: A liquid preparation which, when spread upon a surface, dries by evaporation, forming a hard, lustrous coating that is more or less transparent and that serves as a protection as well as a decorative finish.

Veneer: Thin sheets of fine-grained wood glued together to make plywood or glued to a piece of coarser wood to give it strength, beauty, or a better surface for taking a finish.

Venetian blinds: Inside window blinds made of slats of wood, metal, shade cloth, plastic, etc., which are strung together with tape and used to control light.

Wallboard: A sturdy sheet of pressed fibers used in place of lath and plaster as partitions in a house.

Warm colors: Those colors having a predominance of red and yellow— *i.e.,* red, yellow, orange, yellow-orange, etc.

Warp: The lengthwise threads in a fabric.

Waterproofed material: A fabric that has been treated with a waterproofing solution, such as Pyroxylin, to make it resist water.

Webbing: A strong, woven tape used to hold springs in upholstery.

Weft: The crosswise threads in a fabric. Also called woof or filling.

Welting: A cording or other material inserted in upholstery seams so that it will show on the right side.

What-not: A small wall chest with rows of open shelves.

BIBLIOGRAPHY

Bibliography

GENERAL

BOOKS

Agan, Tessie, *The House.* J. B. Lippincott Company, Philadelphia, 1939.

Burris-Meyer, E., *Decorating Livable Homes.* Prentice-Hall, Inc., New York, 1947.

Draper, Dorothy, *Decorating Is Fun.* Doubleday & Company, Inc., New York, 1939.

Dunham, C. W., and M. D. Thalberg, *Planning Your Home for Better Living.* McGraw-Hill Book Company, Inc., New York, 1945.

Eberlein, H. D., *American Home Book of Decoration: Downstairs.* Doubleday & Company, Inc., New York, 1931.

Eberlein, H. D., *American Home Book of Decoration: Upstairs.* Doubleday & Company, Inc., New York, 1931.

Ford, James, and Katherine Morrow Ford, *Design of Modern Interiors.* Architectural Book Publishing Company, Inc., New York, 1942.

Germaine, Ina M., *Design for Decoration.* Dodd, Mead & Company, Inc., New York, 1948.

Gillies, Mary D., *All about Modern Decorating.* Harper & Brothers, New York, 1948.

Gillies, Mary D., *Popular Home Decoration.* Wm. H. Wise & Company, Inc., New York, 1948.

Goldstein, Harriet, and Vetta Goldstein, *Art in Everyday Life.* The Macmillan Company, New York, 1941.

Hardy, Kay, *How to Make Your House a Home.* Funk & Wagnalls Company, New York, 1947.

Hillyer, Elinor, *Mademoiselle's Home Planning Scrapbook.* The Macmillan Company, New York, 1949.

Koues, Helen, *The American Woman's Encyclopedia of Home Decorating.* Garden City Publishing Company, Garden City, New York, 1948.

Koues, Helen, *How to Be Your Own Decorator*. Tudor Publishing Company, New York, 1940.

Lee, Ruth W., and Louise T. Bolender, *Fashions in Furnishings*. McGraw-Hill Book Company, Inc., New York, 1948.

Merivale, Margaret, *Furnishing the Small Home*. The Studio Publications, Inc., New York, 1940.

Miller, Duncan, *Interior Decorating*. The Studio Publications, Inc., New York, 1937.

Miller, Gladys, *Decoratively Speaking*. Doubleday & Company, Inc., New York, 1939.

Patmore, Derek, *Decoration for the Small Home*. G. P. Putnam's Sons, New York, 1938.

Rockow, Hazel M., and Julius Rockow, *Creative Home Decorating*. H. S. Stuttman Company, New York, 1951.

Rutt, Anna H., *Home Furnishings*. John Wiley & Sons, Inc., New York, 1948.

Sooy, Louise Pinkney, and Virginia Woodbridge, *Plan Your Own Home*. Stanford University Press, Stanford University, California, 1946.

Stewart, R., and J. Gerald, *Home Decoration*. Julian Messner, Inc., Publishers, New York, 1935.

Storrs, Lewis, *The Key to Your New Home*. McGraw-Hill Book Company, Inc., New York, 1946.

Terhune, F. B., *Decorating for You*. M. Barrows & Company, Inc., New York, 1944.

Trilling, Mabel B., and F. W. Nicholas, *The Girl and Her Home*. Houghton Mifflin Company, Boston, 1947.

Trilling, Mabel B., Florence Williams, and B. R. Andrews, *Art in Home and Dress*. J. B. Lippincott Company, Philadelphia, 1942.

Whitman, Roger C., *First Aid for the Ailing House*. McGraw-Hill Book Company, Inc., New York, 1946.

Whiton, Sherrill, *Elements of Interior Design and Decoration*. J. B. Lippincott Company, Philadelphia, 1951.

Wright, Richardson, *House and Garden's Complete Guide to Interior Decoration*. Simon and Schuster, Inc., New York, 1947.

PAMPHLETS *

Decorating Today, by Virginia Jenkins. Archway Press, 41 W. 47th St., New York 19. (1947)

Trends in Interior Decoration. Wildenstein & Co., 19 E. 64th St., New York 21. (1947)

---

* Some of the pamphlets listed are free; the others range in price from 5 cents to 50 cents.

Your Decorating A. B. C., by Gladys Miller. Archway Press, 41 W. 47th St., New York 19. (1946)

SECTION ONE: COLOR IN THE HOME

BOOKS

Abbott, Arthur G., *The Color of Life*. McGraw-Hill Book Company, Inc., New York, 1947.

Burris-Meyer, E., *Contemporary Color Guide*. William Helburn, Inc., New York, 1947.

Burris-Meyer, E., *Historical Color Guide*. William Helburn, Inc., New York, 1938.

Bustanoby, J. H., *Principles of Color and Color Mixing*. McGraw-Hill Book Company, Inc., New York, 1947.

Graves, Maitland, *The Art of Color and Design*. McGraw-Hill Book Company, Inc., New York, 1951.

Graves, Maitland, *Color Fundamentals*. McGraw-Hill Book Company, Inc., New York, 1951.

Hartley, Paul, *How to Beautify Your Home with Color*. McGraw-Hill Book Company, Inc., New York, 1952.

Maerz, A., and M. Rea Paul, *A Dictionary of Color*. McGraw-Hill Book Company, Inc., New York, 1950.

Miller, Duncan, *More Color Schemes for the Modern Home*. The Studio Publications, Inc., New York, 1938.

Vanderwalker, F. N., *The Mixing of Colors and Paints*. Frederick J. Drake & Company, Wilmette, Illinois, 1950.

PAMPHLETS

Color in the Home, by Charlotte B. Robinson. Cornell Bulletin for Homemakers 738, College of Home Economics, Cornell University, Ithaca, New York. (1950)

SECTION TWO: FURNITURE IN THE HOME

BOOKS

Aronson, J., *The Encyclopedia of Furniture*. Crown Publishers, New York, 1938.

Burris-Meyer, E., *This Is Fashion*. Harper & Brothers, New York, 1943.

Cherner, Norman, *Make Your Own Modern Furniture*. McGraw-Hill Book Company, Inc., New York, 1951.

Genauer, E., *Modern Interiors—Today and Tomorrow*. Illustrated Editions Co., Inc., New York, 1939.

Ornstein, J. A., *Decorating Unpainted Furniture*. Greenberg: Publisher, Inc., New York, 1946.

Sloane, Louise, *Revive Your Old Furniture*. The Studio Publications, Inc., New York, 1943.

Spears, Ruth Wyeth, *Make and Remodel Home Furnishings*. M. Barrows & Company, Inc., New York, 1944.

Spears, Ruth Wyeth, *Painting Patterns for Home Decorators*. M. Barrows & Company, Inc., New York, 1947.

Storey, Walter Rendell, *Furnishing in Style*. The Studio Publications, Inc., New York, 1947.

Wenham, E., *Antique Furniture for Modern Rooms*. The Studio Publications, Inc., New York, 1948.

PAMPHLETS

The Identification of Furniture Woods, by Arthur Koehler. Misc. Circular 66, Superintendent of Documents, Government Printing Office, Washington, D.C. (1926)

Use and Care of Furniture. Better Buymanship Bulletin No. 26, Household Finance Corporation, 919 N. Michigan Ave., Chicago 11. (1948)

SECTION THREE: FABRICS IN THE HOME

BOOKS

Blondin, Frances, *The New Encyclopedia of Modern Sewing*. Wm. H. Wise & Co., Inc., New York, 1950.

Spears, Ruth Wyeth, *Make and Remodel Home Furnishings*. M. Barrows & Company, Inc., New York, 1944.

Stephenson, J. W., *Drapery Cutting and Making*. Hall Publishing Company, New York, 1950.

PAMPHLETS

Living with Light. Lamp Division, General Electric Company, Nela Park, Cleveland 12, Ohio. (1945)

1001 Decorative Ideas. Consolidated Trimming Corp., 27 W. 23rd St., New York. (1950)

Use and Care Floor Covering. Better Buymanship Bulletin No. 10, Household Finance Corporation, 919 N. Michigan Ave., Chicago 11. (1948)

Use and Care Household Textiles. Better Buymanship Bulletin No. 2, Household Finance Corporation, 919 N. Michigan Ave., Chicago.

Window Curtains—Planning and Selection. Home and Garden Bulletin No. 4. Bureau of Human Nutrition and Home Economics, U.S. Department of Agriculture, Washington, D.C. (1951)

SECTION FOUR: ACCESSORIES IN THE HOME

BOOKS

Batchelder, Martha, *The Art of Hooked-rug Making*. Manual Arts Press, Peoria, Illinois, 1947.

Biegeleisen, J. I., and E. J. Busenbark, *The Silk Screen Printing Process*. McGraw-Hill Book Company, Inc., New York, 1941.

Biegeleisen, J. I., and Max Arthur Cohn, *Silk Screen Stenciling as a Fine Art*. McGraw-Hill Book Company, Inc., New York, 1942.

Cox, Doris, and Barbara Warren, *Creative Hands*. John Wiley & Sons, Inc., New York, 1951.

Good Housekeeping Needlecraft Encyclopedia. Randolph Publishing Institute, New York, 1947.

Hobbs, H. J., *Ninety-nine One Evening Projects*. Home Craftsman Publishing Corporation, New York, 1947.

Hodkin, Mabel, *Rug Making and Designing in Cross-stitch*. Pitman Publishing Corporation, New York, 1948.

Leeming, Joseph, *Money-making Hobbies*. J. B. Lippincott Company, Philadelphia, 1948.

McClinton, Katherine M., *Antique Collecting for Everyone*. McGraw-Hill Book Company, Inc., New York, 1951.

Robinson, Jessie, *Things to Make from Odds and Ends*. Appleton-Century-Crofts, Inc., New York, 1945.

Starr, Julian, Jr., *Fifty Things to Make for the Home*. McGraw-Hill Book Company, Inc., New York, 1941.

Starr, Julian, Jr., *Make It Yourself*. McGraw-Hill Book Company, Inc., New York, 1938.

Sternberg, Harry, *Silk Screen Color Printing*. McGraw-Hill Book Company, Inc., New York, 1942.

Stieri, Emanuele, *Home Craftsmanship*. McGraw-Hill Book Company, Inc., New York, 1935.

PAMPHLETS

A. B. C. of Embroidery Stitches, by Miriam Rodier. The American Thread Company, 260 West Broadway, New York 13. (1948)

African Violets, by H. V. P. Wilson. Ladies' Home Journal, Independence Square, Philadelphia 5. (1945)

Bear Brand Bucilla Afghans, Vol. 327. Needlework, 30-20 Thomson Ave., Long Island City 1, New York. (1944)

Books about Hand Arts. Mademoiselle Magazine, 575 Madison Ave., New York 22. (1947)

Craft Projects that Can Be Made with Inexpensive and Discarded Materials (A Listing of Projects by Media, MP 256). National Recreation Association, 315 Fourth Ave., New York 10. (1951)

Make It at Home. Universal Distributors, 54 W. 13th St., New York 11. (1948)

Mettle, Clay, and Metal, by Polly Weaver. Mademoiselle Magazine, 575 Madison Ave., New York 22. (1947)

1001 Money-saving Needlework Hints. Hearst Magazines, Inc., New York. (1951)

Weaving and Dyeing Processes in Early New York with a Description of Spinning Fibres, by Virginia D. Parslow. The Farmers' Museum, Cooperstown, New York. (1949)

SECTION FIVE: MANAGEMENT OF THE HOME

BOOKS

Bonde, Ruth L., *Management in Daily Living*. The Macmillan Company, New York, 1944.

 Cushman, Ella M., *Management in Homes*. The Macmillan Company, New York, 1945.

Herald Tribune Home Institute, *America's Housekeeping Book*. Charles Scribner's Sons, New York, 1949.

Kendall, H. W., *The Good Housekeeping Housekeeping Book*. Good Housekeeping Institute, New York, 1947.

Nickell, P., and J. M. Dorsey, *Management in Family Living*. John Wiley & Sons, Inc., New York, 1950.

PAMPHLETS

A Reference Manual on Electric Appliances in the Home. Westinghouse Electric Corporation Home Economics Institute, Appliances Division, Mansfield, Ohio. (1948)

College Budget Calendar. Household Finance Corporation, 919 N. Michigan Ave., Chicago 11. (1948)

Electrical Living—and How to Have It. Westinghouse Electric Corporation, School Service, 306 Fourth Ave., Pittsburgh 30.

Finishing Floors, Walls, and Woodwork, C-112, by Bernice Claytor. A. & M. College of Texas Extension Service, College Station, Texas. (1946)

Home Management Yardstick, by Esther Everett and I. H. Gross. Michigan State College of Agriculture Experimental Station, Lansing, Michigan. (1947)

Home Wiring Handbook. Westinghouse Electric Corporation, School Service, 306 Fourth Ave., Pittsburgh 30.

Household Finance Money Management Booklets. Household Finance Corporation, 919 N. Michigan Ave., Chicago 11.

> Children's Spending. (1948)
> Home Furnishings. (1947)
> The Recreation Dollar. (1948)
> The Shelter Dollar. (1950)
> Your Budget. (1950)
> Your Shopping Dollar. (1950)

Lighting Handbook. Westinghouse Electric Corporation, School Service, 306 Fourth Ave., Pittsburgh 30.

Sleek Closet—Chic Girl! Good Housekeeping Magazine, Bulletin Service, 959 Eighth Ave., New York 19. (1947)

SECTION SIX: PLANS FOR THE HOME

BOOKS

Bottomley, M. E., *New Design of Small Properties.* The Macmillan Company, New York, 1948.

Creighton, T. H., *Planning to Build.* Doubleday & Company, Inc., New York, 1945.

Crouse, William, *Home Guide to Repair, Upkeep, and Remodeling.* McGraw-Hill Book Company, Inc., New York, 1947.

Ericson, Emanuel E., and Roy L. Soules, *Planning Your Home.* Manual Arts Press, Peoria, Illinois, 1938.

Field, Wooster Bard, *House Planning.* McGraw-Hill Book Company, Inc., New York, 1940.

Hawkins, R. R., and C. H. Abbe, *New Homes from Old.* McGraw-Hill Book Company, Inc., New York, 1948.

Johnstone, B. Kenneth, and others, *Building or Buying a House.* McGraw-Hill Book Company, Inc., New York, 1945.

McKennee, O. W., and others, *Prefabs on Parade.* National Firemen's Institute, Deep River, Connecticut, 1948.

Shultz, H., *Housing and the Home.* Appleton-Century-Crofts, Inc., New York, 1939.

Ware, D., and B. Beatty, *A Short Dictionary of Architecture.* Allen & Unwin, Ltd., London, 1944.

Waugh, Alice, *Planning the Little House.* McGraw-Hill Book Company, Inc., New York, 1939.

Williams, Paul R., *New Homes for Today.* Murray & Gee, Inc., Culver City, California, 1946.

PAMPHLETS

Garlinghouse Plan Booklets. (1949) L. F. Garlinghouse Company, 820 Quincy St., Topeka, Kansas.

> All American Homes
> America's Best Home Plans
> Artistic Homes
> Blue Ribbon Homes
> Budget Homes
> Colonial Homes
> Deluxe Small Homes
> New American Homes
> New Brick Homes
> New Duplex Designs
> Our Future Home
> Ranch and Suburban Homes
> Small Homes
> Small Southern Homes
> Sunshine Homes
> Your Home in Brick
> Your New Home Plan

What Kind of Homes Do Families with Children Want? Parents Magazine, 52 Vanderbilt Ave., New York 17. (1946)

INTERIOR DECORATION AS A CAREER

PAMPHLETS

Design for a Modern Career, by Polly Weaver. Mademoiselle Magazine, 575 Madison Ave., New York 22. (1946)

If You Are Considering Interior Decoration, by J. M. Stampe. Vocational Guidance Service, Rochester Institute of Technology, Rochester 8, New York. (1951)

The Interior Decorator, by Anne Harris. Sir Isaac Pitman & Sons, Ltd., Toronto, Canada. (1946)

Opportunities in Interior Decoration, by Suzanne Conn. Vocational Guidance Manuals, Inc., 45 W. 45th St., New York 19. (1951)

List of Visual Aids

The motion pictures and filmstrips listed in this visual bibliography can be used to supplement the material presented in this book. It is recommended, however, that each film be reviewed before using in order to determine its suitability for a particular group.

Both motion pictures and filmstrips are included in this visual bibliography, and the character of each is indicated by the self-explanatory abbreviations "MP" and "FS." Immediately following this identification is the name of the producer; and if the distributor is different from the producer, the name of the distributor follows the name of the producer. Abbreviations are used for names of producers and distributors, and these abbreviations are identified in the list of sources at the end of the bibliography. In most instances, the films can be borrowed or rented from local or state 16-mm film libraries. Unless otherwise indicated, the motion pictures are 16-mm sound black-and-white films and the filmstrips are 35-mm black and white and silent.

For the convenience of film users, the films have been grouped by the subjects treated in various chapters. In some instances the same film may be used in connection with several different chapters. Special attention should be called to the series of 6 color filmstrips prepared by the McGraw-Hill Text-Film Department to correlate and supplement the material presented in Sections One, Two, Three, and Four. See particularly the descriptions of these filmstrips.

This bibliography is suggestive only, and film users should examine the latest annual edition and quarterly supplements of *Educational Film Guide,* a catalogue of some 10,000 films published by the H. W. Wilson Co., New York. The *Guide,* a standard reference book, is available in most college and public libraries.

General

Designing Women (MP, BIS, 24 min). Illustrates, in story form, two methods of furnishing an apartment—one flamboyant and arty, the

437

other in a modern style that is simple, usable, and pleasing. (Sponsored by the British Council of Industrial Design.)

The Fifth H (MP, Venard, 43 min color). Shows how 4-H Club boys and girls can improve the appearance of the interior of a farm home. (Sponsored by Sears-Roebuck Foundation.)

Home Magic (MP, Georgia, 11 min color). Shows how paint, slip-covers, rearrangement of furniture, etc., can transform an ordinary room into an attractive place in which to live.

We Decorate Our Home (MP, Pitts Glass, 28 min color). Shows how to redecorate a home and particularly what to do with cut-up walls, exposed pipes, ugly radiators, etc. Emphasizes the use of plate glass and mirrors.

Section One: Color in the Home

Background for Home Decoration (MP, MTP, 22 min color). Illustrates ways in which wallpaper contributes to interior decoration; explains color, design, and style as elements of room arrangement; and demonstrates how wallpaper can be hung by families redecorating their homes themselves. (Sponsored by the Wallpaper Institute.)

Color in the Girl's Room (FS, McGraw, 38 frames color). Explains the basic factors of color application and demonstrates four kinds of color schemes—monochromatic, analogous, complementary, and triad.

Color Keying in Art and Living (MP, EBF, 11 min color). A study of color relationships. Employs abstract demonstrations of color deceptions followed by practical applications. Color relations are applied to art subjects and to aspects of everyday life.

Introduction to Color (FS, McGraw, 33 frames color). Provides an elementary analysis of color and covers such subjects as primary and secondary colors, the color wheel, neutralization of colors, warm and cool colors, and definitions of hue, value, and intensity.

The Nature of Colors (MP, Coronet, 10 min color). Defines color as mental reactions to varying wave lengths of visible light, and explains the nature of color in physical terms. Includes illustrations of color principles in the arts, color printing, and photography.

Section Two: Furniture in the Home

Arranging Furniture in the Girl's Room (FS, McGraw, 40 frames color). Covers basic principles of furniture arrangement, including the placing of furniture parallel to walls, grouping furniture around focal points, and maintaining balance.

Furniture Films for Homemakers (FS series, NRFA). Seven filmstrips, color, each one with an accompanying $33\frac{1}{3}$ rpm recording with playing times of 10 to 14 minutes. Titles of the individual filmstrips are:

*Room Arrangement; Upholstery Fabrics; Floor Coverings; Color Har-
mony; Styles in Furniture; Furniture Construction: Case Goods; Furniture Construction: Upholstered Furniture.*

Furniture Styles (FS, Filmette, 200 frames). Two filmstrips, 100
frames each, consisting of reproductions of paintings of great artists in
which furniture styles are portrayed: in one, antiques up to the Medieval
Epoch; in the other, Renaissance, Baroque, Rococo, Empire, Biedermeier.

Making Your House Livable (FS, SVE, 43 frames). How to make a
home attractive and livable through the selection and arrangement of
furniture. Stresses the importance of being clean and orderly.

Selecting Furniture for the Girl's Room (FS, McGraw, 41 frames
color). Gives suggestions for fixing old furniture, making or improving
furniture, painting and rearranging furniture, and buying new furniture.
Explains furniture styles—Modern for simplicity, Early American for in-
formality, Eighteenth Century for elegance.

Section Three: Fabrics in the Home

Before and After (MP, MTP, 10 min color). Demonstrates how a
living room that was furnished and decorated twenty years ago is redecorated into a modern room. Emphasizes the use of rugs and carpeting.
(Sponsored by Alexander Smith & Sons Carpet Co.)

Fabrics in the Girl's Room (FS, McGraw, 36 frames color). Explains
the factors to be considered in choosing fabrics; pattern, texture, and
color; balance and harmony with furniture and room characteristics;
strength, weight, and durability.

Fibers, Threads, and Textile Fabrics (FS, Filmette, 110 frames).
Explains through microphotographs the characteristics of various types
of fibers, threads, and fabrics—linen, flax, cotton, silk, damask, satin, mo-
hair, crepe, etc.

Miracle Under Foot (MP, MTP, 16 min color). Shows how a young
couple make their living room more attractive and livable through the
correct use of rugs. (Sponsored by Bigelow-Sanford Carpet Co.)

Nearly Right Won't Do (MP, CCNY, 28 min). Explains the factors
in judging the quality of rugs, the techniques of rug making, and the
selection of appropriate colors and designs. (Sponsored by Alexander
Smith & Sons Carpet Co.)

Section Four: Accessories in the Home

Accessories in the Girl's Room (FS, McGraw, 35 frames color). Gives
examples of good and bad accessories—vases, pillows, lamps, book ends,
etc.—and explains principles governing the choice and use of accessories
in a room.

Section Five: Management of the Home

Research for Better Living (MP, USDA, 17 min color). Shows examples of the work done by the U.S. Department of Agriculture Bureau of Human Nutrition and Home Economics in the fields of food and nutrition, textiles and clothing, housing and household equipment, and family economics.

Step by Step in Everyday Tasks (FS, USDA/Photo, 60 frames). Suggests short and easy methods of doing everyday tasks in the home, stressing the need to eliminate unnecessary motions and steps.

A Step-saving Kitchen (MP, USDA, 14 min color). Demonstrates the features and facilities of a modern farm kitchen scientifically designed and built by the Bureau of Human Nutrition and Home Economics. Similar filmstrip with title, *A Step-saving U Kitchen*, 40 frames color, also available.

What Is Your Shopping Score? (FS, HHF, 64 frames). Explains how and what to buy in order to get more for one's money. Presents shopping problems from the points of view of a career girl, bride, young mother, mother of teen-age daughters, and an older homemaker.

Your Family Budget (MP, Coronet, 10 min). Explains the make-up of a family budget, its operation, and its contribution to family well-being and relationships.

Section Six: Plans for the Home

Building Techniques (MP series, USN/UWF). A series of six motion pictures demonstrating basic principles and techniques of building construction. While not directly related to interior decoration, these films provide background information which may be of value. Titles and running times of the individual films are: *Foundations and Concrete* (26 min); *Framing: Floor Joists and Walls* (25 min); *Framing: Rafter Principles and Common Rafters* (15 min); *Framing: Hip and Valley Rafters* (25 min); *Interior and Exterior Trim* (12 min); *Fundamentals of Stair Layout* (11 min).

What Is a Farm Worth (MP, USDA, 14 min color). Explains the factors to be considered in appraising a farm, illustrated through the experiences of a young couple interested in buying a farm in Illinois.

Directory of Sources

BIS—British Information Services, 30 Rockefeller Plaza, New York 20, N.Y.

CCNY—City College of New York, Midtown Business Center, 430 West 50th St., New York 19, N.Y.

Coronet—Coronet Films, Coronet Building, Chicago 1, Ill.

EBF—Encyclopaedia Britannica Films, Inc., 1150 Wilmette Ave., Wilmette, Ill.

Filmette—Filmette Co., 635 Riverside Drive, New York 31, N.Y.

Georgia—Georgia Agricultural Extension Service, Athens, Ga.

HHF—Household Finance Corporation, 919 North Michigan Ave., Chicago 11, Ill.

McGraw—McGraw-Hill Text-Film Department, 330 West 42nd St., New York 36, N.Y.

MTP—Modern Talking Picture Service, Inc., 45 Rockefeller Plaza, New York 20, N.Y.

NRFA—National Retail Furniture Association, 666 North Lake Shore Drive, Chicago, Ill.

Photo—Photo Lab Inc., 3825 Georgia Ave., Washington 11, D.C.

Pitts Glass—Pittsburgh Plate Glass Co., 632 Duquesne Way, Pittsburgh 22, Pa.

SVE—Society for Visual Education, Inc., 1345 West Diversey Parkway, Chicago 14, Ill.

USDA—U.S. Department of Agriculture, Motion Picture Service, Washington 25, D.C.

USN—U.S. Department of the Navy, Washington 25, D.C.

UWF—United World Films, Inc., 1445 Park Ave., New York 29, N.Y.

Venard—The Venard Organization, 702 South Adams St., Peoria 2, Ill.

Index*

* Definitions for terms pertaining to home furnishings as used in this book are given in the Glossary on pages 415–426.